Red-figure Pottery in its Ancient Setting

Acts of the International Colloquium held at the National Museum of Denmark in Copenhagen, November 5-6, 2009

Edited by Stine Schierup & Bodil Bundgaard Rasmussen

Aarhus University Press

RED-FIGURE POTTERY IN ITS ANCIENT SETTING
© Aarhus University Press and the authors 2012.

GÖSTA ENBOM MONOGRAPHS

General editor:
Bodil Bundgaard Rasmussen.

Editorial board:
Mark L. Lawall, John Lund, Dyfri Williams.

Gösta Enbom Monographs is a peer reviewed series.

Published with support from The Foundation of Consul General Gösta Enbom.

Graphic design:
Nina Grut, MDD.

Printed at Narayana Press.

Typeset with Stone Serif and Stone Sans.

ISBN 978 87 7124 051 1
ISSN 1904-6219

Aarhus University Press
Langelandsgade 177
DK-8200 Aarhus N

White Cross Mills
Lancaster LA1 4XS
England

Box 511
Oakville, CT 06779
USA

www.unipress.dk

Front cover:
Apulian rhyton, tomb 19, La Scala cemetery, Roccagloriosa (Photo: E. Salinardi).

Back cover:
1) Athens, National Archaeological Museum, inv. 12486 (Photo courtesy: National Archaeological Museum at Athens, Ministry of Culture/TAP).
2) Paris, Musée du Louvre, inv. CA 308 (Photo courtesy: RMN, Musée du Louvre).

Amphora attributed to the painter Syriskos, Athens 500-470 BC, Collection of Classical and Near Eastern Antiquities, The National Museum of Denmark, inv.no. Chr. VIII 320.

 NATIONALMUSEET

Table of Contents

5 Per Kristian Madsen
Preface

7 Stine Schierup & Bodil Bundgaard Rasmussen
Introduction

11 Martin Langner
Mantle-figures and the Athenization of Late Classical Imagery

21 Annie Verbanck-Piérard
Herakles and his Attic Pillars: Iconographical Study and Socio-religious Context of the Four Column Herakleion

33 Adrienne Lezzi-Hafter
The Xenophantos Chous from Kerch with Cypriot Themes

43 Athena Tsingarida
White-ground Cups in Fifth-century Graves: A Distinctive Class of Burial Offerings in Classical Athens?

59 Maurizio Gualtieri
Late 'Apulian' Red-figure Vases in Context: A Case Study

69 Helena Fracchia
Changing Contexts and Intent: the Mourning Niobe Motif from Lucania to Daunia

81 Victoria Sabetai
Boeotian Red-figure Vases: Observations on their Contexts and Settings

99 Martin Bentz
Elean Red-figure Pottery from Olympia

109 Thomas Mannack
An Overview of Athenian Figure-decorated Pottery in Southern Italy and Sicily

117 Stine Schierup
A Heroic Emblem: The Cultural Transformation of the Panathenaic Amphora in Southern Italy.

133 Guy Hedreen
Vase-painting and the Narrative Logic: Achilles and Troilos in Athens and Etruria

147 Abstracts

151 Bibliographic Abbreviations

155 Bibliography

177 List of Authors

Preface

BY PER KRISTIAN MADSEN
DIRECTOR GENERAL
THE NATIONAL MUSEUM OF DENMARK

In the early 19th century the Danish Prince Christian Frederik and his wife, Caroline Amalie, undertook a Grand Tour of Europe. In 1820 they settled for a several months in Naples enjoying the rich cultural and social life of the town. The royal couple was soon introduced to Giuseppe Capece Latro, former Archbishop of Taranto and the owner of a fairly large collection of antiquities. The Prince developed a serious interest in the collection and on the advice of P.O. Brøndsted, classicist and 'agent of the Royal Danish Court to the Holy See', he acquired the greater part of it. The acquisition comprised above all vases – a total of around 200 – decorated vases representing the various local styles of Southern Italy, a large group of Gnathia pottery and another large group of black glazed vases and a few Greek vases. The Prince established a Vase Cabinet at the Royal Palace in Copenhagen and spent a lot of time with his collection playing an active role in further acquisitions until his accession to the throne in 1839 as King Christian VIII made this more difficult. Upon the King's death in 1848 the collection was incorporated into the National Museum, where studies into ancient pottery ever since have been a major research field.

In 2008 the research programme "Pots, Potters and Society in Ancient Greece" was launched thanks to a generous grant from The Foundation of Consul General Gösta Enbom. The programme focuses on two main themes: 1) a societal and economic aspect, the production of – and trade in – pottery as a source for understanding the ancient economy, and 2) an ideological/iconographical aspect: vase paintings and other iconographical evidence as a source for understanding the life and thoughts of the ancients. "Pots, Potters and Society in Ancient Greece" seeks to further our knowledge of both themes and if possible to develop new theoretical approaches by combining existing knowledge with fresh ideas. To pursue this goal international thematic colloquia are held at regular intervals and in 2008 a PhD scholarship was launched in collaboration with Aarhus University entitled

Consul General Gösta Enbom (1895-1986).

"Greek Iconography in Southern Italy. Imported Attic and early South Italian red-figure pottery from Lucanian and Apulian sites".

Taking its cue from the theme of the PhD-study the National Museum in November 2009 staged the colloquium "Red-figure Pottery in its Ancient Setting" aimed at highlighting the significance of the various settings and cultural contexts of red-figure pottery be it in Greece or outside Greece.

I wish to thank all contributors to both colloquium and the present publication for accepting our invitation and shedding light on the cultural encounters traceable in the iconography of ancient pottery. My thanks also go to the Foundation of Consul General Gösta Enbom for generous support of both colloquium and publication.

Introduction

BY STINE SCHIERUP &
BODIL BUNDGAARD RASMUSSEN

The study of red-figure pottery is one of the cornerstones of classical archaeology. Thousands and thousands of vessels and potsherds have been excavated throughout the Mediterranean countries, an endless number of publications on the topic have been produced, and scholars have dedicated their lives to the study of figured Greek vases. Yet, we still must face the challenge of trying to understand the meaning of figured Greek pottery through the prism of the present.

Imagery was undoubtedly an important part of ancient Greek society, but ancient written sources remain remarkably silent about pottery, perhaps because figured vases were of a completely different character than other major sources of Attic imagery, including sculpture, wall painting and fine metal ware. First of all the vases were produced in very high quantities and by a great number of different potters, and secondly they were part of everyday life and thus potentially a strong medium for communicating social or political views and messages to a wide audience. Thirdly, they were easily transported far beyond the borders of their place of origin, thus promoting the spread of the iconographical language of Athens and its adaptation in other cultural settings throughout the Mediterranean world. Indeed, in this way they become a means for understanding not only the culture of Athens in the Classical period but also of cultures far beyond the Athenian city-state.

The question presents itself as to how the setting of the pottery, in other words the various contexts in which it appears, can provide criteria for reaching a fuller understanding of its function and iconography, in particular how Attic iconographic themes were altered or absorbed as they entered into new cultural settings.

In the wake of the passionate debate about the study of Greek pottery that dominated the 1990s, in which iconographic, stylistic and socio-anthropological approaches were juxtaposed, especially in the form of connoisseurship versus structuralism, such questions have come increasingly into sharp focus. The more so with the contextual and anthropological approach to figured pottery now becoming one of the most popular fields within this area of research, combining an iconographic study with that of the vessel shape, the function, and the various cultural contexts of use.[1] This approach has clearly influenced the chosen themes for conferences on Greek pottery held within the last decade.[2]

The colloquium in Copenhagen aimed at highlighting the interpretative challenges we face when analyzing red-figure pottery and its iconography within various cultural contexts. Participants were invited to present case studies from within their particular areas of research, which would serve as examples for enhancing our understanding of the variability in the character and value of red-figure pottery and its imagery, whether in a Greek, a colonial Greek, an Etruscan or any other indigenous community.

Turning to the content of this volume, the first papers focus on the way red-figure imagery functioned as a medium for expressing socio-political ideas. Martin Langner introduces us to a neglected field in the study of iconography: the mantle-figures seen mainly on the B-sides of kraters and other large vessels. He offers a deeper insight into the meaning of these figures, which have hitherto mostly been overlooked in the iconographic study of red-figure pottery, despite the fact that they appear on the majority of the kraters from the Classical period. Langner suggests that the theme in Attic contexts serves as a symbol of the ideal citizen and that this view of the Athenian citizen is exported to Italy, where it is later adopted in an altered form in the local red-figure pottery of Southern Italy, where, however, the garments and their patterning are different and where, in some cases, the scenes gain a new ritual meaning. Annie Verbanck-Piérard discusses the representation of Herakles in the setting of a four-columned peristyle, usually known as the four-column Herakleion. The motif is particularly popular at the end of the fifth and the beginning of the fourth century BC, that is during the last phase of the Peloponnesian war. It may, therefore,

---

1 For a discussion of the methodological and theoretical development within the study of figured Greek pottery, see the two recently published articles: Isler-Kerényi 2009; Oakley 2009b.
2 See e.g. the following conference proceedings: Denoyelle *et al.* 2005; De La Genière (ed.) 2006; Nørskov *et al.* 2009; Schmidt & Stähli 2012.

Apulian krater acquired from the collection of Giuseppe Capece Latro, inv.no. CHR VIII 3. From Bari. Copenhagen, The National Museum of Denmark. (Photo courtesy: The National Museum of Denmark).

be seen as a way of promoting common civic-religious behavior and giving new life to cult practices, probably as part of a general religious revival in the final years of the century. Adrienne Lezzi-Hafter introduces us to the complex iconography of one of the works by Xenophantos Athenaios: a chous found in the so-called 'Smeni Tumulus' (Snake Tumulus), near Pantikapaion in the Crimea, together with two lekythoi produced in the same workshop. The chous is a fine example of an imitation of metal ware in a highly skilled workshop. Given the vessel's archaeological context, the interpretation of the depiction of two mythical Cypriot events is unexpected but convincing. It seems that a Hellenized version of an eastern theme was accepted in a territory unfamiliar with its true meaning.

The next three papers deal with the way iconography could be consciously used in the (self)representation of a deceased. There is no denying that tombs provide us with the best evidence for understanding the intended use of red-figure pottery and its iconography. Unlike most other archaeological contexts, tombs are deliberately planned and effected, a fact which allows for the possibility that the pottery was specifically selected by the family of the deceased, or even the deceased himself before death, in order to present specific ideas and values. One particular class might be the remarkable and rare white-ground cups, known from tombs in Athens and in particular from the famous 'Sotades Tomb'. These are the focus of the paper by Athena Tsingarida. The unusual iconographic themes and the elaborate style set them apart from other types of contemporary figured pottery, emphasizing their special status. Athena Tsingarida argues that these cups might have been ordered specifically by distinctive individuals in the Athenian society for burial use.

The Lucanian site of Roccagloriosa in the south-western part of Italy is an example of a recent, well-executed excavation that has provided documented contexts with unique evidence for the use of Italiote red-figure pottery. Maurizio Gualtieri discusses the symbolic meaning of the elaborate mythological themes chosen for the figured pottery in an aristocratic male tomb (tomb 19) and how these themes might be linked to the social status and family connections of the deceased, as a consciously used medium for self-representation. In the same burial group a rich female tomb yielded an amphora showing the mourning Niobe. Taking as a starting point the amphora from Roccagloriosa, Helena Fracchia discusses the changes in the representation and the figurative code of the popular "mourning Niobe" motif from western Lucania to Daunia and the ways in which the motif expresses common religious beliefs among the Italic aristocracies. Maurizio Gualtieri's and Helena Fracchia's contributions both demonstrate how the adaptation of Greek myths is used in the representation of Italic values.

A period of particular relevance to the issues discussed here is the latter part of the fifth century BC, when the Attic pottery market weakened and local red-figure productions were established outside Attica, a development often explained as a consequence of the economic crisis following the Peloponnesian war. The natural consequences of this process were the development of various local styles. These productions mark the beginning of completely new and different opportunities for the consumer. In contrast to previous periods where pottery was imported from Athens, the potters and painters were now in much closer contact with their buyers and with the settings in which their pottery was used. Consequently, new styles and favoured iconographic themes may be traced throughout the areas of use.

The various local regional styles of Greek red-figure pottery have not hitherto been well-studied or published, perhaps due to their not being as abundant as those of South Italy. But Victoria Sabetai's paper on Boeotian red-figure and Martin Bentz's paper on Elean red-figure pottery from Olympia provide us with valuable evidence for two such regional styles in Greece. Set against the social and historical background of the region, Victoria Sabetai argues that the local Boeotian red-figure pottery seems to have been used in the tombs of persons of special status and social standing. The evidence provided from the sanctuary in Olympia indicates, according to Martin Bentz, that the use of red-figure was limited here. It appears that the red-figure pottery in use in the sanctuary was mainly intended for everyday use and did not serve ritual purposes.

From regional styles in Greece, the focus turns again to Italy. Thomas Mannack's paper, 'An Overview of Athenian Figure-decorated Pottery in Southern Italy and Sicily', gives a summary of the published evidence for imported Attic pottery in Southern Italy and Sicily, their contexts, shape and iconography. While some work has been carried out in establishing a general picture of the contexts in which Attic pottery was found in Etruria, similar studies are absent from the study of red-figure pottery in Southern Italy and Sicily, a situation Thomas Mannack's paper helps to remedy. The discussion of context, form and iconography of figured pottery in Southern Italy is taken on by Stine Schierup, focusing specifically on the meaning of the Panathenaic amphora shape through the transitional stage from imported Attic to locally produced red-figure pottery. By combining the evidence of iconography and archaeological contexts various uses for this particular shape of vessel can be traced, indicating that the Panathenaic amphora remained a symbol of heroic importance in the grave cult within the Greek communities, whereas it seems to have been incorporated into symposia ware of the Italic communities.

Finally, we head north to Etruria with Guy Hedreen's paper on the narrative of the Achilles and Troilos motif. He suggests that local productions of red-figure in Etruria occasionally reveal a profound knowledge of the depicted theme, rather than being simply copies of an Attic motif. By means of a structural analysis he emphasizes how the same story can be depicted in different ways through variations of the style and depictions of the theme. This is essential to our understanding of the potters and painters and the buyers of imitations of Attic pottery. Both groups must have had an intimate knowledge of the story behind the image.

In conclusion, the organizers/editors wish to extend our sincere thanks to the speakers who kindly accepted our invitation to take part in the colloquium in Copenhagen and to contribute to this publication. We thank the Thorvaldsen Museum for offering a visit to Bertel Thorvaldsen's collection of antiquities in which Greek pottery plays a major role. Finally, a special vote of thanks is offered to the 'Generalkonsul Gösta Enbom Foundation' for their generous support of both colloquium and publication.

Mantle-figures and the Athenization of Late Classical Imagery

BY MARTIN LANGNER

Mantle-figures and the Athenization of Late Classical Imagery

BY MARTIN LANGNER

Strolling through collections of ancient vases and looking at the abundant pictures of mantle-figures or 'men in conversation' on the reverse of some of these vessels one may wonder what these images are all about. Are they only Side-B scenes, that are not worth looking at in depth, and merely a common or traditional way of decorating the reverse? Is the reverse the place for a boring or (better), inconspicuous image that has to be there to complete the decoration of the entire vessel, an image that the beholder need not pay attention to? That is perhaps the common opinion, and even John Boardman in his handbook, where he listed all the daily-life themes pictured on red-figure vases, did not mention the 'youths in cloaks'.[1]

To support this point of view, one could put forth several arguments. Firstly, compared to the main picture the execution of the reverse is frequently very sketchy. Secondly, it was often done by a minor artist and it seems that through the centuries the quality of the drawings deteriorates. In addition they all seem to be the same, one much like the other, meaningless stereotypes without any narrative content, and therefore in aspects of quality and content not worth looking at.[2] And finally, one could even argue that they were not seen at all, if the krater was placed at the most remote corner of the andron.[3]

I feel uncomfortable however with this approach to 'Side-Bs', because a picture in contrast to pure ornament contains much information and if no meaning had been intended, the idea could simply have been dropped. Furthermore the importance of the motif of draped youths is common on late red-figure cups, skyphoi and jugs, where it is sometimes the main theme of both sides.[4] The following analysis will, therefore, seek to broaden our understanding of these pictures and raise the question as to what exactly is shown in these conventional iconographic themes of 'men in conversation'.

THE THREE MANTLE-FIGURE TYPES
Of the 1,123 preserved kraters of the late fifth and the fourth century BC, more than 80% (900) show youths in cloaks on Side-B (Fig. 1).[5] On calyx-kraters one also finds Dionysos and his thiasos on Side-B, but in general 'draped youths' is the preferred theme. And the same can be said about the growing number of pelikai. Depending on the size of the vessel, two or more – often three – figures are depicted. From these figures three common types can be identified on the basis of clothing and posture. The types can be found in various kinds of combination. They can all be seen together on the reverse of an Attic bell-krater in Berlin[6] (Fig. 2).

The first type is the standing youth in the middle. He is completely wrapped in his cloak, his neck and sometimes also his head is covered. Often he is shown with curly long hair and therefore should be considered younger than the others. This attire is described by ancient authors as an expression of the youthful decency and restraint of an ephebos.[7]

The young man to the left on the Berlin krater can be defined as the second type. He also keeps his arms under his himation, but keeping the cloak under the right armpit while resting the other arm on his hip. This attitude is a typical pose for an orator[8] and is known from portrait sculpture of Attic orators such as Aeschines. In literary sources it is described as a sign indicating that the speaker/orator is keeping his emotions under control while speaking.[9]

The third type is the man on the right. He is making a gesture with his right arm outstretched and the thumb of his hand downwards while reaching towards the youth in the middle as if he is trying to get in contact with him. Various kinds of gesture can be seen associated with this third figure, but in my opinion they all belong to the type, which Heinz-Günter Hollein has named the 'dynamis-type', that is of a powerful man putting his plans into action.[10]

THE SETTING OF THE MANTLE-FIGURES
The setting of these scenes remains mostly uncertain, since it is rarely indicated in the vase-painting. Usually we could assume that the setting was in a street, in the agora or in any other meeting place for citizens,[11] while in the few cases where columns are shown it might define the place as somewhere inside or near a building.[12] If devices occasionally hanging behind the figures (strigilis,

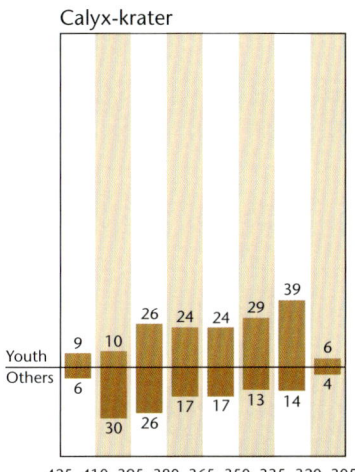 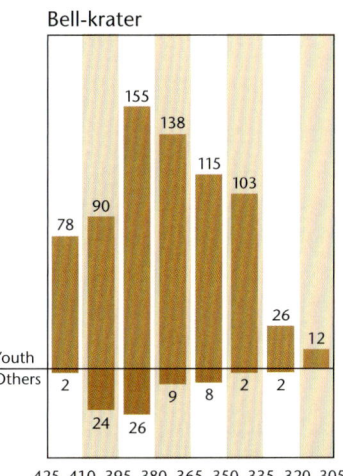 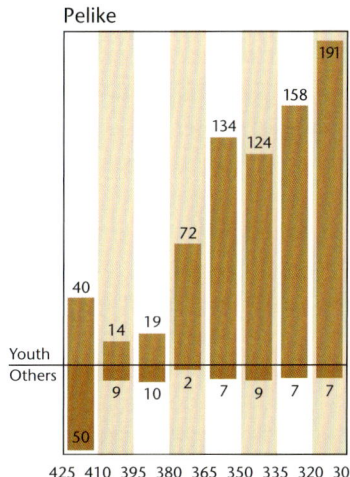

Fig. 1: Frequency of draped youths on side-B of kraters and pelikai.

Fig. 2: Reverse of an Attic red-figure bell krater in the manner of the Dinos Painter. Berlin, Antikensammlung F 2641 (Photo courtesy: bpk/ Antikensammlung, Staatliche Museen zu Berlin/Johannes Laurentius).

aryballos, discus, halteres and writing tablets) are read as location-markers and not as part of a comprehensive visual representation of citizenship, they might indicate that the scenes were set in the gymnasia or the palaestra.[13]

During the fourth century BC draped youths are frequently depicted holding a discus in combination

1. Boardman 1975, 216-222; Boardman 1989, 218-221. The same can be said about Lissarrague 1999. On the other hand F. & I. Giudice counted the mantle-figures under their non-specific heading "Men, women, youths, boys" without any distinction between main and secondary sides of a vessel (Giudice & Giudice 2009, 50).
2. See e.g. Robertson 1992, 212; 242.
3. Fless 2002, 36-38 discusses the find-spots of kraters.
4. *ARV*² 1484-1495, 1515, 1526-1528. As precursors one may note the onlookers or spectators on black-figure vases: Kaeser 1990, 151-156. Stansbury-O'Donnell 2006, 231 and passim interprets them as a means "to transform the image into a model of choral and civic ritual performance, and thereby into a model of social values and behaviour."
5. These figures derive from my *Repertorium spätrotfiguriger Bildervasen aus Athen* which will be published soon in an online-version.
6. Berlin, Antikensammlungen F 2641: *CVA* Berlin 11, 47-48, pl. 45.1-6; *BAPD* Vase 215308.
7. Hollein 1988, 40-43. For a recent discussion of aidos and sophrosyne, see Ferrari 2002, 54-60; 87-90.
8. Shapiro 1993b, 24 with fig. 4.
9. Hollein 1988, 278-280; Zanker 1995, 45-49; Schäfer 1997, 74; Bergemann 1997, 76-77. On gestures expressing self-control and courage (or the lack of those virtues) in general, see McNiven 2000; Rosen & Sluiter 2003.
10. Hollein 1988, 25-36, 46, 59-63. On the importance of the (clothed) body as a medium of representation in Athens: Hawhee 2004; Mann 2009.
11. Hollein 1988, 71-117; Neer 2002, 135-146 (law-court). For possible places to meet, see Shear 1994; Kenzler 1999, 239-303; Hoepfner 2006 (Agora); Raeck 2004, 365; Gehrke 2004; Hawhee 2004, 109-136 (Gymnasion).
12. E.g. *ARV*² 525.45-46, 1027.2, 1029.28, 1125.17, 1186.28, 1333.4, 1431.2, 1432.15, 1451.2, 1456-1460, 1693.2bis.
13. Bérard 1984, 26-31; Bergemann 1997, 78.

with others holding a stick, an aryballos or a strigilis (Fig. 3),[14] but statistically no clear conclusions can be drawn from these combinations. It seems as if these objects are primarily chosen for compositional reasons to fill the space between the heads or bodies, and therefore the four attributes do not have a distinct meaning but should be taken as equally weighted symbols of Athenian public behaviour: a certain way of living that the Athenian citizens practised day-by-day in the gymnasia of the city, where they spent lots of time not only playing sport but most of all debating current political or cultural topics.

THE INTERDEPENDENCE BETWEEN THE SCENES ON SIDE-A AND SIDE-B

From the postures of the mantle-figures and the objects occasionally depicted near them, it seems reasonable to presume that the scenes reflected the typical institutions of the Athenian democracy and the most important activity fields of an Athenian adult. But how were these Side B mantle-figures connected to the decoration on the primary side of the vessel?

At the beginning of the fifth century BC both sides could often have belonged to the same story, showing draped youths together in scenes set in the gymnasium or at a sacrifice in a sanctuary.[15] Or, as seen on a neck-amphora in Berlin, the Athenian youths excitedly debate the outcome of the fight between Theseus and the Minotaur depicted on side-A (Fig. 4).[16]

In all these cases Side-B functions as a motif which guides the beholder to the significant main side of the story. And remarkably, even on a mythological level of story telling, the draped youths are meant to be Athenians as it is shown on the Berlin amphora (Fig. 4). Indeed, the attributes they are holding, a stick to lean on or the set of aryballos and strigilis, reference (as is commonly accepted) the well-known signs of Athenian citizenship,[17] and the painter is employing these symbols[18] in the same way as they are used as signs of citizenship on Attic grave-stones.

As on the contemporary Attic gravestones,[19] these figures comprise in a dense and compact form the ideals of Athenian democratic society: the equality of all citizens, expressed by the undifferentiated, uniform representation of the himation; the youthful energy which appears in the naked breast of their athletic body; the self-control, as it is rendered by the arm held under the cloak and the ability to address a suitable word embedded in the

Fig. 3: Reverse of an Attic red-figure bell krater by the Pourtalés Painter. Berlin, Antikensammlung 31094 (Photo courtesy: bpk/Antikensammlung, Staatliche Museen zu Berlin/Johannes Laurentius).

picture by using gestures of speech. At the same time, the activity fields on which citizen areté is proved, the public gathering and the gymnasia, are alluded to through stick and strigilis.

Such scenes of Athenians meeting and talking could also function as counter-images to the mythological or festive sphere of the main side of the vessels. These scenes show the everyday area in which the Athenian proves himself and demonstrates his virtue, in contrast to the festive mood of sacrifice or banquet, or to the fabulous Dionysiac or erotic world of the gods and heroes. In this sense one can see such civic images as complementary to the main subject of the kraters, deepening the discussion with counter points.

THE RECEPTION OF MANTLE-FIGURES IN ITALY

Along with the red-figure vases, Athenians exported their view of 'behaviour' intensively throughout the Mediterranean world. Therefore, the question that arises

Fig. 4: Reverse of an Attic red-figure neck-amphora by the Kleophrades Painter. Berlin, Antikensammlung 1970.5 (Photo courtesy: bpk/Antikensammlung, Staatliche Museen zu Berlin/Johannes Laurentius).

is: what might such an image of Athenian citizenship have meant to the foreign user of the vessel? Do the depicted mantle-figures remain Athenian citizens or do they become Greeks in general? Or, is it possible that in foreign contexts they were also seen as non-Greeks?

To answer this question we have a good heuristic

14 Berlin, Antikensammlung 31094: *CVA* Berlin 11, 52-54, pl. 52,2; *BAPD* Vase 218149.
15 E.g. *ARV*² 274.44, 275.53, 281.27. Mantle-figures on both sides (leaving aside komos- and courting-scenes): 523.14, 525.34, 543.39bis, 543.42, 544.63-64, 548.46, 563.12 (at a herm), 570.58, 570.65 (with cock on a column), 576.43.
16 Berlin, Antikensammlung 1970.5: *BAPD* Vase 5766; Greifenhagen 1972; Heilmeyer 1988, 108, No. 10, 130 no. 1; Schefold & Jung 1988, 254-255, figs. 304a-b. cf. *ARV*² 257.11, 292.39, 531.38, 563.6, 574.11-13, 593.44.
17 Koch-Harnack 1983, 208.
18 E.g. Boston, Museum of Fine Arts 01.8073: *BAPD* Vase 203543; *ARV*² 342.19; Himmelmann 1994, 13, fig. 7 or Copenhagen, Thorvaldsen Museum 105: *BAPD* Vase 203386; *ARV*² 329.131.
19 Bergemann 1997; Scholl 2002.

Fig. 5 Two Attic red-figure skyphoi and an Alto-Adriatic jug from a grave at Numana (Photo: after Berti, Bonomi & Landolfi 1996, 92, fig. 4.3-4 and Landolfi 2000, 123, pl. X 2).

tool: the local red-figure productions, which can be seen to depend on – even to clearly imitate – Attic red-figure vases,[20] for such vessels are also commonly decorated with youths wearing cloaks as on the Attic B-sides (Fig. 5-10). The originally Athenian expression of civic identity seems, however, to become so generalised that a specific explanation of the side-B pictures is difficult. I will, however, try to give three different examples of the reception of this Attic image in Italy by Greeks and non-Greeks, starting with the Etruscans and the Piceni, and then moving to Apulia, Lucania and Paestum.

On the Adriatic coast the range of locally produced pottery comprises bell- and calyx-kraters, stamnoi, skyphoi, jugs, lekanides and stemmed plates.[21] Most of them, especially the later ones, do not have figured but only ornamental decoration. The most common motifs are not full figures but simply male and female heads; and even the reverse of the kraters shows heads more often than figured scenes. Only occasionally do figures in cloaks appear. [22]

A grave-context from Numana – for example, where imported Attic pottery, a bell-krater and three skyphoi were found together with an Alto-Adriatic red-figure jug (Fig. 5)[23] – makes it easy to study how the local imitation converted the Attic picture. All the vases show a similar figure-type completely wrapped in a cloak. The sketchy and rough execution seems to be copied from the Attic way of rendering these figures. There is only one difference. On the Alto-Adriatic jug the cloak has an ornamental border with dotted lines, a feature not known in Attic red-figure.

Here, as in other cases, it is not easy to decide whether the depicted figures are male or female. On a krater from Spina it is surely a woman with her hair put up in a knot.[24] Furthermore, if we look closely at the lower part of the figures, it seems as if a second garment is worn underneath, a feature which cannot be identified on the imported skyphoi.[25] There are only two known early imitations that can be securely said to depict men wearing no second garment underneath the cloak (Fig. 6).[26] On both of these vases this is made explicit by leaving a large blank space between the legs. These are not locally actualized versions but correct imitations of the Attic pictures. Here the patterning of the cloak is also absent.

For the Piceni in Numana and the Etruscans in Spina the mantle-figures on the imported Attic pottery would not have been taken generally as men (or women) in cloaks as they appeared in their daily experience. Indeed, it is probable that they understood the youths primarily as Athenians and the pictures as some kind of quality guarantee of Attic origin. Since they did not seek to imitate Attic costumes and customs, they cannot have seen the images on Attic vase paintings as depictions of their own way of living. Thus, on Alto-Adriatic vases one can search in vain for images of men leaning on their sticks or holding a strigilis and aryballos.

Placed together with other pots beside the deceased in the Numana grave the Attic pottery seems to indicate that he was a man of wealth, who used the best pottery on the market for his drinking parties.[27] But the stereotypes on the skyphoi and jugs function not only as quality-markers for the Attic origin, they serve also as a guide for the viewer. The generic and stereotyped motif of the picture and also the hasty and sketchy drawing give the image on the

Fig. 6: Reverse of an Alto-Adriatic red-figure bell krater. Numana 2916 (Photo: after Landolfi 2000, 123 pl. III 2).

Fig. 7: Reverse of an Apulian red-figure bell krater by the Rodin Painter. London, British Museum F60 (Photo courtesy: Trustees of the British Museum).

level of execution, a conceptional value. In other words, since the motif is easily understood there is no need for the beholder to look for a deeper meaning. And so these images on the reverse, or on minor vessels, are meant as agents in a visual hierarchy giving way to other pictures like that on the main side of the krater, which is usually more elaborate.[28]

And the consumer preference of only one main picture was growing: In the fifth century BC almost every red-figured vessel that Athens produced for drinking parties, including kraters, cups and jugs, was decorated with a great variety of motifs. But at the beginning of the fourth century BC the range of motifs on cups, skyphoi and jugs was limited to easily readable figures of athletes, women, and citizens. Now it is often only the krater that has an important image, while other vessels are secondary. And some thirty years later they were totally replaced by black-glazed pottery. At that time, during the second-half of the fourth century, there was usually only one red-figure vessel deposited in the Etruscan tombs.[29] This development shows that also the beholders in the first half of the century

20 On this method (exemplified by Bosporan watercolor-pelikai) see Langner 2005. For an recent overview on the South-Italian red-figure, see Denoyelle & Iozzo 2009; Hoffmann 2002; Denoyelle 2005; Lissarrague 2008.
21 Felletti Maj 1940; Desantis 1993; Berti, Bonomi & Landolfi 1996; Landolfi 2000.
22 E.g. Berti, Bonomi & Landolfi 1996, 37. 97-101 no. 5.01; 8.01; 9.01; Landolfi 2000, 99-100; 130 pl. X 1-4; 170 pls. II-III.
23 Numana 27082 from the Area Davanzali, grave 195: Berti, Bonomi & Landolfi 1996, 91-96 no. 04.05; Landolfi 2000, 125 pl. VIII 1-2.
24 Ferrara 12153 from Spina grave 197C: Berti, Bonomi & Landolfi 1996, 40 fig. 9.
25 Cf. also Landolfi 2000, 127 pl. X 1-3.
26 Numana 3389: Felletti Maj 1940, 63 no. 1 pl. IV 1; Landolfi 1988, 352 fig. 308; Berti, Bonomi & Landolfi 1996, 25 fig. 5. 91; Landolfi 2000, 123 pl. III 1-2. Numana 3665: Landolfi 2000, 123 pl. III 3-4.
27 Cf. Nilsson 1999.
28 This combination of vessels to sets, used during the banquets, is not limited to Spina, but can also be seen elsewhere. One may mention the burial offerings in a Scythian barrow in Novovasilevka: Fialko 2004. Even in Athens fragments of bell-kraters from houses near the north slope of the Kolonos Agoraios were found together with fragments of skyphoi decorated only with mantle-figures: Moore 1997, nos. 427 and 535 together with no. 1305 [well C 12:2]; nos. 462, 477, 480 and 492 together with no. 1298 ['foundry-pit' E 2:3]; nos. 361 and 408 together with no. 1330 [well E 13:5]; no. 400 together with no. 1275 [well B 15:1].

Fig. 8: Reverse of a Lucanian red-figure bell krater by the Amykos Painter. London, British Museum E501 (Photo courtesy: Trustees of the British Museum).

Fig. 9: Reverse of a Paestan red-figure bell krater by the Asteas Painter. London, British Museum F152 (Photo courtesy: Trustees of the British Museum).

tended to concentrate on one main picture, i.e. that of the main side of the krater, while they took the others as secondary. Therefore the typical and common decoration with youths in cloaks had two main functions: to declare the pottery as an Attic import and to direct the eye to the more important picture.

Next we will take a brief look at the development of the mantle-figure type in Apulia and Lucania (Fig. 7-8).[30] Only in the early phase of Apulian red-figure production we find some attempts to actualise the image, for example in expanding the range of objects (e.g. phiale or plates, wreaths and fillets) or persons (women, children).[31] All in all, however, the Attic way of depicting citizens was taken over and accepted. On the main sides, mantle-figures (as well as athletes) only seldom appear, and nearly always in connection with a woman. Thus a specific role model of a youth or a man as a citizen, athlete, or at a sacrifice, was mainly articulated in this context and in comparison and interaction with women.[32] For this reason the depiction of mantle-figures conversing was not seen as a typical Apulian behavior but as an adopted symbol of Greekness that was not specified any further. And the same should be stated for the red-figures from Boeotia, Corinth and the Chalcidice.[33]

In Campania and Paestum, called Poseidonia at that time, things were different. At first the Greeks living there adopted the Athenian image of being a citizen. Thus, the youths on the reverse sides are similarly depicted as in Athens, wearing their cloaks in a comparable way. Following the Athenian example the clothing is shown without embroidery (Fig. 9),[34] though on the main picture of the same vases mythological figures like Dionysos were always shown with patterned garments.[35] But nearly a generation later the figures on the reverse were given dotted borders as well (Fig. 10),[36] which Trendall called 'one of the distinguishing features of the developed Paestan style'.[37] Furthermore, they are shown wearing shoes, a feature that Attic mantle-figures usually do not have. Occasionally they look like Athenian impostors,[38] but most of them with their long curly hair and the slightly changed drapery have a totally different character, emphasizing the age

Fig. 10: Reverse of a Paestan red-figure bell krater attributed to the Python Painter. Richmond, Museum of Fine Arts 81.72 (Photo courtesy: Virginia Museum of Fine Arts, Richmond. Arthur and Margaret Glasgow Fund).

and behaviour of the youths as decent epheboi even more explicitly than was the case in Athens, where this iconographic formula is only used in certain contexts: during a sacrifice or sacrificial procession.[39] Stick and strigilis appear seldom in Paestan red-figures and are to be seen only at that early stage. More often the youths are shown holding twigs in their hands for ritual purposes, indicating that it is the religious and not so much the political aspect of civic life that is shown.

On later Paestan pottery the motif was changed, being replaced by naked youths, sitting women, or youths and women conversing.[40] Here the scenes of public behaviour were transformed into intimate scenes with some erotic content. This means that the Attic image was accepted first as the best way of presenting Greeks, as those Greeks in Apulia and elsewhere did. However, later they preferred

29 This can easily be seen in looking through the plates of Massei 1978 and the contexts given in Berti & Guzzo 1993, 267-334.
30 London, British Museum F 60 (1978.4-14.32): *RVAp* II, no. 6/196. London, British Museum E 501 (1856.12-26.8): *LCS*, no. 1/169.
31 E.g. *RVAp* II, pls. 22.2, 27.4, 37.6, 62.3, 69.2, 72.4, 80.4, 81.2, 87.4, 89.6, 90.6.
32 Hoffman 2002, 166-167.
33 E.g. Lullies 1940; Sparkes 1967; Avronidaki 2007, pls. 1-3, 83; *CVA* Berlin 11, 71, pl. 71; Herbert 1977, pls. 7-17, 32; McPhee 1981; McPhee 1983.
34 London, British Museum F 152 (1824.5-1.40): Trendall 1987, 73 no. 2/54.
35 E.g. Trendall 1987, pls. 17; 20-22; 25-31; 38a-b; 39.
36 Richmond, Museum of Fine Arts 81.72: Trendall 1987, 160 no. 2/285, pl. 104d.
37 Trendall 1987, 12, 15, fig. 2.
38 E.g. Trendall 1987, pl. 121d
39 Moore 1997, no. 22 pl. 9; Gebauer 2002, figs. 263-292.
40 E.g. Trendall 1987, pls. 194; 204-206. For the change in motifs in the Lucanian red-figure, see: Söldner 2007, 65.

their own image – that of being a Campanian or a Paestan Greek citizen – until finally they felt no need at all to broach the issue of citizenship on their vessels.

CONCLUSIONS

In his book *Hellenicity*, Jonathan Hall proclaims that the feeling of being Greek (and not an Athenian, Argive or Spartan) did not arise until the Persian Wars and that the name 'Hellenes' first occurred in this meaning during these years.[41] Indeed, it was Herodotus and the Athenian tragic poets, who proclaimed this new feeling of togetherness. But as we know from Thucydides' reports, this really meant under the hegemony of Athens.[42]

'As a city we are the school of Hellas', the Athenian statesman Perikles stated at the beginning of the Peloponnesian War (Thucydides 2.41.1), and with these words he confirmed not only the political but also the cultural primacy of Athens.[43] This self-proclaimed leadership finds its confirmation in many areas. In the course of the fifth century BC Athens took in all the leading artists, writers and philosophers. In this highly stimulating climate art-forms developed, which were motivated by the special situation in Athens. They became a classical standard in their well-balanced and suitable form, even beyond Athens: the art-form of the tragedy, for example, the creation of the Parthenonian type of temple, and the typical figure style of the Attic relief sculpture. To mention only two examples of the Athenian influence on foreign style and content, one can point to a grave-relief from the Taman Peninsula, which has obviously been done in an Attic manner and employing Attic iconography. However, the way of holding the weapons and wrapping the cloak finds no parallel on Attic tomb reliefs.[44] In addition to the style, the influence of the tragedies of Euripides on Apulian vase-painting should be remembered.[45]

The same is true, if we look at the Attic red-figure. It was considered of such extraordinary quality that it had squeezed all competition out of the market from the beginning of the fifth century. In so doing, the Athenian understanding of the gods and heroes, and their way of telling myths about them, reached to the very edges of the known world. And with them, also the way the Athenians led their lives, was exported and received.

We cannot say exactly if all Greeks wore their himatia in public all the time instead of lighter clothing, or with a second garment underneath. Nor if they regularly went out barefoot keeping their stick or their sports gear with them. But they are depicted like this, surrounding themselves – not only in public but also in their private sphere – with a huge number of pictures concerning their public life and civic mentality.[46] And that model seems to have conquered the world as Attic tragedy did. So, what we have been looking at was not the real life of a Greek citizen, but the way citizenship was put into pictures and the symbols that were connected with it.[47] In my opinion the reverse side of Attic red-figure pottery helped to spread this Attic view, until it became for most Greeks an image of all Hellenes, as the gymnasia became more and more important as symbolic places of Greek identity.[48]

---

41 Hall 2002. On the construction of Athenian civic identity see Connor 1994; Cohen 2000.
42 Zumbrunnen 2008; Low 2008.
43 Cf. Loraux 1986. On the 'cultural revolution' in Athens at the end of the fifth century see Osborne 2007.
44 Clairmont 1993, 355-356 no. 2.354; Savostina & Simon 1999.
45 Trendall 1991; Taplin 2007 with literature.
46 Hölscher 1998.
47 On the pictorial construction of reality with vase-paintings see generally Berard 1984; Hoff & Schmidt 2001.
48 Delorme 1960; Hesberg 1995; Groß-Albenhausen 2004; Hoff 2009.

Herakles and his Attic Pillars:
Iconographical Study and Socio-religious Context of the Four-column Herakleion

BY ANNIE VERBANCK-PIÉRARD

Herakles and his Attic Pillars:
Iconographical Study and Socio-religious Context of the Four-column Herakleion

BY ANNIE VERBANCK-PIÉRARD

During the last decade, Herakles has become a little old-fashioned. Several studies were published and conferences were held on Herakles and his representations in the 1980s and 1990s.[1] However, since that time, interest seems to have dwindled. Personally, I do not mind old-fashioned subjects and I have decided to come back to our good old friend Herakles for this article. Indeed, some red-figure vases and votive reliefs from the late fifth and first half of the fourth century BC with a specific Heraklean scene will enable me to develop two main topics: one is the relation to the context of production and to the cultural and religious setting of the vases and the other is the symbolic value of the iconography.

These vases and reliefs represent Herakles resting or standing in a strange and puzzling architectural setting: a four-column edifice, sometimes called the four-column Herakleion, or the four-column Heroon – which is actually worse. Since 1911, the theme has been often described and studied.[2] Unfortunately, most of the previous interpretations base themselves on a literary perception of Herakles' biography, relying on texts and not on iconographical criteria, and they often consider a priori Herakles as a hero, the hero of the Labours. In my opinion, this is a preconception and it is too restrictive when working on the many sources about Herakles in Attica[3] or other Greek cities.

A survey of the various documents on the subject of the so-called four-column Herakleion is very complex.[4] Even the iconographic definition of the edifice is problematic, since it is sometimes truncated. Moreover, the images do not answer all the questions. Is it a temporary, a permanent or a semi-permanent structure? What size is it? Is it a ritual or a scenographic element? What kind of existing building could be connected with it? Is it even a real building, or is it fictive architecture? And what would an accurate name be? As a result, I simply point out here the main trends from

Fig. 1. Calyx-krater, Caltanissetta, Museo Archeologico, inv. S 46/T28 (Photo: after Sedita Migliore 1991, fig. 85).

this interesting research, dealing first with the vases, then with the sculpture, and ending with the context.

THE VASES

The corpus[5] consists of about twenty Attic red-figure vases, some of them fragmentary, dating from approximately 420 to 350 BC. But, as noted in the previous paragraph, it is difficult to include in the list the representations of a simple white architrave with four capitals and four abridged columns hanging from it in a line, without perspective, which appears in the background of some of the scenes.[6] This element seems to have a more general meaning.[7] Among the Herakleion corpus, only five vases present a distinctive and complete tetrastyle edifice. I have selected three of them[8] for a preliminary description:

The first one is an amphora of Panathenaic shape attributed to the Talos Painter and dates around 400 BC.[9]

On side A, a young and wreathed Herakles is seated (or rather floating) in front of a four-column Doric shrine on the left of the image. This building is seen in foreshortened view and is roofed with diagonal beams. It has no pediment or doors and is topped with branches and fillets. Moreover, we can distinguish something odd on it: an inverted lebes. Athena is standing on the right, looking at Herakles. On the other side, Herakles and Iolaos are in a rushing chariot, supposedly on the way to Olympus. Linking the two sides are two wonderful Nikai under the handles of the vessel. One is flying before the chariot; she carries a thymiaterion towards A, indicating a place of a ritual action. The other Nike is about to tie a long leafy wreath.

The second is a calyx-krater from the end of the fifth century BC, which was found in the necropolis of Sabucina (grave 28) and has been attributed to the Lugano Painter (Fig. 1).[10] On the krater we find the same kind of edifice in the centre of the image, but here with Ionic columns. A young Herakles is seated on it, or in front of it, his left arm leaning on his club, which looks rather thin and unusual. On the left, a bearded man is looking at Herakles. On the right, a young woman presents a phiale to a young man with chlamys and spear. On the other side of the vase, Dionysos as a child is portrayed in a very rare (initiation?) iconography.

The third one is a calyx-krater from the beginning of the fourth century BC, which was found in the necropolis of Kanapitsa and attributed to the Plainer Group.[11] Though fragmentary, this krater offers impressive iconography. I refer here to the description by Victoria Sabetai in the *CVA*.[12] The figures are arranged on two levels. In the upper part of the scene, a young Herakles is in his columnar shrine. On the left, we can see Zeus and Hermes; above the handle, a rushing satyr. On the right are Athena and Apollo, then a satyr and a maenad. In the lower level, on the left, there is part of a naked figure painted in white, near a chest, probably Eros.[13] In the centre, just under the tetrastyle, a pile of rough stone is surrounded by laurel or olive branches and shoots; on the right is a flying Nike. Note the tripod just above her: it is related to the Pythian Apollo, of course, but it refers also to the more general idea of victory in a contest.[14] On side B, there are three naked youths shown as filleted athletes.

An initial discussion of these three large vases and then of the whole corpus will help us to determine the general scheme of the images especially the structure that has traditionally been considered a four-column Herakleion, their similarities and their main iconographical indications:

The Shrine

The scenery is dominated by the tetrastyle open shrine, most often adorned with branches. On the top, beams are shown, but there are no walls, no doors, no roof, nor a

---

1. See e.g., among many, Boardman 1972; Bérard 1987; Vollkommer 1988; Verbanck-Piérard 1989; Verbanck-Piérard 1995; Bonnet & Jourdain-Annequin 1992; Bonnet & Jourdain-Annequin 1996; Bonnet 1998. Yet, there is a recent revival.
2. Frickenhaus 1911; Walter 1937. For more recent studies, see Tagalidou 1993; Froning 1996; Carabatea 1997.
3. Verbanck-Piérard 1995.
4. I am preparing a more exhaustive study of the tetrastyle Herakleion. On the occasion of research workshops, I have had the opportunity of discussing this topic with A. Muller, at the University of Lille III, and with P. Jacquet-Rimassa, V. Pouyadou and H. Guiraud, at the University of Toulouse-le-Mirail (see *Pallas* 65, 2004, 12). I would like to thank them here for their advice and comments.
5. The most convenient list is *LIMC* IV, s.v. Herakles, nos. 1368-1374, to which can be added a krater in Caltanissetta (here fig. 1 and n. 10); a krater in Samos: *LIMC* IV, s.v. Hades, no. 69; and a fragment of an amphora in Bucarest: *CVA* Bucarest 1, pl. 32, 1.
6. As on the krater in Rome, Villa Giulia 3619: *BAPD* Vase 260023; *LIMC* IV, s.v. Herakles, no. 1372.
7. This kind of truncated façade can be found in other contexts, for example on the so-called Pourtalès krater (London, British Museum F68), devoted to the Eleusinian deities and initiates: *BAPD* Vase 218148; *ARV*^{2} 1446.1, 1693.
8. The other two vases are Ferrara, Museo Nazionale T1B VP: *LIMC* IV, s.v. Herakles, under no. 1374; and the most famous of the series Athens, National Museum 14902: *BAPD* Vase 5556; *LIMC* IV, s.v. Herakles, no. 1372.
9. Taranto, Museo Archeologico Nazionale 143544: *BAPD* Vase 41697; *LIMC* IV, s.v. Herakles, no. 1368. The names of the figures are inscribed.
10. Caltanissetta, Museo Archeologico S 46/T 28: *BAPD* Vase 28005; Froning 1996.
11. Thebes, Archaeological Museum 190: *BAPD* Vase 44252; *LIMC* IV, s.v. Herakles, no. 1370.
12. *CVA* Thebes 1, 89-91.
13. Compare other contemporary figures of Eros, for example, just near Herakles, see *LIMC* IV, s.v. Herakles, no. 3409; cf. also *LIMC* V, s.v. Herakles, 172-176 ('Herakles with Eros'). It cannot be interpreted as Hebe, who is never nude in Greek art. But the chest, Eros and the bird allude to a nuptial context.
14. The tripod, I believe, does not refer here to the Delphic struggle between Herakles and Apollo, as said in the *CVA* Thebes I, 90. The representation of a tripod has many other meanings, such as oracular power, athletic success or precious offering. In Athens, tripods were displayed either in or near the sanctuary of Dionysos as choregic monuments, after a dithyrambic victory.

Fig. 2. Bell-krater, Paris, Musée Rodin, inv. Co. 217 (Photo courtesy: Musée Rodin).

pediment, what I consider to be a discriminant criterion. The base or *krepis* consists of one or two steps, probably made of stone, but the upper part of the structure seems lighter, with wooden(?) columns and architrave.

The Vase
On a few representations, a large vase appears either on the top of the shrine or near it. It is a kind of lebes on a high stand, sometimes turned upside down. A closer observation makes it possible to discern at least two different vessel shapes: a large and rather flat open shape (Fig. 7), without handles or with small horizontal handles near the rim, and a vessel with high vertical handles, a vessel which could not be inverted. Exact parallels are not easy to find[15] and the vase could be of bronze. Names like lebes, lebes gamikos, dinos, even louterion have been suggested.

Herakles
Herakles is seated in the centre of the scene, or in the upper part. Naked and crowned, he is presented 'in glory', like a

statue. There is no narration, no movement nor action: it is a kind of epiphany.

The Attendants

Among the attendants, we can find other gods such as Athena, Zeus, Hermes, Hebe, Dionysos or Selene;[16] Nike, who is important as a symbol of victory and success; satyrs and maenads with offerings placed around Herakles; Iolaos as charioteer on the way to the Olympus; young men and women. The latter are generic figures belonging to an ideal sphere in the Meidian manner. I do not think we can always identify them as heroic figures. Young men with spears could be the Dioskouroi, but they are more than the Dioskouroi, they are the ideal of young men. Females could be Hebe and heroines, but not in the legendary meaning: they are another expression of the Heraklean gift of eternal youth. Less often we find mortals, as worshippers in some ritual action. In a single example we find a young citharist playing music in front of the shrine.

Surroundings

Some vases suggest a place like the 'land of happiness', full of bliss and light. It could be Olympus, especially if gods are present, but not necessarily. There is just a subtle celestial atmosphere; nothing is dark nor suggesting death.

Sometimes, there are clear indications of a sanctuary: not only the shrine itself, but also a column for the entrance, an altar with flames and offerings on plates. The setting seems rustic, as suggested by branches on the shrine or by sprigs growing from the ground. Moreover, the altar can be built out of a pile of rough stones, or it is just a large low block of irregular shape (Fig. 2).[17] It is not an *eschara*,[18] but just a quickly-made or improvised *bomos*. All this evokes a temporary installation and a local festival in a rural *temenos*, not well fitted out. Again, there is nothing to do with chthonic cults, *sphagia* or holocausts.

It is important to note here that these vases with the columnar shrine are just one part of a larger iconography related to Herakles' apotheosis: they belong to the many representations of Herakles as a god, or among the gods. On red-figure vases of the same period and workshops, the motif of the court scene, most often without any architectural structure, but sometimes with a *bomos*, is usual for Herakles but also for other deities, especially Dionysos, Apollo or Demeter. This is the fashionable way in which major gods are represented.[19] In the corpus studied here, the tetrastyle just seems to add a special flavour to this kind of image. Our small series does not differ from it and is not inconsistent with it. The most relevant feature of the red-figure representa-tions with the Heraklean shrine is their very close relation to contemporary votive reliefs, and they give us a good link to the study of the context.

THE RELIEFS

Attic figured votive reliefs for Herakles are not very numerous.[20] Their typology is the same for Herakles as for the other gods, with the representations of votaries (on a smaller scale) in front of the god, the victim or victims for the sacrifice (*thusia*) and sometimes an altar, more often of the *bomos* type. On a few of these Heraklean reliefs, we easily recognize our architectural structure, a kind of four column shrine. Of course, the link with cult practices is undeniable here. I have selected four reliefs from a list of nine (some of them fragmentary).

The first is from Marousi in Attica, it is made from Pentelic marble and dates to the early fourth century BC (Fig. 3).[21] The four-column Doric shrine seen in perspective view stands in the middle of the relief. Herakles is on the right and holds out his hand, or a vase (cup or kantharos), to a nude youth with a himation on his left arm, followed by a bearded worshipper.

---

15 For a fifth century lebes or dinos on stand by the Achilles Painter see Boardman 1989, fig. 116. In some images of the Adonia, we can see very large vases on stand, as on a squat lekythos in Karlsruhe, Badisches Landesmuseum B39: *BAPD* Vase 361; *CVA* Karlsruhe 1, pl. 27. See also *infra*, for the vase represented on the relief in Boston (fig. 5), on the krater in Copenhagen (Fig. 7) and on the inscribed stele found in Eleusis (n. 39-40).

16 On a fragmentary hydria in London (British Museum E 252) Selene appears as a sky-goddess: *LIMC* IV, s.v. Herakles, under no. 1374. In assemblies of gods or together with Helios, she symbolizes eternity, much more than night or chthonic powers: *LIMC* VII, s.v. Selene, 713.

17 Bell-krater, Paris, Musée Rodin Co 217 (TC1): *BAPD* Vase 218050; *ARV*² 1436, 2, Painter of Louvre G 508; in *LIMC* IV, the vase is listed s.v. Hedone no. 4, but there is no inscription to justify this association, see Laurens 1987, 69.

18 See infra n. 44.

19 Metzger 1951; Boardman 1989, 221.

20 Tagalidou 1993, 7-85; for the reliefs with tetrastyle see *LIMC* IV, s.v. Herakles, nos. 1375-1380.

21 Athens, National Archaeological Museum 2723: *LIMC* IV, s.v. Herakles, under no. 1379.

Fig. 3. Votive relief to Herakles, Athens, National Archaeological Museum, inv. 2723 (Photo: Annie Verbanck).

Fig. 4. Fragment of a votive relief to Herakles, Athens, National Archaeological Museum, inv. 1404 (Photo: Annie Verbanck).

The second fragment also dates to the early fourth century BC and is said to be from Athens or from Ithome (Fig. 4).[22] Standing on the left, Herakles is leaning slightly on his club, which rests on the upper step of the shrine. The perspective of the architrave is suggested by engraved lines. A bearded man in himation is in front of Herakles in a devotional attitude; he is leading a bull and a ram to the sacrifice. As the relief is broken, it is impossible to guess who was following this worshipper.

The third relief is said to come from Attica (Peiraeus?) and is from the early fourth century BC (Fig. 5).[23] The composition is different. Herakles in front view is indicating his small shrine. On the left part, a handsome young man with petasos and chlamys is represented. He is generally considered to be Hermes, because he is on the same scale as Herakles. His caduceus could have been painted in his left hand. But could he be the personification of an ideal ephebe? The shrine looks like a high pedestal and features a lebes with its stand, presented in a normal position, not inverted. The vase with its two horizontal curling handles recalls the shape of some sixth-century lebetes,[24] and not the contemporary lebetes gamikoi with very high double handles. So it could be an old traditional vessel. On the base, an inscription[25] mentions *Herakleou Alexikakou*, which could refer to the well-known Herakles cult in Melite, a deme in the centre of Athens, but it could have a more general meaning as well.

The fourth relief is from the mid-fourth century and is said to come from Athens (Fig. 6).[26] On the right side of the relief, Herakles is seated in front of his columnar shrine. A naked youth is standing. His left arm[27] is raised (holding a spear?). He is sometimes considered to be Theseus, but there is no decisive iconographic indicator. Between them there is an impressive plunging bull, a perfect offering for Herakles.

Let us again observe the organization of these images, together with the other examples. According to the repetitive composition of the votive reliefs, there is no detailed scenery, just the god, his votaries and some basic cultic elements:

The Shrine
The base, two front columns, sometimes the four columns, and the architrave stand out clearly against the background. Other important elements to notice are the lebes in the shrine on the Boston relief and a low altar on the Eretria relief.[28]

Fig. 5. Votive relief to Herakles Alexikakos, Boston, Museum of Fine Arts, Catharine Page Perkins Fund, 96.696 (Photo courtesy: © 2010 Museum of Fine Arts, Boston).

Herakles

Herakles is always represented as a young Polycleitan athlete. Either standing or seated, he is in close relation with the tetrastyle.

Votaries

Among the votaries (on the most complete examples), we find exclusively an elderly man with a young man, sometimes also with a male child, surely a father and his son(s).

This last observation is one of the main keys for proposing a tentative interpretation. Indeed, Herakles is shown – here and elsewhere – as the patron of young men. Moreover, the presence of the impressive vase on the Boston relief and on some vases of our corpus has suggested to many scholars a link between these representations and a special offering to Herakles, called the *oinisteria*, which is part of the famous *Apatouria* festival.

VASES, RELIEFS AND CITIZENSHIP FESTIVALS

The *Apatouria* was a very ancient festival in Attica,[29] celebrated by the phratries in the month of Pyanopsion. It was devoted to the usual tutelary gods of the phratries, Zeus Phratrios, Athena Phratria, and Apollo Patroos, and we could add Herakles, as shown on our vases and reliefs.

Fig. 6. Votive relief to Herakles, Rome, Museum Barracco, inv. 1114 (Photo: E. Richter (no. 742), Roma).

---

22 Athens, National Archaeological Museum 1404: Tagalidou 1993, 208; *LIMC* IV, sv Herakles, no. 1377.
23 Boston, Museum of Fine Arts 96.696: *LIMC* IV, s.v. Herakles, no. 1378; dimensions: 53 x 67,5 cm.
24 Boardman 1974, fig. 293. It could be a bronze vessel.
25 The inscription could have been added later, but the letters are from the same period as the relief.
26 Rome, Museum Barracco 1114: *LIMC* IV, s.v. Herakles, no. 1380.
27 Or both arms? The relief is broken here. The position is similar to the Diadoumenos statue: Boardman 1985, fig. 186a.
28 Eretria, Archaeological Museum 631: *LIMC* IV, s.v. Herakles, no. 1379.
29 Parker 1996, 104-105; Lambert 1998, 143-189.

Even if many details are controversial, the general pattern of the festival is as follows. All the related families in the different phratries gathered during three days, called *Dorpia*, *Anarrhusis* and *Koureotis*. On this last day, the children, the young men at the age of puberty (*epheboi*), and the newly-married wives were enrolled in the phratry and three specific sacrifices were offered, the *meion*, more likely for the children, the *koureion* ('haircut' or 'for the *kouroi*') for the ephebes and the *gamelia* for the young wives. Thus this was a very important day for the definition of citizenship and family links in Attica, throughout the whole history of the city.

A close link between Herakles, the *koureion* sacrifice and the *oinisteria* is well attested by a few texts and the most ancient source is a fragment by Eupolis (*Demoi*, fr. 135 Kock). According to Athenaeus (XI, 494f)[30]: *"There is the oinisteria too. The ephebes, when they are going to cut their hair, says Pamphilos,*[31] *fill a large cup with wine, and bring it to Herakles; and they call this cup an oinisteria. And when they have poured a libation, they give it to the assembled people to drink."* That the offering of 'a large cup of wine' to Herakles happens during the last day of the *Apatouria* seems to be proved by the mention of the future ephebes together, the haircut and the meeting of people assembled for this occasion. According to many scholars,[32] *oinisteria* could be the name for the large vase shown on some of the vessels and reliefs discussed here. However this is not certain, for the texts mention a large drinking cup, (*poterion*),[33] or a measure of wine, or a libation, and not a mixing vessel, like a lebes or a krater.

In the Archaic period, membership of a phratry was the sole test of citizenship, based on the principle of descent and kinship. Moreover, with his admission to the phratry, each new male Athenian was introduced not only into civil society, but also into the military contingent. Cleisthenes' democratic reforms introduced a new topographical criterion, that of deme-membership. During the Classical period, membership of demes and phratries overlapped. Each citizen, the legitimate son of a citizen, was recognized as a member of his deme and of his phratry.

However, in the second half of the fourth century, the main source concerning the official definition of an Attic citizen, Aristotle's (or the Aristotelian) *Athenaion Politeia*, XLII, only refers to the selection and inscription of the ephebes by the *demotai* and the *boule*, that is to say by the political democratic body, and not by the *phrateres*.[34] The last part of chapter XLII depicts the new organization of the ephebia by the state, for military purposes, in relation to the reforms of Lycurgus.

I believe that, even if this well-known text is later than most of our Heraklean scenes and even if Attic society has changed in the meantime, the comparison with the iconographical corpus could be significant. The written description of the Athenian Constitution does not take into account the role of the phratries. By contrast, the images never show the 'legal' selection of the ephebes, but favour the religious traditions, with a special liking for the Herakles festival, and more particularly for the four-column Herakleion. Once again, we can easily detect how Attic iconography works. Political life, with meetings, debates, and votes, never seems to have been an iconographical theme. Citizenship is described through many other themes such as war, symposion, athletics and festivals.

THE CONTEXT AND SYMBOLIC VALUE

The date, and thus the context of the vases and reliefs with the Herakleion, is another interesting aspect. As noted before, most of the representations showing the tetrastyle date back to the last decades of the fifth and the first half of the fourth century BC, that is to say during the last phase and after the Peloponnesian War and its disasters: a period during which Athens had to rebuild its identity and its social values. One of the better means to restore a coherent city, a polis, was to promote common civico-religious behaviour and to put new life into the cult practices, not only in the main sanctuaries, but even more in the small local *temene* and sacred places. Regional and family cults developed all over Attica, generally on a more modest and economic scale than for the state cults. Archaic traditions, *ta patria*, were renewed or even created in an archaistic manner. Ancient networks or brotherhoods, related to the definition of citizenship, were reinforced.

This religious revival can be detected in many documents: in literary texts as well as in inscriptions, such as the Nikomachos code (403-399 BC); in the sacrificial calendars, such as the Great *Demarchia* in Erchia (375-350 BC); or in decrees concerning phratries, like the *Demotionidai* motions (396/5 and 370-350 BC).[35] In vase-painting, cult scenes with festivals, sacrifices, feasts, court scenes around gods and goddesses, mysteries and games like the *lampadedromia* became more important.[36] The number of votive reliefs obviously increased, especially for protecting and healing gods, such as Apollo, Asklepios, Herakles, or for local heroes. All these documents illustrating beliefs and rituals reflect in their own way the political reorganization and restored civic life.

In view of this context, our vases and reliefs representing Herakles in his sanctuary are good witnesses to their contemporary setting. Some of them could have been special commissions in order to celebrate one of the most important moments in an Athenian citizen's life. They could preserve the good memory of a family feast in a little phratry *temenos* fitted for the occasion with wooden columns and beams on a stone base, and a cover of branches, near a rough altar. On a number of our vases and reliefs, the presence of an ephebe is particularly apposite (Figs. 1, 2 and 3). Moreover, on the Rodin and on the Louvre kraters, the proximity of a young woman identified as Hebe reinforces this interpretation, not only as a goddess of *ephebia* and coming of age, but as a bride, and we have noted that young wives were also celebrated and introduced during the *Koureotis* day. Concerning the monopteros, many questions remain. Is "Herakleion" a sound name for this kind of naïskos? What could have been its function? To shelter an image of the god? To invite him to the *Theoxenia*?[37] Is it suited to a rustic or urban setting, or to both?

Drinking a lot of wine would have been part of the fun, as attested by the emphasis on the old revered lebes, sometimes turned upside down when the symposion and the celebration were over. The conspicuous and prominent position of this vase, always set in the upper part of the scene, mostly on or inside the tetrastyle, is inconsistent here with the assumption of a chthonic ritual, which has sometimes been suggested because of the reversal of the vessel.[38] On an important inscription discovered in Eleusis (332/31 BC),[39] a similar vase[40] on its stand is carved in the centre of a large wreath of olive-tree leaves, and is related to two texts mentioning a *thusia* for the *theos* Herakles.[41] This epigraphical document dissociates the vase from our family Herakleion and attests its use not only in the gatherings of the phratries but also in deme-festivals for Herakles.[42]

As I have said previously, the position of the famous lebes and the visual evidence of all our images tend to prove that the Heraklean cult described here is construed as divine and not as heroic. I consider that even the low altars can be interpreted as rustic altars, made on the spot with a rock or with piled up stones.[43] We do not know what the low mound on the Eretria relief would have been called by the worshippers, but eschara is not a suitable name:[44] the Greek word implies a hole in the ground, a hearth with ashes, and not an omphalos-like hummock.[45] Even if, as for other gods, some ritual peculiarities here and there could have implied burnt offerings on a true *eschara*, the aim of the painters, sculptors and purchasers of the works presented in this case-study was to express Herakles' divine powers and triumphal destiny.[46] An objective analysis of our documents seems to rule out for good the designation of the little pergola as a heroon or fictive tomb.

---

30 Athenaeus, *The Deipnosophists*, vol. V, Books XI-XII (Loeb Classical Library), transl. C.B. Gulick.
31 Pamphilos of Alexandria, lexicographer of the first century AD.
32 See e.g. Walter 1937; Tagalidou 1993; Froning 1996; Carabatea 1997.
33 In some images, Herakles holds a cup or a kantharos; on the krater Athens, National Museum 14902 (supra n. 8), a satyr brings a Sotadean kantharos to him. Scheibler (2000) suggests that the '*mega poterion*' is a large skyphos.
34 The only allusion to the family of the ephebes is the mention of the fathers gathered by tribes in order to designate candidates for the sophronistes, see Ath.Pol. XLII, 2.
35 Verbanck-Piérard 1998; Parker 1996, 52-53, 218-220, 321-322; Lambert 1998, 95-141.
36 Boardman 1989, 167; Bentz 2007.
37 Verbanck-Piérard 1992.
38 Froning 1996, 116. On a hydria by the Washing Painter (Berlin, Antikensammlung 2394: Boardman 1989, fig. 210) with a representation of a woman on a swing, a large vase seems to be turned upside down, but here it has been put directly on the ground.
39 Coumanoudis & Gofas 1978.
40 For an illustration, see Van Straten 1979, 195 fig. 1. With high vertically attached handles, as on a krater in Athens, National Museum 14902: *LIMC* IV, s.v. Herakles, no. 1372 (supra n. 8).
41 Coumanoudis & Gofas 1978, 290-291, II, Text, l. 4-5 and passim.
42 Even if the sanctuary was located in Eleusis, there is no link with the Mysteries, nor with the sanctuary of the two Goddesses. It is a normal deme-cult. Van Straten 1979, 190-191, suggests an Eleusinian connection, which is not attested here.
43 Victoria Sabetai has judiciously suggested that the rock and the stones could refer to the idea of primitiveness and very ancient time, or even to the Golden Age or to a moment of foundation. I thank her for this interpretation.
44 Ekroth 2002, 25-59.
45 For a *thusia* on a similar omphalos-like altar: Van Straten 1995, fig. 144; ibid. 166.
46 The assertion of Froning 1996, 116: 'nella nostra serie di rappresentazioni di questo *mischkult* domina l'aspetto ctonio' cannot be accepted. I do not wish to return to the old discussion of the "pseudo-dual cults", see e.g. Lévêque & Verbanck-Piérard 1992.

Fig. 7. Bell-krater, Copenhagen, National Museum, inv. 3760 (Photo courtesy: The National Museum of Denmark, Copenhagen).

Whatever the cult practices may have been, the corpus of vases and reliefs showing a four-column building perfectly expresses the symbolic values of the Heraklean iconography in Athens, connected with youths, with athletes and with important ritual transitions. Herakles' patronage of the ephebes, during their integration into the civic and military community, was long-standing, and it continued for a long time, as proved by the famous Ephebic Oath,[47] in which he is evoked as one of the main gods of the ephebia.

The relation to a specific historical and religious context could also explain the paucity of the representations of the tetrastyle without pediment in Athens and in other Greek cities, either for Herakles or for other deities, in different periods. We can find only very few examples outside our corpus of vases and reliefs. Two other gods, Hermes and Apollo, seem to be connected with a similar structure, but the occurrences are even more exceptional and more difficult to understand.[48]

For example on a bell-krater in Kiel by the Nikias Painter[49] (420-410), a small and light canopy on a stone base is seen as a protection for a quadrangular Hermes. A sacrifice is offered in front of it. Also another puzzling case is the famous 'man in need' on the Copenhagen krater (Fig. 7).[50] The date and workshop of this vase are the same as for our Heraklean corpus. On the right edge of the image, 'our' columnar shrine, with an inverted lebes on it, is empty: does it mean the Herakleion in the deme of Melite, as an interesting article by Marilena Carabatea has argued?[51] However, the god represented as a herm in the centre of the scene is Hermes.[52] This god is not directly linked with phratries in Attica, but his patronage of athletes is well attested, side by side with Herakles, and his close iconographical relationship with the 'ephebe-figure' is often striking, especially on the Boston relief (Fig. 5), where he is depicted as an athletic youth, with short hair, wearing the ephebic garment (*petasos*, *chlamys*, even boots). Moreover Hermes is known in many Greek cities as a god who protected transitions, comings of age and initiations.[53] So, like Herakles in his four-column Herakleion, he could be related to some family or local festivals, celebrating the god of youth, integration and good luck in a modest sanctuary with a cheap temporary shelter for the herm.

A few well-known Attic classical red-figure vases and reliefs feature Apollo receiving sacrifices.[54] On the famous krater from Spina by the Kleophon Painter⁵⁵ (440-430 BC), Apollo is welcoming the procession, seated on a throne with a base, in his temple, which is depicted as a kind of sumptuous tetrastyle (two columns on the left, two columns on the right, and a simple horizontal epistyle, without roof and pediment).⁵⁶ On a bell-krater of the same date in Agrigento, Apollo is looking at the preparations of the sacrifice in his *temenos*. He is seated on a throne in his temple, suggested by two columns and a light epistyle.⁵⁷ But the most impressive example for our subject is given by an interesting Lucanian amphora of Panathenaic shape in Taranto: both sides are devoted to what seems to be a shared festival for Apollo (side A) and Artemis (side B).⁵⁸ The deities are welcoming young men and women in a rural setting or an *alsos*, perhaps for *rites de passage*. Apollo is standing on a base between two massive Doric columns carrying a heavy lintel, like a monumental doorway, without any indication of perspective. Such a propylaion would be strange and we are here surely shown the frontal view of a tetrastylon edifice. On different levels all around the shelter are: a youth with a spear, a woman with a hydria, young men and women, Erotes, laurels, deers, a tripod and two louteria, one of them just level with the architrave of the building. On the other side, a veiled woman with a torch is approaching a little shrine with a *xoanon* – in the shape of a herm – of a goddess wearing a long richly decorated chiton and a polos, likely Artemis (or maybe a nymph?⁵⁹ or Aphrodite?). This chapel, with two pilasters, is simpler and smaller than Apollo's (on the other side). Other attendants are present, with Dionysos reclining and a statue of a goddess with a torch. The general meaning of the image seems to refer to a nuptial ceremony and/or to the worship of water deities. But the presence of Apollo and the special building could suggest the role of the local Dorian phratries in transition rituals, especially for young men being integrated into the community and for young girls getting married.

Including this last vase in our corpus enables us to enlarge the argument and an exhaustive study concerning this kind of monopteros in Greek art and architecture could help to demonstrate that it is not restricted to Herakles, nor to the sole Melite sanctuary in Athens. Our four-column edifice could have existed in different places as a peculiar temporary structure linked with family gatherings and festivals more than with state cults, but not exclusively. By reviving old (or supposedly old) customs and kinship with common offering and sacrifices, such a context is in keeping with the tradition of the *frairies antiques* extolled by the French anthropologist Louis Gernet.⁶⁰

But, as I have suggested, *showing* these festivals – or a specific moment in these festivals, or a specific tutelary god – on vases and reliefs, depends on historical context and setting. In Attica, the red-figure painters and the sculptors of the last part of the fifth and first half of the fourth century had to answer the needs of the social classes

---

47 Known from a few texts and an epigraphic version, the stele found in Acharnes dates from the year 334/3 BC: Pélékidis 1962, 110-113. For the Archaic origin and meaning of the Oath: Siewert 1977. Even if the "official" organization of the Attic ephebia dates back to 336/5 BC, it is generally agreed now that it is not a creation *a nihilo*, and that, in former periods, Athenian youths (*neoi* or whatever the name) were trained before becoming hoplites and were selected by a scrutiny before their admission into the citizen body.
48 A columnar shrine is also carved on an Attic relief of the end of the fifth century (or Neo-Attic?) found in Rome and now in the Torlonia Museum 433: Boardman 1985, fig. 145. Unfortunately, the upper part of the relief (and of the edifice) is not preserved. In the shrine, the lower part of a statue of a draped god, sometimes said to be the cult statue of Asklepios, can be seen on the base between two columns.
49 Kiel, Antikensammlung B54: *BAPD* Vase 217475; *ARV*² 1334.14; *LIMC* V, s.v. Hermes, no. 121.
50 Copenhagen, National Museum 3760: *BAPD* Vase 215311; *ARV*² 1156.11, Manner of the Dinos Painter.
51 Carabatea 1997.
52 *LIMC* V, s.v. Hermes, no. 168.
53 Costa 1982. Could it be the meaning of the Copenhagen krater?
54 *LIMC* II, s.v. Apollon, nos. 952-964. Van Straten 1995, 363, Index s.v. Apollo.
55 Ferrara, Museo Nazionale 44894 (T 57 CVP): *BAPD* Vase 215141; *ARV*² 1143.1; Boardman 1989 fig. 171.
56 Because of the omphalos and the tripods, most scholars suggest the temple in Delphi, but it could refer to any temple or shrine for Pythian Apollo in Attica. There is no stylobate here to isolate the building as an independent tetrastyle. Is it supposed to suggest a pronaos? But Apollo is sitting inside.
57 Agrigento, Museo Archeologico Regionale 4688: *BAPD* Vase 30321, Kleophon Painter?; Van Straten 1995, fig. 30.
58 Taranto, Museo Archeologico Nazionale I.G. 8275, from Ceglie del Campo: Trendall 1967, p. 72, no. 369, Hamburg Painter, c. 410-380; *LIMC* II, s.v. Apollon, no. 242.
59 Compare a hydria showing a woman or deity inside a columnar structure on a high podium with offerings, which was found in a deposit of the extra-urban sanctuary of Heraklea Lucana (località Masseria Petrulla); according to M. Osanna, the sanctuary could be devoted to a nymph, Osanna 2010. I thank M. Osanna for having sent me a photograph of this vase.
60 Gernet 1928; for ritual banquets, see Walter 1937.

who ordered and used their productions in a very troubled and changing period. These people, symposiasts and worshippers, fathers of future citizens, deliberately chose to throw light on the traditional patronage of Herakles, shown as a god, either in an Olympian idyll or in a religious scenery, and decided sometimes to feature the old phratric ritual of a wine-offering to him and the evocative tetrastyle. Once again, the iconography balances the texts in a very useful way and helps us to understand more deeply, completely and subtly the cults of Classical Attica.

ACKNOWLEDGEMENTS
I would like to warmly thank Bodil Bundgaard Rasmussen for her generous invitation to the Enbom Conference, Stine Schierup and all the Copenhagen staff for their help, and the participants for their references and support. For the photographs, I am obliged to the Rodin Museum in Paris (D. Vieville, B. Garnier and A.-M. Chabot); to the Museum of Fine Arts in Boston (J. Riley); to the Caltanissetta Museum and Soprintendenza (C. Guzzone), to the National Museum of Denmark (B. Bundgaard Rasmussen). I also thank M. Osanna, Università della Basilicata, for valuable information, M. Podevin for revising my English text, A. Quertinmont (Mariemont) for the drawing of the Boston relief and S. Verbanck for his filial digital support.

The Xenophantos Chous from Kerch with Cypriot Themes

BY ADRIENNE LEZZI-HAFTER

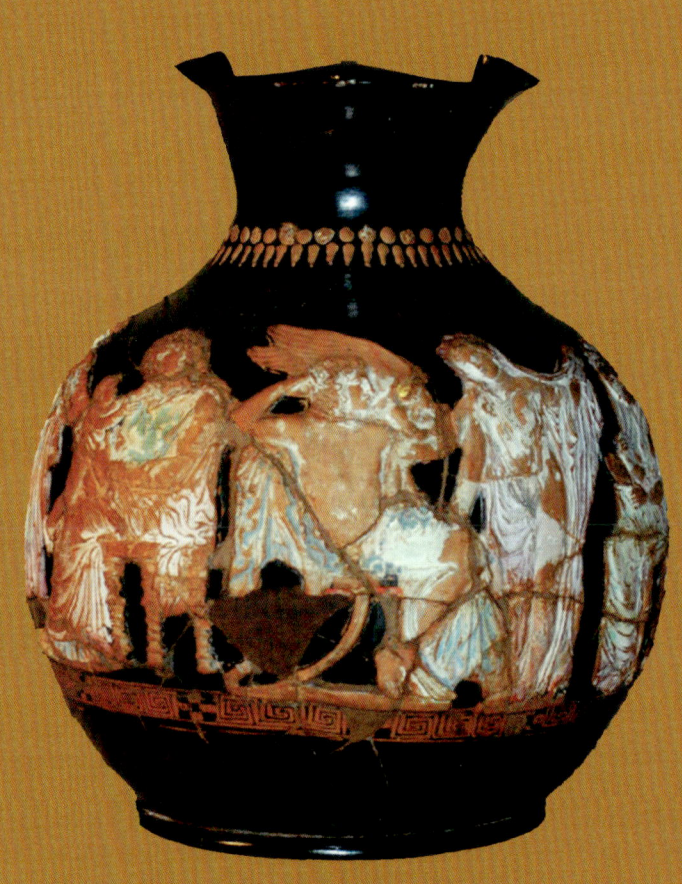

The Xenophantos Chous from Kerch with Cypriot Themes

BY ADRIENNE LEZZI-HAFTER

In addition to the two squat lekythoi signed by 'Xenophantos Athenaios' (Figs. 1-2), there is a third vase without signature (Fig. 3): a chous with figures added in relief. It was found in 1883, together with the smaller of the two signed lekythoi, in a place called Smeni Tumulus, 'Snake Tumulus', on the southern outskirts of ancient Pantikapaion (modern Kerch) in the Crimea. All three are in the Hermitage in St. Petersburg.[1]

As, at least to my knowledge, a signed chous – be it by a potter or by a painter – has not yet been found, our particular vase has not attracted the same degree of attention as its siblings. Examining the three vases – the tall squat lekythos also came to light near modern Kerch, about fifty years earlier – we recognize that the lekythoi have some relief-figure-types in common, and, as a result, depict the same theme. They are both partly painted in red-figure, whereas on the chous the red-figure technique is reduced to a mere band of maeander, and all of its figures are applied in mould-made relief. It shares with the tall lekythos only a necklace of beech-nut-like pendants, added in gilded clay.

At this particular time, the late fifth century BC, such full-size choes, over 20 cm in height, can only have been made in one Attic workshop, which I call the EAM choes-and-lekythoi workshop, after the Eretria Painter, Aison, and the Meidias Painter, and their potters respectively.[2] Consequently, it should now be called the EAMX-workshop, since the two squat lekythoi by Xenophantos and the chous were also produced in this workshop.

The chart gives an idea of how I imagine the different painters and potters to be interconnected (Fig. 4). The Eretria Painter and Aison stand as partners at the apex, but they give rise to different pupils. On the side of the Eretria Painter follows the Meidias Painter, with much Aisonian influence. In so far as the Meidias Painter seemed promising, he must have died early or have left the business for some other reason. Meidias the potter, however, is not easy to trace. Aison, having joined this workshop as a pupil of the Kodros Painter, by whom we know only one chous,[3] taught his art to the Painter of the

Fig. 1. Squat lekythos (H 38.5 cm) signed by 'Xenophantos Athenaios'. St. Petersburg, State Hermitage Museum, inv. P 1837.2 (Photo: Museum).

Frankfort Acorn and to Aristophanes who, in their turn, passed it on to the Xenophantos Painter (for the red-figure on the big squat lekythos in Fig. 1) and the Painter of the New York Centauromachy.[4] We know the names of three potters of his painter-pupils: Phintias fashioned a special shape of lekythos, the name-piece of the Painter of the

Fig. 2. Squat lekythos (H 24.6 cm) signed by 'Xenophantos Athenaios'. St. Petersburg, State Hermitage Museum, inv. SM 3. Smeni Tumulus, Pantikapaion, Crimea (Photo: author).

Fig. 3. Chous (H 22 cm) attributed to the Xenophantos workshop. St. Petersburg, State Hermitage Museum, inv. SM 4. Smeni Tumulus, Pantikapaion, Crimea (Photo: author).

Frankfort Acorn; Xenophantos signed two squat lekythoi and probably was also responsible for our chous, as the last generation of the EAMX workshop. Erginos, together with Aristophanes followed another line of Aison, the production of cups, outside our workshop.

The EAM-workshop, a generation before the addition of the X, already exported full-size choes to the Black Sea. There is a commissioned chous by the Eretria Painter found in Apollonia Pontica. It is special in regard to its shape, and in particular for the handle's plastic snake. Yet, it is still painted in an Athenian vase-painter's technique.[5]

1 a) Squat lekythos (H 38,5 cm), St. Petersburg, State Hermitage Museum P 1837.2: *ARV*² 1407,1; *BAPD* Vase 217907. b) Squat lekythos (H 24,6 cm), St. Petersburg, State Hermitage Museum SM 3: *ARV*² 1407 bottom; *BAPD* Vase 217908. c) Chous (H 22,0 cm), St. Petersburg, State Hermitage Museum SM 4: Zervoudaki 1968, 32, no. 59 with older lit., 49 and pl. 3,1-2, pl. 4,3 (she speaks of it as a 'Choenkännchen', that is a small chous meant for children, which it is not); Kopcke 1969, 545-551, 547, Abb. 2-5. About 400 B.C. For the findspots: of a) see Gerhard 1856, 163, n. 1: "Gefunden 1836 im Garten Dubrux, anderthalb Wersten nördlich von Kertsch." Of b) and c) see Tiverios 1997, 269-284, 281, n. 2: "Von Kondakow bei Ausgrabungen in Zminyj Kurgan südlich von Pantikapaion entdeckt, vgl. A. Wassiltchikoff, CR Pétersbourg 1883/1884, XXXVIff."
2 Lezzi-Hafter 1988, chapters VII (choes) and VIII (squat lekythoi).
3 Oxford V 534, Lezzi-Hafter 1988, 190-191, pl. 195a, there attributed to the Kodros Painter, whereas Beazley, *ARV*², 1258,1 put it "more or less akin to the Eretria Painter."
4 See Kathariou, 2007a.
5 Lezzi-Hafter 1997, 353-369, especially 353-359.

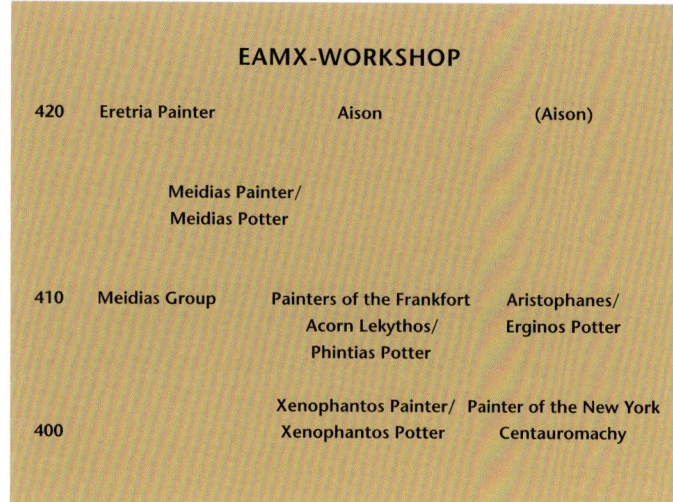

Fig. 4. Proposed scheme of EAMX-workshop.

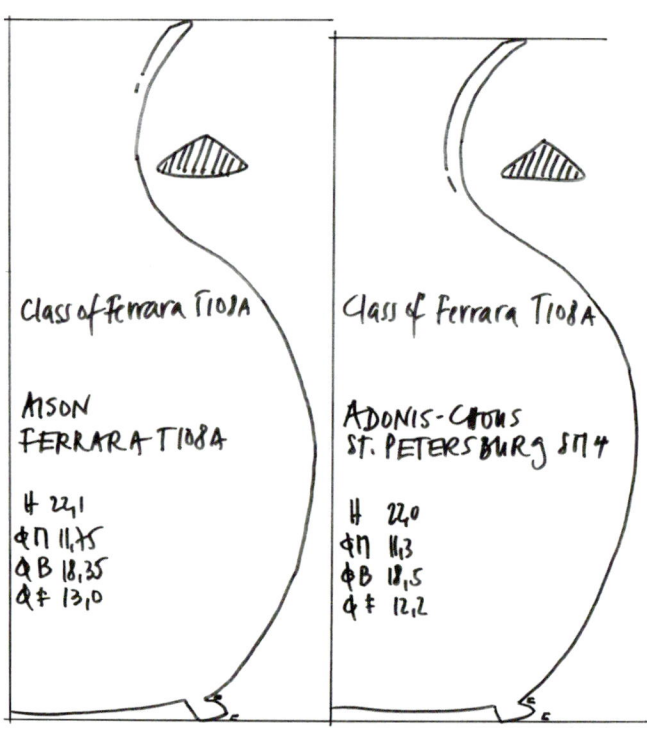

Fig. 5. Profiles of a chous by Aison in Ferrara and the Xenophantos chous in St. Petersburg (Drawings: author).

If we compare the Pantikapaion chous with one from Spina painted by Aison, the similarity in their proportions is evident, although they are about twenty years apart in date. As for the profiles, they have in common the small foot, a mark of this workshop, and the extreme lightness of fabric (Fig. 5).[6]

Once the clay figures adhered firmly to the surface of the vase, they were covered with a white slip and the garments decorated with turquoise, red and pink (Fig. 6a). The exposed flesh remained white: black for eyes, red for lips, and golden hair. Starting on the left, a beardless man stands leaning on a stick and contemplates calmly the scene before him. A maternal woman sits on a stool. She leans over to welcome a boy of about two or three years of age into her arms. The boy seems to be naked and rests one knee in her lap. Both the man and the boy have their names written in white above their heads: it is uncle and nephew, TEUKROS and EURYSAKES. Teukros was a (half-)brother of the Salaminian Ajax, who, while besieging Troy, had a son, Eurysakes, by Tekmessa. As Teukros returned from war with Eurysakes, but without Ajax, he was expelled by their father Telamon from Salamis. As a result, he made his way to Cyprus to found another Salamis and took the boy with him.[7]

Ever since this chous was first mentioned in a publication, the *Meisterwerke der griechischen Plastik* by Adolf Furtwängler in 1893, who described the figures as "von wunderbarer Schönheit und einem dem Parthenonfriese gleichartigen Stile", and who proposed to identify the seated woman as Tekmessa, the widow of Ajax, this name has lasted through the years. As logical as this proposition may seem, we know little about the fate of Tekmessa after the Trojan War.[8]

When I studied the vase in the Hermitage, I saw that the woman had a name of her own, which is not Tekmessa (Fig. 6b): it starts with a kappa and ends with omikron and sigma. At first, I thought that it might be a late, but very rare occurrence of a kalos-inscription, possibly praising Teukros. I left the question open until the visit of Ian McPhee, who, without hesitation, proposed to restore the name as KYPROS, as the personified island. The spacing seems to adapt much better to a word of five instead of four letters. And it makes sense. The little child will find a new home (and kingdom), greater than his native Salamis: indeed, were we to imagine Kypros as standing, she would tower over all the other persons present. Personifications were popular at that time: numerous are the personifications of abstract ideas, less common the

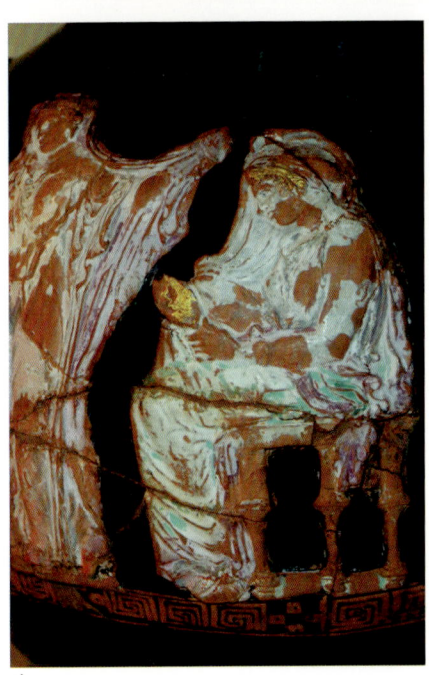

Fig. 6a-d. Details of the Xenophantos chous in St. Petersburg (Photo: author).

personification of an island, let alone the far away Cyprus, which, as a female figure, is rarely attested.[9] Our Kypros seems to be the earliest occurrence.

to give it to Aison.

7 For Teukros and Eurysakes, see *LIMC* VIII, 1195, s.v. Teukros II (O. Touchefeu-Meynier).

8 Furtwängler 1893, 487; *LIMC* VIII, 1197, no. 12, the Xenophantos chous; cf. also *LIMC* VII, 1994, 852, s.v. Tekmessa (J. Boardman).

9 For Kypros, see *LIMC* VII, 166, Pl. 77 (V. Tatton-Brown) and *LIMC* Suppl. 1, 318 with two more examples (D. Michaelides). The New York calice: Bühl 1995, 122-123; for 'Kypris' as an epitheton for Aphrodite, see e.g. the pelike by the Dareios Painter, ex Malibu, J. Paul Getty Museum: *CVA* 4, pls. 198,1 and 200,1; Godart & De Caro 2007, 100-101 (reference owed to J.R. Guy).

---

6 See Lezzi-Hafter 1988, 197 and the scheme on 190, Class of Ferrara T 108A. For the chous in Ferrara T 108A, see 195, no. 222; in *ARV*² 1313,12 Beazley attributed the chous to the Meidias Painter, I prefer

Fig. 7. Paris, inv. MNB2109 (Photo: author).

Fig. 8. Berlin, inv. F2705 (Drawing: by author after AZ 1879, pl. 10).

With the personification of Cyprus dominating the scene, it does not come as a surprise that the remaining figures are imbued with a Cypriot flavour.

Teukros, once in Cyprus, married into the family of king Kinyras. That king had an incestuous liaison with his daughter Myrrhe, who, having been turned into a Myrrh tree, gave 'birth' to the great hunter Adonis. Teukros and Adonis became brothers-in-law, and uncle and nephew at the same time.

When the goddess of love, with a keen eye for beautiful young men, saw Adonis, she decided to seduce him. The tradition goes that the meeting took place in the hills of Mount Lebanon, but on this Attic vase the location must be Cyprus, her island.

On the right side of the chous we see Aphrodite (ΑΦRODITTH) sitting on a stool, elaborately made up, anxiously inspecting herself in a mirror (Fig. 6d). Meanwhile she has sent out her other self, Peitho (ΡΕΙΘΟ), the personification of persuasion, to convince the young man to meet the goddess (Fig. 6c). In an inviting gesture she points towards her mistress, revealing the physical beauties of a woman's body shining through her closely fitting chiton. She is assisted by Eros, confidently leaning on the arm and hip of Adonis, looking towards her and the goddess – the affair has already taken wing. Adonis (ΑDΩNIOS) sits leisurely on a klismos awaiting the advances to come.[11]

This three-figure relief is closely interwoven in a way rarely

Here, workshop connections reveal their importance. On a cup in Warsaw by the Eretria Painter we find, in a Dionysiac context, isles personified: Euboia, Lemnos and Delos, a mixture of male and female. The notion of personifying an island was thus not exceptional to this vase-painter, nor was it, as we now propose, to the coroplast of the Xenophantos chous.[10]

Fig. 9. Ex Berlin, inv F2706 (Drawing: after Wehgartner 1987, 189).

Fig. 10. Adonis paired with Aphrodite. Florence, inv. 81948 (Photo: after Esposito & De Tommaso 1993, 80).

seen in vase-painting, and gives an intimate picture of three people touching each other tenderly: Peitho's hand rests on Adonis's knee, Adonis's left arm lies on her shoulder, and Eros, in his primary role as god of love, embodies the very essence of the scene. He is the only participant who is not named.

Again, the figures are richly coloured over a white slip: turquoise, pink, red, gold, and touches of black glaze other than eyes (as on the klismos) which show the novelty of the procedure.

The moment the coroplast chose to depict is the amorous encounter. The premature death of the youth is still in the future; there is not a hint of any cult practices so familiar in Athens during the last decades of the fifth century. It is the best of all moments in Adonis's life.

Five contemporary vases depict this agreeable moment, including ours. Needless to say, the five were made in the same EAMX- workshop. Aison first (Fig. 7): Aphrodite and Adonis in eye-contact, served by Eros, in the company of two women, one of whom is labelled Paidia, the playful. The second, by the Painter of the Frankfort Acorn (Fig. 8): Adonis in close mouth-contact with Eros, in the company of Eunomia and Eukleia, good law and good fame; Aphrodite is absent. The third, sadly lost, by Aristophanes (Fig. 9): Adonis with Eros on his lap, in the company of two women. According to old publications, there are no inscriptions.[12] The most elaborate illustration of this mythical moment is, of course, by the Meidias Painter (Fig. 10). By now, the goddess and Adonis must already be lovers, enjoying one another's company in the presence of Aphrodite's retinue. Nearby Pannychis (through the whole night) speaks for herself.[13]

At the end of the fifth century, Adonis is quite popular and seen as a Greek: there is nothing oriental about him.

---

10 See Lezzi-Hafter 1988, pl. 57c-d.
11 Aphrodite with two tt's, and Adonis written Adonios. Adonios appears as such on the kalpis by the Meidias Painter, see below, n. 13. For Adonis in general, see *LIMC* I, 222, s.v. Adonis (B. Servais-Soyez), as Adonis 9 our chous; Borg 2002, 172-187; Shapiro 2009b, 236-263, especially 238-250. For Peitho, see Shapiro 1993a, 186-207, s.v. Peitho.
12 Aison: squat lekythos Paris, Louvre MNB2109: *ARV²* 1175,12, *LIMC* I, pl. 161, Adonis 8. Painter of the Frankfort Acorn: Tallboy lekythos, Berlin, Antikensammlung F2705: *ARV²* 1317,1; Wehgartner 1987, 185-197. Aristophanes: ex Berlin F2706: *ARV²* 1319,5, Wehgartner 1987, 189, fig. 4.
13 Meidias Painter: Kalpis Florence, Museo Archeologico Etrusco 81947: *ARV²* 1312,1. See Borg 2002 and Shapiro 2009b. Verbanck-Piérard & Massar 2008, 207-210.

Fig. 11. Golden necklace from Seven Brothers Kurgan in comparison with detail of the Xenophantos chous (Photo: after Williams & Ogden 1994, 129).

Teukros, on the other hand, appears only here – he and Adonis are paired uniquely on this chous. The common element is KYPROS, both as a mythical figure and as the location of the scenes depicted.

We have put the Adonis-chous in its ancient context, with regard to workshop tradition. The potting, the painting, the iconography are all still conceived from the point of view of a traditional vase shop-owner of the fifth century. Elements remain of the 'old' style, as in the maeander employed in the EAMX-workshop.[14] Its outer appearances, however, have changed, perhaps as a concession to the 'Barbarians' of the Black Sea who adored silver and gold vessels with embossed decoration. The figures were taken from moulds, creating thereby a wholly new species. It remains an open question though, whether the coroplast is identical with either Xenophantos or the Xenophantos Painter or might have been an artist of his own.

Our workshop already had some experience in three-dimensional figures and terracotta-like additions: the examples are a late figure-lekythos with the workshop's red-figure ornament, the plastic part painted in a way similar to that of the plastic head of Aphrodite on the epinetron by the Eretria Painter, that is, not yet with the full range of matt colours as seen on our chous.[15]

In her study of the relief vases, Eos Zervoudaki has the Xenophantos workshop continue well into the fourth century.[16] The shapes, squat lekythoi and choes, are somewhat altered in profile and much diminished in size. Soon, also the themes, with Xenophantos rather elaborate, are being reduced to a small number of repeated relief-figure scenes. A subject such as ours is not to be found among them.

As I noted at the beginning of this paper, the three vases by Xenophantos were found in the 19th century in the area of Pantikapaion in the Crimea (Fig. 1-3). Unfortunately the exact circumstances are not known, at least not to me. All three are exceptional vases and must have found their way together to the East around 400 BC. The figures on the lekythoi tell us of a hunt in a Persian *paradeisos* – involving historical figures of the time, those on the chous of two mythical Cypriot events. The iconography of our three vases, though obviously taken from the East, is thoroughly Attic of the latest fashion. The vase shapes do not hint at Persian or Cypriot models; they, too, are thoroughly Attic. As far as I am able to judge from the other Attic finds from the Crimea, the vase shapes, as a rule, do not adopt any Eastern features, as they sometimes did further west in Bulgaria, ancient Thrace.[17]

Our three vases were purchased in Pantikapaion, the major city of the Bosporan kingdom. The people of this Black Sea town were neither Persians nor under Persian dominion, let alone that of Cyprus. The people of

Pantikapaion, as inhabitants of a Milesian colony, were partly Greek, and, as we are told, must have also been of Scytho-Thracian extraction, albeit strongly Hellenised. The Bosporan kings even sent their sons for education to Athens. The Panticapaians who bought, on the one hand, the big tallboy-lekythos and, on the other, the smaller squat lekythos together with the chous, wished to possess exclusive Attic products, in accordance with their conspicuous wealth.[18]

The fame of the gilded silverware with chased figure work and the beautiful jewellery which was made along the shores of the Black Sea, often by Greek silversmiths, had spread to Athens, where, in the EAMX-workshop, now presided over by Xenophantos, it was decided to imitate silverwork of the East in clay.

The workshop in the Kerameikos did not stint in adding gold leaf and applied a wide range of matt colours after firing. By adding matt colours they moved away from the elegant, but somewhat cold feel of gilt silver vessels, finding a style of their own.

A last look at the necklaces: the chous and the big lekythos both feature imitations of gold necklaces which are found in graves on both sides of the Crimean Bosporus (Fig. 11).[19] Both vase shapes were used by men and women. A necklace made for a woman combined with a hunt, a necklace on top of the heads of Kypros and Adonis? This, in my opinion, is an eccentric 'gift' for wealthy Easterners, to make the vases look richer.

There remains the question of the signature.[20] Xenophantos signed the big lekythos as 'epoiesen', stressing the point of being 'Athen(aios)'. He signed the smaller lekythos likewise.

The 'Athenaios', discussed now for over a century, was taken as a sign of Xenophantos having moved to the Crimea and having produced the three vases there. In fact, there are no other vases or vase-fragments from this workshop-phase known to me. The succeeding products have proveniences ranging from the Black Sea to Greece to Italy, and they are not signed. Between the Xenophantos vases and the smaller and later versions there must be a time gap.

The 'Athenaios' of Xenophantos has in the meantime been joined by another 'Athenaios', a generation earlier, this time applied to a lekythos painted by the Painter of the Frankfort Acorn: PHINTIA I ATHENAIOI I EPOE I, the Athenian Phintias potted [this]. Xenophantos, the 'one who appears as stranger', may have needed the epithet 'Athenaios', certainly more than Phintias with his Athenian name, whose vase probably never left Attica in antiquity.[21] Imagining Xenophantos with his entire team loading a ship with clay – and the clay of the three vases is thoroughly Attic – with all his tools and moulds, is not convincing. In my mind, Xenophantos must have stayed at home and executed this challenging order from the East in his accustomed environment; the same way as this workshop functioned a generation earlier, as is attested by its exports to eastern Thrace. In late fifth century Athens, Persians and images of Adonis were 'in the air'. If Xenophantos had travelled all the way to Pantikapaion, he probably would have chosen a local theme, his new abode for example, or disclosed his being abroad in some other way.

The Kerameikos artisans clearly knew their customers' taste, be they in the West or in the East. Here, the EAMX-workshop imitated metalwork and spared no expense. For depiction it chose Eastern themes and expressed them in its own Greek stylistic language, enhanced further by the addition 'Athenaios' in the signature. Some Bosporans, probably members of the Royal family, were enticed to accept an iconography which was not theirs, but made them dream an Attic dream of a vast and thrilling world abroad.

---

14 Cf. for the meander the tallboy lekythos by the Painter of the Frankfort Acorn in Malibu, J.P. Getty Museum 91.AE.10: *ARV*² 1317,3; Cohen 2006, 133-134, no. 34.
15 Epinetron in Athens, National Museum 1629: *ARV*² 1250,34; Lezzi-Hafter 1988, pl. 168, and 255 for the description of its colours, when found, and 256 for the conservative style of the bust. Figure lekythos in London, British Museum 1893.11-3.4: Lezzi-Hafter 1976, pl. 173c-d. For the interaction of metal and clay, see e.g. Barr-Sharrar 1990, 31-36; idem 32, fig. 20 is our chous.
16 Zervoudaki 1968, 49-50.
17 See above, n. 5. and Oakley 2009a.
18 See, e.g. Fornasier & Böttger 2002, 26-29; Trofimova 2007, especially 131-134.
19 For such a necklace, see Trofimova 2007, 216-217.
20 See Tiverios 1997, 275-276; Viviers 2006, 141-154, especially 147-148, 150, 152.
21 Frankfort, Liebighaus 538: *ARV*² 1319,1; *CVA* 2, pl. 81, and 33 (drawing of the signature); Flashar & Wohlfeil 2003, no. 187. I thank M. Flashar for looking up Furtwängler's lists of his collection: unfortunately there is no provenience given, but Greece seems likely. For the older Phintias, see Cohen 2006, 266-267; signature on the rim.

ADDENDUM

In spring 2011 I was shown (in photographs) an Attic red-figure pelike on the market. Stylistically it belongs to the Meidian workshop and can be dated 420 B.C. It is some 30 cms high and in perfect shape. On its obverse there is, on two levels, the depiction of Adonis and Aphrodite, banqueting together, yet another moment in their relationship.

Above, from left to right, stands a woman holding an open wreath, hidden by a tree which, together with a second tree growing symmetrically from the other side, marks a shady pergola (as on the Meidias kalpis) in which is situated a kline. The goddess is seated at its end, turning around towards the leisurely outstretched Adonis who is tuning his lyre. He is wreathed by a hovering Eros. On the right of the grove, sits a woman holding a chest.

Below, five more women of the goddess's retinue are busy tying a sandal, proffering a chest; one carries a plate full of fruit (as on the Berlin tallboy), one holds an open wreath. In the centre, with a thymiaterion in her back, sits one, taller than her companions, and holds out a broken twig of myrtle. This, according to the studies of Erika Kunze (Myrte als Attribut und Ornament auf attischen Vasen, 2006, 70-84), symbolizes the unhappily ending love affair between Aphrodite and Adonis. Apparently, there are no inscriptions.

ACKNOWLEDGEMENTS

I would like to thank Bodil Bundgaard Rasmussen for inviting me to take part in the Enbom Workshop; Stine Schierup for preparing this publication. My warmest thanks go to the curators of the Hermitage in St. Petersburg, Alexander M. Butyagin and Dimitri Chistov. I also thank Anastasia Mikliaeva for permission to publish the Hermitage vases. I plan to write an essay on the three 'X-vases.' Robert Guy patiently corrected my English, for which I am much indebted to him.

White-ground Cups in Fifth-century Graves: A Distinctive Class of Burial Offerings in Classical Athens?

BY ATHENA TSINGARIDA

White-ground Cups in Fifth-century Graves:
A Distinctive Class of Burial Offerings in Classical Athens?

BY ATHENA TSINGARIDA

Following the increasing scholarly interest in archaeological contexts and the distribution of ancient Greek figure-decorated pottery, several recent studies have laid emphasis on the reception of images on Greek vases in local and export markets.[1] Most scholars have agreed on the large variety of meanings that might be given by customers to the iconography of the widely distributed Attic vases, the latter often seen as part of intercultural exchanges. Yet, since the study of T.B.L. Webster,[2] the part played by the image in the deliberate choice made by the purchaser for specific pots has been the subject of wide debate.[3] Common subjects on vases are not seen to respond to any special demand on either the home or the export market, and most studies acknowledge that shape is more important when catering overseas markets.[4]

While it might be difficult to demonstrate special commissioned iconography for vases found in areas distant from their place of production, the question becomes relevant when it concerns pottery with subjects outside the usual range addressing a local clientele. A few Attic white-ground cups, decorated in outline technique by red-figure painters and dated from the early to the third quarter of the fifth century BC, serve as special offerings in some Attic graves. Because of their rare iconographical themes and their elaborate style and technique, they form a coherent group of really individual, and thus potentially personal, objects from grave contexts. In this paper, I would like to discuss their iconography and shapes to understand the reasons for their funerary use, and investigate if these vases were specially made, or even commissioned, for such a purpose.

THE 'SOTADES TOMB'

Any study on Attic white-ground cups has to deal with the delicate polychrome (white-ground, black-glazed and coral-red) vases found together in one and the same Athenian tomb, named the 'Sotades Tomb' after the potter who signed at least four of these vessels.[5] Since the seminal article of Lucilla Burn, who reconstructed and discussed the archaeological assemblage of the grave,[6] which was dispersed at the van Branteghem sale in 1892,[7] several studies focused on different aspects of this exceptional burial.[8] For the purpose of this paper, it is worth recalling here the known components of this pottery service, while also summarizing the conclusions of previous authors about the distinctive iconography and shapes of the vases, and, eventually, their deliberate links.

In the 1892 sale, nine pieces were initially associated with the find: five white-ground cups with wishbone handles, two horizontally fluted phialai and two horizontally fluted mastoi. Following documentary evidence, it was further possible to add to this original assemblage a sixth white-ground cup with wishbone handles, once adorned with a nineteenth-century picture inside that is now partially removed.[9] Thus, as far as we know, the tomb contained ten vases, attributed to the Sotades workshop on the basis of drawing, potter's work and signatures.[10]

In terms of the potter's work, all vases display special shapes and techniques of decoration. The pair of mesomphalic phialai, signed *Sotades epoie*, do not simply derive from Near Eastern metallic models, as generally this shape does in the Greek repertoire, but the phialai also display horizontal ribbing that suggest strong connections with foreign, most probably, Achaemenid metalware (Fig. 1).[11] The phiale in Boston further bears an exceptional feature: a clay cicada, mold-made and worked with handle-tooled details on its surface, is perched on the omphalos.[12] The pair of mastoi are made according to the same principles as the two phialai: horizontal flutes on the outside painted red, white and black, and added white-ground on the inside.[13] The cups, three stemmed and three stemless, use combinations of white-ground and coral-red techniques. They are all designed with the same thin walls, delicate and distinctive wishbone handles with purple studs. These features are extremely rare in Attic pottery, and also clearly allude to metallic prototypes.[14]

---

1 See the third part 'Formation', in: Schmidt & Oakley 2009, 135-177; Paleothodoros 2009, 45-62; Rystedt 2006, 499-506.
2 Webster 1972.

Fig. 1. Ribbed phiale. London, British Museum (Photo courtesy: British Museum, London).

Fig. 2. Polyeidos and Glaukos. London, British Museum GR 1894.7 - 18.2 (BM Cat. Vases D5) (Photo courtesy: British Museum, London).

3 Supporting the idea of iconography shaped by a specific demand: Maggiani 1997. Contra, J. Boardman's summary on the question (Boardman 2001, 226-239), and the discussion by Stissi (Stissi 2009, 21-36).

4 For the importance of shape in the Etruscan market see for instance, Spivey 1991, 131-150; Reusser 2002.

5 The name was first applied by Burn 1985, 100.

6 Burn 1985, 93-105.

7 Fröhner 1892, nos. 159-167.

8 Williams 2004, 95-120, especially 106-112; Williams 2006, 291-300; Tsingarida 2002, 245-273; Tsingarida 2003, 67-74.

9 Boston, Museum of Fine Arts 13.4503: ARV^2, 771.bottom; *BAPD* Vase 209541, and most recently Cohen 2006, no. 91, 302-303. For the addition of the tenth cup, see Tsingarida 2003, 67; Archives Stiftung Weimarer Klassik GSA 107/228 [2]: Letter of A. Van Branteghem to W. Fröhner, where he reports that the cup comes from the same grave as the nine vases, formerly in his collection; cf. Williams 2004, 107-108 (independently, on different evidence).

10 For a discussion on the workshop connections, see Williams 2006, 296-298.

11 Miller 1997, 38-139 and n. 17, pl. 37.

12 Boston, Museum of Fine Arts 98.886: ARV^2, 772; *BAPD* Vase 209544; Cohen 2006, no. 96, 311-131.

13 London, British Museum GR 1894.7-19.4 (BM Cat. Vases D10) and 1894.7-19.3 (BM Cat. Vases D9): ARV^2, 773.top; *BAPD* Vase 209549-50; Cohen 2006, 315-316, nos. 98-99.

14 For parallels and a brief history of the development of the shape in Attic pottery see Ramage 1983, 453-460, pl. 454; Hoffmann 1997, 119.

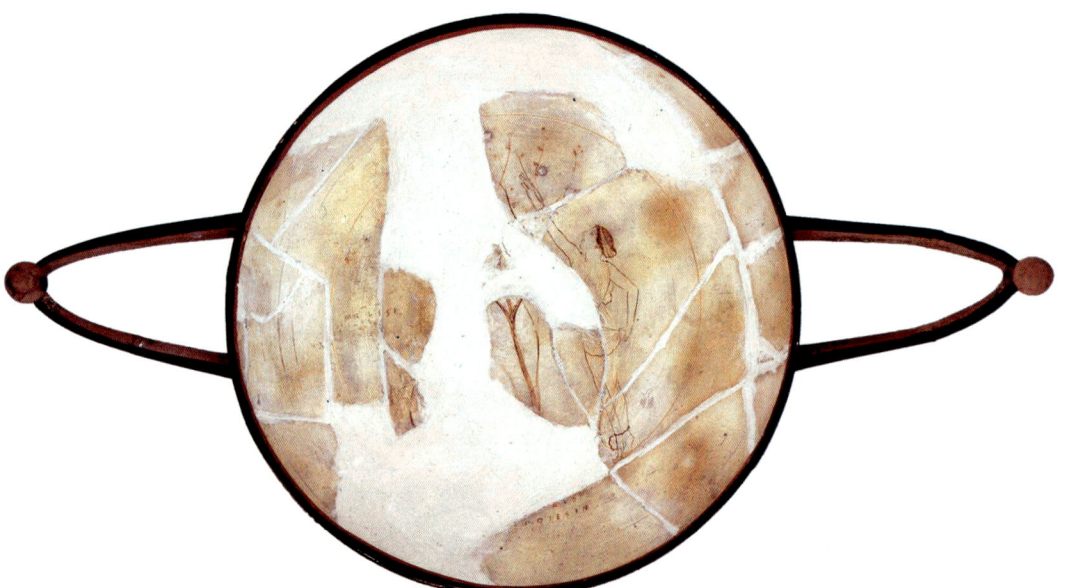

Fig. 3. Melissa picking up apples. London, British Museum GR 1894.7 - 18.1 (BM Cat. Vases D6) (Photo courtesy: British Museum, London).

Following their shape and use of special techniques, the vases fall into two trios and two pairs.[15] The trios are made from three stemmed and three stemless cups that display a similar exterior colour combination, one cup is black-glazed and the two others are coral-red. The pairs of phialai and mastoi are designed with black, white and red ridges. Evidence also suggests that iconographical choices may be significant, deliberate and linked. Three cups, now in the British Museum, do not form a group regarding their shape (two stemmed and one stemless) but are clearly related through iconography. In her article, L. Burn pointed to the honey, death and afterlife connections of the scenes:[16] Glaukos drowned in honey is reanimated by Polyeidos (Fig. 2);[17] Melissa, the honey-nymph picking up apples, often identified as the Hesperides (Fig. 3);[18] and Aristaios, the first bee-keeper, with the dying Eurydice, wife of Orpheus, also clearly alludes to the hope in the afterlife (Fig. 4).[19] The identity of the latter scene, previously disputed, is now confirmed by Dyfri Williams through the reading of two remaining letters that might spell the beginning of the name Aristaios.[20] The two cups in Brussels are also complementary since they share rare genre scenes of a woman with a baby (Fig. 5) and a girl with a spinning top (Fig. 6).[21] They have been seen as evidence of the female gender of the deceased. Regarding the imagery of the Sotades cups, already studied by L. Burn, I would like to add another link: the allusion to oracular practices and to divination. The main figures are known as seers, mantes. Polyeidos finds Glaukos through the art of divination and transmits it to him, Aristaios and Melissa are both known for their oracular abilities.[22]

The various views of death, afterlife, divination and honey of the imagery find further echoes in some aspects of the potter's work. It was convincingly noted that the ribbed mastoi had to be displayed up-side-down on their rims and might, therefore, have looked like beehives.[23] The three colours – white, red and black – of the vessels recall the changing colours of the calf in the story of Glaukos, symbolically explained by Polyeidos in terms of the life-cycle of the mulberry.[24] The cicada perched on the Boston phiale is generally acknowledged as a reference to Athenian *autochthony* but also to afterlife since it is born from the earth.[25]

Such underlying connections throughout the pottery assemblage of the Sotades Tomb suggest that it was, at least, chosen if not commissioned as a set to be deposited in a grave. This question will be discussed in a later section of this article.

Fig. 4. Aristaios and Eurydice. London, British Museum GR 1894.7 - 18.3 (BM Cat. Vases D7) (Photo courtesy: British Museum, London).

OTHER WHITE-GROUND CUPS AS BURIALS OFFERINGS

Scholars laid emphasis on the distinctive features of the Sotades Tomb for its material strongly differs from the vases characteristic of contemporary Attic burials such as the white-ground lekythoi, or the standard domestic vessels (e.g. black-glazed or plain cups, bowls or jugs).[26] Yet, the Sotades tomb is not unique. Setting to one side the white-ground cups from Etruscan burials, which certainly respond to the taste of the Etruscan elite for rare and exceptional pieces to be offered to the dead,[27] from around the 480s several cups and phialai were deposited in tombs located in mainland Greece.[28] Most known vessels come from Attica and its environs,[29] while I know of only one piece that has, until now, been found far from this area, in a grave in Kameiros (Rhodos) (Fig. 7).[30]

Although we lack information about the rest of the archaeological assemblage of these tombs, the vases also appear to be special offerings in terms of potter's work, techniques of decoration and vase-painter's achievements. From the known cases, iconography seems to be specifically chosen to show mythical figures closely related with oracular practices and mystery cults.

15 Williams 2004, 109.
16 Burn 1985, 93-105.
17 London, British Museum GR 1894.7-18.2 (BM Cat. Vases D5): ARV^2, 763.2 and 772; *BAPD* Vase 209459; Cohen 2006, 304-305, no. 92.
18 London, British Museum GR 1894.7-18.1 (BM Cat. Vases D6): ARV^2, 763.1, 772a and 1669; *BAPD* Vase 209458; Cohen 2006, 300-301, no. 90.
19 London, British Museum GR 1894.7-18.3 (BM Cat. Vases D7: ARV^2, 763.3; *BAPD* Vase 209460; Cohen 2006, 306-307, no. 93.
20 Williams 2004, 110-112; Williams 2006, 294-295.
21 Brussels, Musées Royaux d'Art et d'Histoire A891: ARV^2, 771.2; *BAPD* Vase 209537; Cohen 2006, 308-309, no. 94. Brussels, Musées Royaux d'Art et d'Histoire A890: ARV^2, 771.1; *BAPD* Vase 209536; Cohen 2006, 310-311, no. 95. For a discussion about the scenes, see Tsingarida 2003, 70-71.
22 Tsingarida 2003, 70; for the allusion to divination in the iconography of the Sotades Painter, see Hoffmann 1997, 119-140.
23 Williams 2004, 112.
24 Burn 1985, 100.
25 Thucydides I, 6; Aristophanes, *Knights* 1331; Suidas s.v. Tettigophoroi. Further see Hoffmann 1997, 116-118.
26 Kurtz & Boardman 1971, 100-105.
27 About exceptional Attic vases in Etruscan graves, see Reusser 2002; Tsingarida *forthcoming*.
28 For the distribution of white-ground cups, see Tsingarida 2008, 199-204.
29 For the location and references of the vases located on the distribution map, see Tsingarida 2008, 200-201.
30 London, British Museum GR 1864.10-7.77 (BM Cat Vases D2): ARV^2 862.22, and 1580.bottom; *BAPD* Vase 211350.

Fig. 5. Woman with a baby. Brussels, Musées royaux d'Art et d'Histoire A891 (Photo courtesy: MRAH, Brussels).

Apollo, the master of divination *par excellence*,[31] occurs on two cups. The earlier example was discovered in a deposit at Delphi associated with funerary material.[32] It shows the god seated on a *diphros*, his lyra in one hand and a phiale in the other, pouring a libation in front of a black bird. The combination of several features clearly alludes to the oracular character of the divinity. The phiale, often associated with the iconography of Apollo, is generally seen as an attribute of his mantic powers.[33] Moreover, here, the god does not simply hold the phiale, but he is actually performing the *sponde* assisted by a raven. The latter is clearly reported as one of the god's mantic birds by Plutarch,[34] while the phiale and the libation might also refer, in this case, to the practice performed before the oracle was given.[35]

The other cup, dated to ca. 470-450 is reported to come from a grave close to Cape Zoster in Attica (Fig.8).[36] It belongs to the rare class of lidded cups introduced into the Attic pottery repertoire in the second half of the sixth century and occasionally produced in black- or outline technique on white-ground.[37] This distinctive shape suggests that it was specially made for ritual, most probably for a libation purpose. It bears a fixed lid with only a small opening, while, as has been shown from X-ray photographs, it contains an internal tube which allowed it to be filled with the liquid from underneath the foot. Such a system was most probably conceived for performing the *sponde* since it was possible to pour only a small quantity of liquid through the opening made in the lid.[38]

It is decorated with Apollo's epiphany before a Muse holding a lyre. A red-figure laurel wreath encircles the white-ground tondo. Although the mantic allusion is less explicit on this vase, several features support the reference. The laurel around the scene is the acknowledged attribute of Apollo but is also clearly linked with his mantic practice in Delphi, even though its precise use during the performance is still disputed.[39] Muses are acknowledged to be patrons of education through the arts, especially music and poetry, and to inspire poets and musicians. Many years ago, E.R. Dodds showed the close relation between poetic inspiration and prophetic revelation in antiquity.[40] Through music, Muses also benefit from a direct connection with Apollo, and evidence shows that they might become a prophetic instrument in his hands, at least in Delphi. In his seminal article on Apollo and the Muses, H.W. Parke noted that it is probably significant that oracular responses, notably those of the Pythia, are reported to have been made in verse (epic hexameter) in the Archaic period.[41] Plutarch, when he mentions Apollo's primal hexameter, describes the cult of the Muses in Delphi, which he sees

Fig. 6. Girl with a spinning top. Brussels, Musées royaux d'Art et d'Histoire A890 (Photo courtesy: MRAH, Brussels).

as directly connected with the use of verse in the oracle. Quoting Simonides, Plutarch ends: 'They settled the Muses as assessors of divination and guardians of the place by the fountain and the sanctuary of the Earth Goddess, to whom the oracle-centre originally belonged, because of the uttering of responses in metres and melodies.'[42] Although Apollo and the Muses are often related in literature and vase-painting, Delphi is the only place where there is evidence that they were worshipped together since early times, while nowhere else is there a shrine of the Muses in an Apolline oracle-centre. If we accept this association (Delphic Apollo – Muses – divination), the Boston cup probably alludes to the prophetic practice of the Muses in Delphi. It shows the Delphic Apollo, crowned and surrounded with laurel leaves, inspiring a young Muse not only in the art of music and poetry but also in that of prophecy.

---

31 As already attested in the *Homeric Hymn to Apollo*, verses 131-132. On the Hymn, see Clay 1989, 17-94. But also Aeschylus, *Eumenides* 61-63. There is an important literature on Apollo and divination, see most recently with extensive earlier bibliography, Monbrun 2007.

32 Delphi, Archaeological Museum 8140: Konstantinou 1970, 27-46.

33 See *LIMC* II, s.v. Apollo, 317 [Palagia, O.]; *THeSCRA* I, Libation, 243 [Simon, E.]; Simon 1953. On the representations of Apollo with the tripod and a phiale clearly alluding to the oracular sanctuary of Delphi, see Amandry 1950, 66-77.

34 Plutarch, *The Oracles at Delphi are no longer given in verse*, 21. 405c. On the discussions about the identity of the bird and arguments against a direct link between the iconography and the place of discovery (Delphi), see Metzger 1977, 421-428.

35 No aspect of Greek divination has drawn as much scholarly attention as the Delphic oracles, for the performance of the Pythia, see most recently with previous literature, Graf 2009, 587–605; for the phiale in the oracular practice at Delphi, see *THeSCRA* III, Divination, 1. Delphes, 27 [Suàrez de la Torre, E.]; more generally, on libations performed for divination and necromancy, see Ogden 2001, 169-171.

36 Williams, 2004, 117, n. 66 : "found in a tomb near Cape Zoster". The funerary context and provenance of both cups, Boston 00.356 ans 00.357, purchased by P. Warren, were mentioned by him in a list of his acquisitions kept year by year. I warmly thank Dyfri Williams for telling me about this evidence and the list, he consulted in Lewes House.

37 For a list of these vessels, see Beazley 1944, 44-46, updated for the white-ground by Mertens 1977, nos. 18-19, 157 and nos. 32-33, 171.

38 Cohen 2006, no. 31, 127, fig. 31.3.

39 For the symbolic association of the laurel and the Delphic mantic with the ancient literary sources that refer to it, see *THeSCRA* III, Divination, 1. Delphes, 26-27 [Suàrez de la Torre, E.], see also among a large literature, Amandry 1997, 195-209.

40 Dodds 1951, 82.

41 Parke 1981, 103-105.

42 Simonides, fr. 72 (Page) [=Plutarch, *Moralia* 3.402C], quoted in Parke 1981, 104.

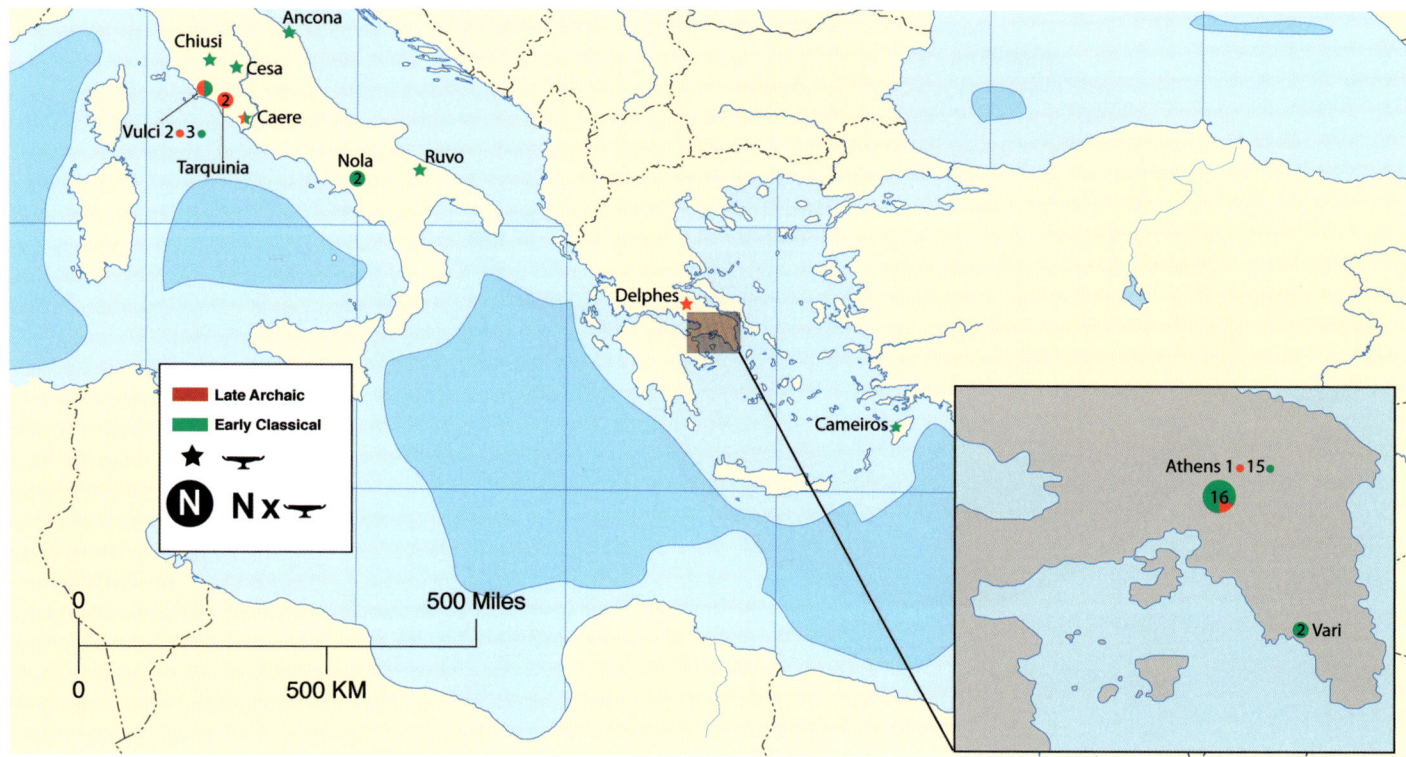

Fig. 7. Distribution map of Attic white-ground cups in funerary contexts (map by the author, designed by N. Bloch, CReA-Patrimoine, ULB).

This cup was paired in the tomb with another one (Fig. 9).[43] The latter bears a red-figure tondo, framed with a large white-ground zone recalling that of the Hegesiboulos cup from the Sotades Tomb. It features a young woman, with loose hair fanned out in the air. She gestures towards a vase settled on the ground. Although puzzling, the scene did not raise any discussion in previous scholarship. J.D. Beazley describes it as 'woman with hydria (at fountain)'.[44] Yet, there is no trace of a fountain, and one sees neither liquid nor spout in the background. In this context, the choice of a hydria, with tall neck and articulated handles, might be significant for the understanding of the scene. It most probably alludes to a metallic or stone version of the vessel, a type known to be often used as a grave marker.[45] The hairstyle and gesture of the young woman might point to a ceremonial activity. Although in Athenian iconography, mourning women often claw at their tattered hair,[46] the loose strands moving backwards and the dignified attitude of the young female on the Boston cup does not suggest a grieving pose. This distinctive rendering of the hair finds a close parallel on one other known example where it suggests the movement of a girl playing ball.[47] Yet, the figure on the Boston cup adopts a motionless pose that excludes such a meaning. The extended right arm towards the vase rather recalls a gesture of valediction. Does then the fanned out hair suggest the presence of the so-called pneuma or mantic wind, which is mentioned during divination in ancient sources. In this case, is it possible to relate the untied hair with the coiffure occasionally prescribed at certain magical or religious ceremonies? Several texts,[48] including a fragment of Sophocles and the poet Alexis in reference to Medea,[49] report that witches or necromancers must avoid bindings of any kind on their head or feet while performing rites related to chthonic or funerary contexts. J.G. Frazer, followed by others, noted that this rule was probably based on the same fear of trammelling or impeding the action in hand by any knot or constriction whether on the head or the feet.[50] If this interpretation is correct, the extended arm might then allude to a prayer towards the deceased or an incantation

Fig. 8. Apollo and Muse – lidded cup. Boston, Museum of Fine Arts 00.356 (Photo courtesy: Museum of Fine Arts, Boston).

over a grave monument suggested by the hydria, both practices well attested during necromantic rites, when the dead are called up to advise about future events.[51]

Two other white-ground cups in the Louvre, decorated with female musicians generally identified as Muses,[52] are reported to come from a grave located either in Attica or in Eretria (Fig. 10-11).[53] Beyond the specific relation between divination, oracular Apollo and the Muses, already mentioned above, we have also seen that scholars point to a more general association between Muses and oracular practice. They recall the familiar picture of Greek and Latin literature where an inspired prophet or prophetess usually breaks into verse utterance, a poetic form inspired by the Muses. The latter are often linked also with two famous seers, Orpheus (son of the Muse Calliope) and Musaeus (literally the man of the Muses), who are mythic poets and allegedly authors of oracular books.[54] Poet and seer might, therefore, be the same man taking his inspiration from the Muses or from a god to perform his art. Regarding funerary contexts, Muses and Orpheus play a role in Mysteries, cults,

43 Boston, Museum of Fine Arts, 00.357: for the provenance see Williams 2004, 117, n. 66 and above note 36.
44 ARV^2, 772.
45 Hydria as a grave marker, see Pontrandolfo *et al.* 1988, 181-202.
46 For a summary of the mourning gestures on vases, Oakley 2004, 76-87.
47 Tübingen, Eberhard-Karls-Universität, E112: I warmly thank Dyfri Williams for drawing my attention to this vase.
48 Apollonius Rhodius, *Argonautica* 3.1026 - 1062 (ca. third century BC); Orphic Argonautica 950-987; Horace, *Satires* 1.8.2-5 (Dido and Medea); Ovid, *Metamorphoses* 7.179-185 (Medea).
49 Alexis F93 (ca. fourth century BC) [K-A/Arnott]; *Rhizotomoi* F543 TrGF (Nauck).
50 Frazer 1927, 310-311; Deonna 1935, 68-69 (I thank Didier Viviers for these references); Ogden 2001, 189.
51 Ogden 2001, 175. Among other passages quoted by Ogden about utterances to the dead, see *Odyssey* 11.34; Aeschylus, *Persians* 627-680.
52 About the identity of the figures, *LIMC* VI, s.v. Mousa, Mousai, 657-681 [Querel, A.]. Contra for Musée du Louvre CA 483, see Kaufman-Samara 1997, 286-288.
53 Paris, Musée du Louvre CA 482 and CA 483: ARV^2, 774.2 and 774.3; *BAPD* Vase 209596. For the provenance, see Pottier 1895, 41.

Fig. 9. Woman and hydria. Boston, Museum of Fine Arts 00.357 (Photo courtesy: Museum of Fine Arts, Boston).

and beliefs about life after death.[55] Moreover, initiates are referred directly to the Muses' mother, Mnemosyne, in order to find their way in the Underworld journey.[56]

Although fragmentary, a white-ground cup that came to light near the Dipylon Gate, also provides us with a distinctive tondo scene.[57] It shows Demeter and Persephone performing a libation. The former is seated, holding a phiale in one hand and a sceptre in the other, the latter holds a sceptre and pours the liquid into the phiale with an oenochoe. An inscription identifies Persephone as *Pherrepha[tta]*, a rare Attic version of the name meaning the one to whom we offer or dedicate. On the inside, around the medallion, are the remains of a draped figure holding a sceptre, most probably part of a larger group of figures, while a similar scene adorned the outside. Both have been generally recognized as an assembly of gods. The subject on the medallion is clearly linked with the Eleusinian Mysteries, while the name *Pherrephatta*, further associates Persephone with the Underwold and with two Attic festivals,[58] the Thesmophoria[59] and the Lesser Mysteries,[60] which allude to her death and revival. But Persephone is also linked to oracular practices. The two main Underworld divinities, Hades and Persephone are included in necromantic prayers already in early texts such as the Iliad and the Odyssey,[61] but it seems that it was the prerogative of the goddess to assemble and scatter the shades for interrogation.[62] Archaeological evidence suggests that she also presided over the ghostly prophecies of the Acheron *nekuomanteion*, located in Thesprotia.[63] She was, with Hades, the patron goddess of the area and a dump, close to the site, yielded Persephone terracottas dating from the seventh to the fifth century BC, and attest to her cult in the surrounding area.[64]

A. Shapiro already noticed the association between divination and the cult of Demeter and Kore. He pointed out that both sources of oracles, such as Orpheus and Musaeus, and their interpreters like Onomakritos, when they were not practising their mantic arts, were most deeply involved with the particular cult of the two goddesses.[65] To quote but a few examples mentioned by Shapiro:

Fig. 10. Woman playing kithara. Paris, Musée du Louvre CA 482 (Photo courtesy: Musée du Louvre, Paris).

Pausanias thought that Musaeus was the author of a *Hymn to Demeter*[66] and that Onomakritos wrote a poem about the ancient cult of Demeter and Kore in Lykosoura in Arkadia,[67] while Euripides considered Orpheus to be the founder of the Eleusinian Mysteries.[68] Scholars explained this link through several common patterns that might exist between necromancy and the Mysteries of Demeter and Kore.[69] In

---

54 About Orpheus: Graf & Iles Johnston 2007, 165-184 (with references to ancient texts). About Musaeus: Herodotus VII.6; Plutarch frg. 24, Them. 1; Pausanias 1.22.7 and West 1983, 39-41; Both Orpheus and Musaeus, mentioned as authors of books, Plato, *Republic* 364c-e.

55 See Hardie 2004, 11-37. For Orpheus and Mysteries, see Graf & Iles Johnston 2007, 155-164 and 171-172.

56 Initiates are instructed to obtain refreshment in Hades from the 'Lake of Memory (Mnemosyne)': Gold tablet from Hipponion (Calabria) ca. 400 BC, gold tablet from Petelia (Calabria) fourth century BC: Graf & Iles Johnston 2007, 4-7, nos. 1-2.

57 Athens, National Museum 2187: Furtwängler 1881, 112-118, pl. 4; *BAPD* Vase 3937.

58 For the ancient sources quoting Pherrephatta, LS 1395 [under the entry Persephone], 1922 [under the entry Phersephassa]. E.g. among the gods of the Lower World, Aeschylus, *Choephori* 490; Platon, *Cratylus* 404c-d; for the Thesmophoria, see Aristophanes, *Thesmophoriazusae* 287; Clement of Alexandria, *Protreptikon* 11; *IG2²* 1437.58.

59 The Thesmophoria (as the Eleusinian Mysteries) invoke the myth of Demeter and Persephone, and metaphorically link human and agricultural revival, see Stehle 2007, 165-188.

60 The Lesser Mysteries celebrate the return of Persephone to Earth and prepare the participants to the main initiation at the Great Mysteries in Eleusis: Mylonas 1961, 239-240; recently with earlier bibliography, Clinton 2003, 50-60.

61 *Iliad* 9.568-572; *Odyssey* 11.633-637

62 *Odyssey* 11.385. Persephone also occurs in the spells of Imperial period necromancy: second spell cf. Stehle 2007, 177.

63 The Acheron *nekuomanteion* is mentioned by Herodotus 5.92; Pausanias 9.30; Scholiast Homer, *Odyssey hypothesis* p. 5 Dindorf; L. Ampelius, *Liber memorialis* 83. For a recent discussion on the site and its function, Ogden 2001, 43-60.

64 Dakaris 1993, 27-29.

65 Shapiro 1990, 335-345, especially 342-344.

66 Pausanias, I.22.7

67 Pausanias, VIII.31.3

68 Euripides, *Rhesos* 943

Fig. 11. Woman playing kithara. Paris, Musée du Louvre CA 483 (Photo courtesy: Musée du Louvre, Paris).

fact, initiates and necromancers alike received advance access to privileged knowledge about the afterlife. As with mysteries, revelations made in necromancy were often a matter of secrecy, and the idea of *Nekyia* – the descent to the Underwold and return – finds a perfect parallel with the concern with death and the promise of afterlife the initiate displayed in Orphic poetry and Eleusinian Mysteries.

A few other white-ground cups might have been deposited in Attic tombs.[70] However, the fragmentary preservation state of most of them prevents an accurate reading of their iconography. Among miscellaneous finds from the area of a necropolis in Lenormant Street, a white-ground sherd bears a funerary scene, which was associated with a grave context.[71] It displays the head of a dying youth, identified by the excavator as Orpheus trying to ward off a blow with his lyra, a figure also related to Mystery cult and divination. A complete piece, now in Berlin, is also said to come from Athens, but without any further information about its context.[72] If it came from a tomb, it is important to note that the figured decoration focuses on a ritual practice: a woman is adding a leafy sprig to a second sprig and a fruit already on an altar.

SPECIAL OFFERINGS ADDRESSED TO A SPECIAL DECEASED?

If one accepts the reading proposed above, the iconography of white-ground cups from Attic graves reveals an underlying connection with mantic and, occasionally, with Mystery cults.[73] An excursus into some other features that occur in the pottery assemblage may further confirm such associations.

L. Burn mentioned the honey reference in the subject scenes of three cups from the 'Sotades Tomb'. It is acknowledged that honey is connected with funerary rituals. It is mixed with milk (*melikraton*) in the libations over the grave for 'it brings soothing and life',[74] and it is applied as a part in the embalming process.[75] Yet, scholars also point to a number of significant associations between bees and the art of seeing.[76] According to the Homeric Hymn to Hermes, bee-creatures taught the young god the art of prophecy.[77] Following Aristotle,[78] bees had prophetic powers of their own, while Pausanias tells us that they had revealed the necromantic oracle of Trophonius.[79] And it is also probably not mere coincidence that in one extant account of a supposedly historical consultation at the *Nekuomanteion* of the Acheron, reported by Herodotus,[80] the Corinthian tyrant Periander evokes the ghost of his wife, named Melissa.

Likewise, it is interesting to note that the cicada on the omphalos of the Boston phiale not only alludes to the afterlife and Athenian autochthony, but may also have potent associations with divination. According to D. Ogden,[81] the cicada is already related to divination through a fragment of Anakreon: 'it (the tettix) sang as a prophet, just like a ghost, it derived from the earth, it was ancient and bloodless and it was wise'.[82] Furthermore, there is the connection with the *Nekuomanteion* at Tainaron, mentioned in literary sources. Following Anakreon[83] and Plutarch,[84] the mythical figure of the Tettix (the Cicada) was buried in the *Nekuomanteion*, while Hesychius called the place the 'Seat of the Tettix'.[85]

The choice of special shapes in a pottery assemblage also suggests ritual practices and requires a little discussion. Mesomphalic phialai are, indeed, the regular shape for libations, and we have seen that the Boston lidded cup most probably had the same function. Phialai are further mentioned in later sources as being used in 'lekanomancy', that is prophecy through the reading of water often carried in a phiale or in a bowl.[86] The rare type of 'merrythought' cup, introduced in Attica from about the middle of the sixth century BC, is acknowledged as following bronze prototypes and is also generally associated with sanctuaries in ancient contexts.[87]

This possible combination of elements – ritual shapes and scenes or motifs that refer to the afterlife – with mystery cults and divination, might be related to the status of the deceased. If we accept the idea of conscious choice behind a meaningful imagery and special shapes, it should indicate that the deceased once practised an important *techne* or fulfilled a prestigious function within ancient Athenian society. Following on from the underlying iconographical reference to divination, it might be supposed that such special offerings were addressed to a seer. A seer played an important role in the conduct of daily life, political decisions, and military campaigns that justified the need for a distinctive class of burial material.[88]

The distinctive status of the deceased might be further confirmed by the special use of the vases during either the funerals or the visits to the grave, as it is attested by their distinctive state of preservation. Although we lack accurate information from the archaeological record, close examination of the cups shows that they were reassembled from numerous fragments, often small and worn, therefore suggesting that they were most probably shattered in antiquity. Following the extensive cleaning and restoration carried out on this material in the late nineteenth – early twentieth century, it is impossible to say if the vases bore traces of second burning caused by being thrown into the pyre, even though several pieces display yellow discolorations and black deposits that might result from a contact with fire.[89] Nevertheless, even if we take

---

69 Ogden 2001, 126; Shapiro 1990, 343-344, with further associations.
70 Amsterdam, Allard Pierson Museum 8200: fragment with white-ground and coral-red, *ARV²*, 771.5; *CVA Amsterdam* 1, pl. 37, 8. Copenhagen, National Museum 1635: with coral-red, without interior decoration, *ARV²*, 771.2; *BAPD* Vase 209542. Athens, Agora Museum P10357 (fragment with a head of a youth), Agora Museum P10411 (fragment with a drapery fold beside a chest or a basket): Boulter 1963, nos. 10-11, pl. 47, and Athens, Agora Museum P22326 (fr.): uncertain subject but with chthonian and eschatological references, Moore 1997, no. 1633, pl. 153.
71 Boulter 1963, no. 10, 131. About the uncertain funerary provenance of the material, *ibid*., 113.
72 Berlin, Antikensammlung V.I. 3408: *ARV²*, 774; Cohen 2006, no. 14, 69-70.
73 Already suggested by Tsingarida 2003, 73.
74 'Melikraton': *Odyssey* XI. 633-637; mentioned, among other offerings in funerary rituals: Aeschylus, *Persae* 609-610; a prayer to Hades preceded with a libation of honey: Euripides (Nauck F912).
75 Xenophon, *Hellenica* 5.3.9: used for the body of Agesipolis, king of Sparta. See Ogden 2001, 59
76 Ogden 2001, 7-8, 54-55, 169-170. Iles Johnston 2008, 111-113.
77 *Hymn to Hermes* 470-472, 534, 556.
78 Aristotle, *History of Animals* 627b.10
79 Pausanias, IX.40.
80 Herodotus, V.92
81 Ogden 2001, 38.
82 Anakreon, *Anakreonta* 34.10-17
83 Suidas, s.v. Anakreon
84 Plutarch, *Moralia*, 560e-f
85 Suidas, s.v. *Tettigos hedranon*
86 *Papyri Graecae Magicae* IV.930-1114, V.54-69; see discussion with further references, Ogden 2001, 191-194.
87 For the origin and life of the Attic wishbone cup: Callipolitis-Feytmans, 1979, 195-215; Ramage 1983, 435-460.
88 Flower 2008, 240-247.

into account only the fragmentary state, it is reasonable to think of a ritual 'killing' of the pottery, a practice attested in Attica for other shapes, such as loutrophoroi and some drinking vessels, from the seventh to the late fifth century BC.[90] The earliest known and unique other example of a black-figure 'merrythought' cup from a funerary context might further confirm this custom. It was found in the Kerameikos, and, according to the excavators, it was smashed in an offering place (*Opferplatz*) located in front of a pit grave with incinerated remains.[91] In a recent article on loutrophoroi,[92] V. Sabetai noted that when this practice was applied the broken vases were used (through their shape or iconography), to recall the special value of the deceased, while Houby-Nielsen commented in her study on the *Opferrinen*: 'the vases were not merely gifts to the dead but rather a material expression of a quality of the dead'.[93]

The archaeological record of the white-ground cup decorated with Apollo and the raven may also further point to the special status of the deceased to whom it was addressed.[94] It was discovered in a pit together with other funerary material (bones, pottery and terracotta figurines), located within the temenos of Apollo, underneath the modern archaeological museum. The material, covering a large chronological span from the seventh to the fourth century BC, was carefully deposited during a period of reorganization of the sacred area dating to the fourth century BC. The decision to assemble such burial offerings and bones in a pit within the sanctuary might also reflect the special status of the graves from which the material came.

On three cups, two from the Sotades Tomb and one now in Berlin,[95] the scenes concentrate on women. Most scholars have considered this gender-oriented iconography as evidence for the female identity of the deceased.[96] If this view is correct, it does not contradict the possible connection with divination. Ancient literary evidence attests a long line of female practitioners in prophecy both mortal and mythological.[97]

SPECIAL COMMISSIONS OR A TARGETED PRODUCTION?

The distinctive features of white-ground cups brings me to the last question discussed in this paper. Are they special commissions or the result of a workshop targeting a specific market? Most scholars acknowledge them as objects carefully selected for the tomb,[98] while a few consider them as special commissions.[99]

Although the organization of Early Classical workshops bears further investigation, a close look at the proposed attributions might shed new light on the part played by the producer and the purchaser in the development of this special class of vases. Interestingly, when information is available about the archaeological record, it seems that several white-ground cups were produced in pairs (coupled by scenes, shapes and techniques of decoration), and deposited accordingly in tombs.

The latest known pair, from a grave in Cape Zoster (Fig. 8-9) and dated to the middle of the fifth century, might be related to the Villa Giulia Painter's workshop. The white-ground painting on the lidded cup in Boston has been associated with either the ambit of the Villa Giulia[100] or the Penthesilea Painters,[101] and the red-figure decoration of the vase's exterior with that of the Karlsruhe Painter.[102] No study examines the potter work. Beazley noted with regard to the second cup that its shape is 'like the Sotadean' but the drawing 'somewhat recalls' the Danae Painter,[103] a craftsman also occasionally associated with the Villa Giulia Painter's workshop.[104]

A more significant number of the white-ground cups from burials date to the early Classical period. Most of them originate in the ambit of the Sotades-Hegesiboulos workshop.[105] While J.D. Beazley attributed the two cups in the Louvre (fig 10-11) and the third one in Berlin V.I.3408 to the Hesiod Painter,[106] B. Cohen has recently associated them with the Sotades – Hegesiboulos workshop.[107] On technical grounds, she notes the use of coral-red and its application in the handle zones and in the foot ring, both features displayed by the workshop.[108] Regarding the decoration, she also points to the common style between the woman in the Berlin cup and the top-spinner in Brussels. The attribution of the Berlin and the Louvre cups to the Sotades – Hegesiboulos workshop may confirm a distinctive pattern of organization, already visible from the cups' assemblage in the Sotades Tomb. One or more painters, such as the Sotades and the Hesiod Painters, draw mythological and complex themes in a polychrome technique with gilded and relief details, while another vase-painter, often associated with the potter Hegesiboulos,[109] works in red-figure or in a monochrome outline technique, occasionally enhanced with gilded or relief details. The 'Hegesiboulos' side of the Sotades workshop, experienced in the coral-red technique,[110] might also be responsible for, at least, another pair of delicate cups with merrythought handles. They are said to have been found together in a tomb at Hermione and are not decorated in white-ground but employ coral-red.[111] Beazley attributed them to the ambit of Sotades.[112] Like the Hegesiboulos cups from the Sotades Tomb and the white-ground vessel in Berlin, the two red-figure medallions are decorated with female imagery: the young woman on the Leipzig cup is seated next to an altar and holds an unidentified object on her knees, while her companion in Boston throws astragaloi in the air.

This earlier series of tombs might suggest that the painting of white-ground and coral-red cups for graves might be attributed to two different members of the Sotades workshop: the Sotades Painter decorates white-ground cups with an elaborate subject matter and outline/polychrome technique, while a second painter (associated with the Hegesiboulos potter) uses red-figure or simple monochrome outline, combined with coral-red to draw female oriented iconography. Such a regular distribution of the work might further suggest that the vases were made to respond to an expected but occasional demand, rather than to a special commission, which for practical reasons of time, might also have been difficult to fulfil after a death.

ACKNOWLEDGEMENTS

I am most grateful to the organizers for inviting me to the Copenhagen congress and for their patience in awaiting my paper. For their advice and stimulating discussions I would like to warmly thank Susanna Sarti, Alan Shapiro, Vicky Sabetai and Dyfri Williams. Many thanks are also due to the anonymous reader for constructive criticism. I wish also to acknowledge the help of curators and institutions for providing me with photographs of vases from their collections: A. Coulié (Paris, Musée du Louvre), M. Fodor (Boston, Museum of Fine Arts), N. Massar (Brussels, Musées royaux d'Art et d'Histoire) and D. Prudames (London, The British Museum, Web team). I am happy to acknowledge the talent and kindness of my friend Nathalie Bloch (CReA-Patrimoine, ULB) in preparing the illustrations of this article.

89 See London, British Museum GR 1892.7-18.3: Cohen 2006, 306 ('Condition: yellow discolorations'). Boston, Museum of Fine Arts 13.4503: Cohen 2006, 302 ('Condition: ... spotted gray and black incrustations'). London, British Museum GR 1892.7-18.2: Cohen 2006, 304 ('Condition: white-ground cracked and pitted with yellow discolorations and a scattered black deposit on surface'); Boston, Museum of Fine Arts 98.886: Cohen 2006, 311 ('Condition : ... yellow discolorations, brown deposits...').
90 Kistler 1998, and for examples dated to the fifth century see Houby-Nielsen 1996, 49-51.
91 Kraiker 1934, 1-20
92 Sabetai 2009, 291-306.
93 Houby-Nielsen 1996, 49-54.
94 Konstantinou 1970, 29-28.
95 Brussels, Musees Royaux d'Art et d'Histoire A890 & A891; Berlin, Antikensammlung V.I. 3408. For the latter, see most recently with previous bibliography, Cohen 2006, no.14, 69-70.
96 See most recently, Williams 2006, 295.
97 Such as Manto and Daphne, the daughter of Teirisias, Themis, and the Pythia, to mention but a few, Flower 2008, 211-239.
98 Burn 1985, 100-102; Robertson 1992, 186; Tsingarida 2003, 73; Williams 2004, 106-107 and 108-109.
99 Mertens 1974, 107-108.
100 Beazley 1918, 154; Robertson 1992, 172-173: attributed to the Methyse Painter.
101 Wehgartner 1983, 163-165, 162 no. 2.
102 ARV^2, 741. Recent publication in Cohen 2006, no. 31, 125-127.
103 ARV^2, 772.
104 Robertson 1992, 172.
105 I am following the name given recently to the workshop by Williams. About the possible family links between Sotades and Hegesiboulos, see Williams 2006, 296.
106 ARV^2, 774.2–3 and a stemless cup 'inferior'. For the Hesiod Painter, see also Mertens 1977, 176-177, and for the Berlin cup, see Cohen 2006, n°14, 69-70.
107 Cohen 2006, 51-52.
108 Coral-red on the handle zone is also found on the Hegesiboulos cup in Brussels.
109 For Hegesiboulos, named Hegesiboulos II, see Williams 2006, 296-297.
110 Williams 2006, 296 with previous references.
111 Leipzig, Antikenmuseum der Universität T954: *CVA* Leipzig 3, 92-93, pl. 54, 1-3. Boston, Museum of Fine Arts 03.791: ARV^2, 771.4. For the findspot, Williams 2004, 109.
112 ARV^2, 771.3-4.

Late 'Apulian' Red-figure Vases in Context:
A Case Study

BY MAURIZIO GUALTIERI

Late 'Apulian' Red-figure Vases in Context: A Case Study

BY MAURIZIO GUALTIERI

'I miti esprimono l'identità, ponendo in rapporto reciproco il mito e il presente.' (Hölscher 1999, 12)

A recent overview of the late Apulian red-figure pottery found in Lucania, carried out with the goal of defining the modality and the chronology of the circulation of Apulian vases in the southeast of the peninsula (in particular the 'frontier' areas of eastern Lucania, Peucetia and Daunia), has provided some evidence about the contexts of those same vases.[1] In many respects, the general picture of a limited occurrence of these vases in the Lucanian area is still warranted, especially for the large vases with mythological scenes dated to the second half of the fourth century BC.[2] Nonetheless, there are some local situations in which this very pottery assumes a role of primary importance in the composition of funerary offerings.

On the one hand, it is certainly true that the large vases of late Apulian red-figure, are not numerous in the area between the Val d'Agri and the area immediately to the east of this very important commercial corridor. On the other hand, it is also true that a good number of vases found within the Val d'Agri, which have been attributed by Trendall to the circle of the Varrese Painter and to the circle of the Darius Painter, exhibit stylistic peculiarities and share various elements that permit one to think that these vases are part of a distinct and characteristic production. Such evidence accords well with what we know about the organization and location of Apulian red-figure workshops in the second half of the fourth century BC, which was much more articulated and spread out than it had been generally thought until just a few decades ago. It is now clear that we are dealing with workshops that were decentralized with respect to those areas that have been generally considered (by A.D. Trendall, in the first place) as the production centers for late Apulian pottery. In what we are now accustomed to refer to as 'the Trendall era', these were generally thought to have been mostly located on a narrow strip of the Ionian coast of Apulia and Lucania, at Metapontum and Tarentum.[3]

In this respect, a pioneer study by E.G.D. Robinson, already 20 years ago, on the location of various stylistic groups of late Apulian red-figure[4] identified by Trendall and the related archaeometric analyses[5] carried out in the Sydney Archaeology Lab, have provided encouraging results. Most recently the accurate statistics worked out by Ettore De Juliis[6] have provided added evidence for a massive presence of late Apulian red-figure vases in Peucetia and Daunia to cater for the needs of the local aristocracies.[7] Thus, it is now generally accepted that a number of production centers of late Apulian red-figure are to be located, without any reasonable doubt, in the vast hinterland between Daunia and Peucetia, but we should not automatically exclude the possibility of more localized production centers also in other districts of inland and western Lucania. Unfortunately, given the almost complete lack of provenience and contextual data on late-Apulian red-figure vases, it is not possible at this stage to provide a more detailed picture of the situation. A notable exception to the fairly bleak picture of late Apulian red-figure vases in context is the work undertaken some time ago by Marina Mazzei. Before her untimely death, Mazzei published a series of studies about the chamber tombs in the Daunian area (especially Arpi and Canosa) that attempted to reconstruct from archival data the provenience of many of the vases found in uncontrolled excavations during the last two centuries which, for the most part, had ended up in major local collections (notably the Jatta collection in Ruvo) and the antiquity market.[8] Much remains to be done, however, to carry on the pioneer work of our sorely missed colleague.

NEW EVIDENCE FROM WESTERN LUCANIA
Against the background picture just outlined, namely of a noticeable spread of late Apulian red-figure workshops, and with specific reference to the problem of the kind of clients to whom such vases would be directed, the documentation provided by a monumental chamber tomb from the cemetery area at Roccagloriosa in western Lucania is of particular relevance. Thanks to the restoration recently undertaken by the Department of Antiquities of Salerno[9] of the tomb groups from the La Scala cemetery[10] it is now possible to analyze in detail a group of large

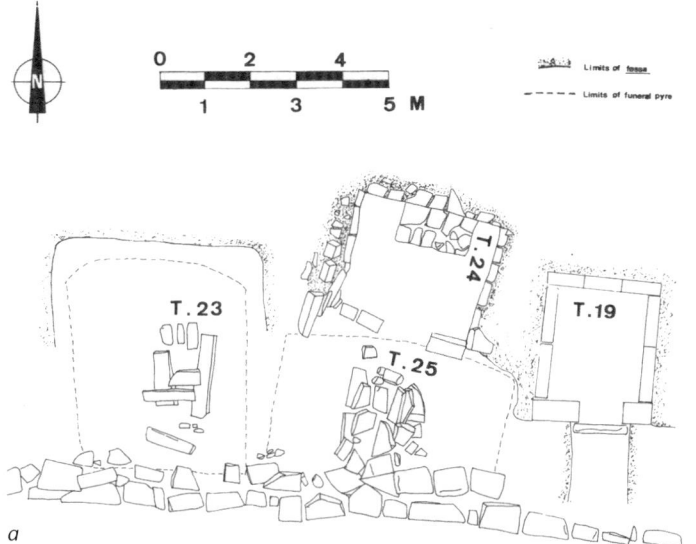

Fig. 1a-b: Tomb 19, 24 and 25. La Scala Cemetery, Roccagloriosa (Drawing: C. Lanzara & D. Girardot. Photo: Maurizio Gualtieri).

vases in the ornate late Apulian style found in tomb 19, a chamber tomb in ashlar masonry (Fig. 1a-b) with a gabled roof excavated in the 1980s, in the context of a large scale exploration of this western Lucanian site.[11] The tomb group in question, albeit before the restoration of the vases, had already been the object of a preliminary study which provided a first definition of the funerary ritual (including the identification of the gender of the deceased – an adult male) and of the chronology of the burial. Chamber tomb 19, dated to ca. 330 BC, was part of a group of burials found in the northern enclosure of the cemetery area which pertained to an extended family group. The systematic excavations conducted in the 1980s have enabled us to document both the general plan of the burials and the composition of the grave goods in relation to the type of tombs. A preliminary publication[12] in the *American Journal of Archaeology* of the two cremation burials (tombs 23 and 25) found within the enclosure in question, the subsequent analysis of the osteological remains[13] and, not least, the recent restoration of the large red-figure vases included in the funerary offerings, have enabled us to delineate a sufficiently precise chronology of the burials found within the northern enclosure in terms of the age and sex of the deceased. In turn, the combined evidence of grave goods and osteological remains has enabled us to postulate the possible reciprocal relationships existing among the

1 Mugione 1996.
2 Mugione 1996, 217-218.
3 *RVAp*, passim.
4 Robinson 1990.
5 Robinson *et al.* 1997.
6 De Juliis 2004.
7 See also, on this particular aspect of late Apulian red-figure, the overview by Torelli (2004, 190-193).
8 Mazzei 1990; 1992c; 1995.
9 I am most grateful to the late Dr. A. Fiammenghi, Director of Antiquities for the Roccagloriosa area and to Dr. M. Cipriani, Director of the Paestum Museum with the annexed Restoration Lab where the vases have been restored. Special thanks are due to Dr. M.L. Nava, present Superintendent at the Department of Antiquities for the Provinces of Salerno, Avellino Benevento and Caserta, who has facilitated in many ways continuing research at this important Lucanian site: the recent 'musealization' of the site, in the context of the Parco Nazionale del Cilento, has also triggered new research and restoration of the finds from the earlier excavations.
10 It is the major cemetery area at the site, located in a saddle of the Capitenali ridge immediately outside (to the south) of the fortified enceinte. The upper sector of the cemetery area has been the object of a 'blanket' excavation in the 1980s and has provided a fairly complete plan of the tomb distribution given the exceptional state of preservation of the area which was given to rough grazing. See Gualtieri 1993, 140-142 and 341-342.
11 Preliminary analysis and formulation of the problems posed by the new ceramic evidence in Gualtieri 2007.
12 Gualtieri 1982.
13 An in-depth osteological analysis of the bone remains from the Roccagloriosa cemetery has been later conducted by M.K. Jackes (formerly in the Department of Anthropology, University of Alberta, Edmonton) and generously funded by a SSHRCC Grant. See the detailed discussion and publication of the sample in Gualtieri & Fracchia 1990, 164-185.

Fig. 2: Apulian Rhyton from Tomb 19, La Scala Cemetery, Roccagloriosa (Photo: E. Salinardi).

Fig. 3: Apulian Rhyton from Tomb 19, La Scala Cemetery, Roccagloriosa (Photo: E. Salinardi).

individuals buried in the north enclosure of the cemetery area.

Tomb 19, at the northeast extremity of the northern enclosure, was the burial of an adult male whose grave goods clearly indicate, on the basis of the horse trappings,[14] that the deceased belonged to an aristocratic group who held the privilege of fighting from horseback, as also suggested by the depiction of the horseman within the naiskos represented on the large mascaroon krater from the same tomb (see below).[15] The chronology worked out for tomb 19 dates the tomb ca. 30-35 years later (hence, most likely a generation later) than that of contiguous tomb 24, which is dated to ca. 360 BC. Thus, the evidence provided by the grave goods and the chronology of tombs 24 and 19, taken together with the location of the two chamber tombs and their position side by side (Fig. 2) within the burial ground of the northern enclosure, warrants the hypothesis that the two tombs may have been those of mother and son. This not only, as already indicated, on the basis of their respective location within the north enclosure (clearly a family plot), but also on account of the chronology indicated by the pottery: Tomb 24 (female) is ca. 30-35 years earlier than Tomb 19 (male).

THE LARGE RED-FIGURE VASES FROM THE ROCCAGLORIOSA (SA) NECROPOLIS

The ceramic goods include, in addition to the three large vases that will be discussed in detail, two elegant *rhyta* (Fig. 2 and 3) of Apulian manufacture,[16] with evident 'heroic' overtones: on a first reading, they can be linked, in their heroizing overtones, to the representation of the deceased with spear, at the side of his horse, inside the *naiskos* depicted on face A of the a large volute krater (Fig. 4a).

The mascaroon krater, a typical form of the late Apulian production, was the object of a preliminary inspection by A.D. Trendall a short time after the excavation. Trendall, who saw some of the larger and more representative sherds of both the krater in question and of the large

b

Fig. 4a-b: Volute krater from Tomb 19, La Scala Cemetery, Roccagloriosa (Photo: E. Salinardi).

a

loutrophoros, had no hesitation in attributing both vases - the two identifiable ones even before restoration, among the concentration of large red-figure sherds at the foot of the deposition – to the production of the Darius/Underworld circle.[17]

The ornamental motifs of the large mascaroon krater (Fig. 4b) have more recently been analysed by Th. Morard, in order to compare it with a krater depicting a scene from the Ilioupersis, which was used as a sema in the territory of Metapontum and is decorated with an almost identical ornamental decoration.[18] A careful study of the black gloss has, however, indicated that the Roccagloriosa vase is certainly not of Metapontine origin, (as a direct inspection

14 It is to be underlined that they are significantly matched by a number of pointed small bronze cylinders found on the central plateau which have been generally interpreted as elements for horse harnessing (Gualtieri & Fracchia 1990, 319 no.663 and fig. 205). See the recently published specimens used as votive offerings at an intra-mural sanctuary in Kroton: Marino & Corrado 2009, 48 and fig.4.

15 An analysis of the iconography – with discussion of the probable aspects of self-representation of the deceased depicted with horse within the naiskos on large late-Apulian kraters and the related overtones of heroization – has recently been published in Castoldi 2004, with updated bibliographic references.

16 See Hoffman 1966. I owe some very helpful suggestions on their unquestionable Apulian provenience to A. Pontrandolfo, on the occasion of a visit to the Roccagloriosa Antiquarium in December 2007.

17 *RVAp*, 531-532.

18 Morard 2002, 37-38 and Pl. 6.

19 Morard 2002, 49, n.81.

Fig. 5. Loutrophoros from Tomb 19, La Scala Cemetery, Roccagloriosa (Photo: E. Salinardi & L. Vitola).

by Antonio De Siena has later confirmed).[19] It is thus no surprise that Th. Morard in his M.A. Thesis defended at Lausanne under Jean-Marc Moret and now published with the title *Le Troyens à Metaponte* has re-assessed the general idea of *'figuli vagantes per Maiorem Graeciam'*.[20]

The thorny problem regarding areas of production of the large red-figure vases found in Tomb 19 still needs to be left open however, for the sake of caution. At this stage we would still prefer to indicate 'Apulian' in quotes when referring to them, especially as regards the location of the workshop.[21] Passing on to the loutrophoros (Fig. 5a), it is to be underlined at the outset that we are dealing with an extremely elaborate shape, of truly monumental dimensions (the height is over 90 cm), which can hardly find parallels outside of Apulia,[22] although it becomes quite popular in late Apulian red-figure as a field for mythological representations. The upper register (Fig. 5b), as proposed years ago by H. Fracchia,[23] on the basis of joining fragments put together before restoration, is a rare depiction of the marriage of Herakles and Hebe at the moment of Herakles'

apotheosis into Olympos. Trendall was in agreement with such an identification, to judge from a brief comment on the vase included in the latest *Supplement to Red-Figure Vases of Apulia*, under the heading of the Darius/Underworld circle. The representation of Herakles, at the crucial moment of his career as a hero, has also suggested possible connections with the already mentioned depiction of the deceased represented as a hero within the funerary naiskos of Side A of the large krater. The connection between the two is perhaps made more plausible by the inclusion of the two rhyta[24] among the grave goods.

More elaborate and much more complex is, however, the scene on the neck of the large oinochoe (Fig. 6a) which develops on two registers. The lower register (Fig. 6b), more easily understandable, refers to the destinies of the royal house of Thebes. Laius, driving a four horse chariot, is shown at the very moment of the abduction of the young Chrysippos who stretches out his arms invoking aid from his father, Pelops, shown behind the chariot in Eastern dress and with a Phrygian type cap (Fig. 6c). The

Fig. 6a-c. Oinochoe from Tomb 19, La Scala Cemetery, Roccagloriosa (Photo: L. Vitola).

rape will be the cause of the curse invoked by Pelops on the Theban dynasty (with the well known consequences for the son of Laius, Oedipus, and for the grandsons Eteocles and Polynices). Furthermore, the family and dynastic connection with the scene of Niobe (sister of Pelops and herself queen of Thebes by marriage) on the amphora in

---

20 Morard 2002, 45-50. See also the related discussion in Denoyelle *et al.* 2005, 216-218, figs. 1-2 and the later comments on this problem by Morel 2009, 248.
21 See a detailed discussion on this aspect in Gualtieri 2007.
22 Leblond 1990: at Table 1 shows that it is the only specimen with known context to have been found outside of Apulia. Furthermore, he rightly points out that the Roccagloriosa loutrophoros is of exceptional dimensions when compared with the average size of known loutrophoroi. Fundamental remarks in *RVAp* Suppl. II, 164, n.327a1 'If the vase is not by his own hand then it is by a very close follower…' (e.g. of the Underworld Painter). See also comments in Schauenburg 1988.
23 Fracchia 1984, 299-300.
24 Discussion on the ritual connotation of rhyta in tombs, with possible 'heroic' overtones in Dolci 2004.

Fig. 7: Niobe amphora (detail) from Tomb 24, La Scala Cemetery, Roccagloriosa (Drawing: A. Kubo Hemingway).

the nearby tomb 24 (Fig. 7) are fairly evident. The upper register of the jug is harder to interpret upon a first reading of the figured decoration. The scene seems to be another mythological episode of love with tragic consequences: the winged figure of Eros between the two registers can be understood as creating a link between the two scenes.[25]

ICONOLOGICAL CONSIDERATIONS

Considering together the scenes depicted on the two vases just discussed, i.e. the loutrophoros and the large oinochoe, one can observe that the two episodes of love with tragic consequences, in particular that of Laius and Chrysippos on the large oinochoe, find a significant counterpoint in the already discussed representation on the loutrophoros which refers instead to marriage and, more generically, to the continuity of the lineage or gens. Such connections between the various mythological episodes shown on the vases from Tomb 19, especially the recurring representation of episodes related to the Theban dynasty, in tomb 19 and on the scene involving Niobe on the amphora in the contiguous Tomb 24, provide an explicit referential background to the events of a regal genealogy. The depiction of the myth, as has been convincingly argued by A. Pontrandolfo for a number of funerary contexts at Paestum,[26] and more generally by A. Rouveret with specific reference to late Apulian red-figure,[27] contributes in certain instances to the construction of a genealogy for the local emerging aristocratic groups. The well documented contexts of Tomb 19 and Tomb 24 in the La Scala necropolis at Roccagloriosa allow us to propose that, in this particular case, the elaborate mythological representations on the large funerary vases found in the tombs may be tied to the specific requests of the Italic clientele[28] – clients of unquestionable high social standing. This hypothesis is further supported by the specific choice of two episodes of the Theban saga (the mourning Niobe, in Tomb 24, and the rape of Chrysyppos by Laios, in Tomb 19). Furthermore the repeated reference to the destiny of a royal dynasty may well be part of an attempt at self-representation in order to present or consolidate the genealogy of a family group. Recently Margot Schmidt[29] cautiously proposed this as one among several possible interpretations of such a variety (literally a 'boom') of new and sometimes rare mythological scenes depicted on later Apulian red-figure.

All of this becomes even more plausible when the depiction of Laius and Chrysippos on the oinochoe from Tomb 19 is considered in relation to the already mentioned neck amphora in the contiguous Tomb 24, representing a particular aspect of the Niobe saga which, in many respects, constitutes the prototype of many analogous depictions dated to the second half of the fourth century, as illustrated by Helena Fracchia.[30] The Niobe story as depicted on the vase in question, with the heroine surrounded by her family group, seems to betray an implicit reference to the deceased in Tomb 24. That deceased, a woman of more than 40 years old who, thanks to the transparent ritual value of the bronze phiale at her feet, is to be understood as a major figure with a specific role as a priestess within the local community.[31]

Undoubtedly, the exceptional find of the two recently excavated and intact chamber tombs from the Roccagloriosa necropolis still requires us to be somewhat cautious in interpreting the significance of elaborate myths that repeatedly refer to the episodes of the Royal house of Thebes, in particular because the group of tombs in the north enclosure still needs to be studied in its entirety once the restoration of the full context of grave goods in the northern enclosure is complete. Nonetheless, already at a first reading, it certainly does not seem coincidental that the depiction of the same figure, Pelops the son of Tantalos, is to be found in both the Niobe scene in Tomb 24 (holding his father who is beseeching his daughter to stop her mourning) and in the contiguous Tomb 19. Here Pelops appears on the lower register of the oinochoe in regal dress and with a Phrygian type cap behind the chariot that is carrying off his son, Chrysippos. The representation of Pelops constitutes within the narrative context a probable link between the two episodes that happened at two distinct moments in the saga of the descendants of Tantalus. Pelops, who as a young brother of Niobe piously holds his old father Tantalos on the scene in Tomb 24, has become a mature regal man to whom his own son Chrysippos begs for help on the oinochoe in Tomb 19.

CONCLUDING REMARKS

One point that emerges in a sufficiently clear manner from this first analysis of the group of red-figure vases in Tomb 19, when set in relationship with the already published amphora with a representation of the Mourning Niobe in the nearby Tomb 24,[32] is the noted correspondence – it would be hard to interpret it as pure coincidence – between the depictions of two different episodes of a royal dynastic saga (the Theban cycle) and the familial relationship that the archaeological evidence allows us to infer for the people ordering these vases, the owners of Tomb 19 and Tomb 24, belonging to one of the families at the very top of the local Lucanian community. What is even more relevant, the cumulative evidence provided by a close reading of the figured scenes in their reciprocal relationships and by the observations on the production of some of the large red-figure vases from Tomb 19, formulated above,[33] strengthens the hypothesis of a probable phenomenon of transfer of craftsmen from the main workshop (in this particular case Metapontum or Tarentum) to the Roccagloriosa site, or, more generally the wider area where there existed a qualified demand for such elaborate mythological representations.[34]

In a very recent comment focussed on the specific case of Tomb 19 from Roccagloriosa, J.-P. Morel aptly underlines '...la possibilité qu-auraient eue des artisans d'aller à l'occasion à travailler dehors de leur officine habituelle et, le cas échéant, d'en créer quelque 'succursale' ou quelque concurrent'.[35] In the case of the Roccagloriosa site, under consideration, such a hypothesis is much strengthened by the well documented tomb context, which allows us to envisage a commission made by the buyers of the vases and presumably even a specific request made for the scenes represented. To this purpose, we should not overlook the fact that, as already mentioned, more conclusive evidence of an actual 'figurative program' might emerge from a more comprehensive study of the entire group of burials in the northern enclosure of the Roccagloriosa cemetery (once restoration is completed) and from a deeper analysis of the mythological representations on the individual vases included in Tomb 19. Such evidence might further strengthen the hypothesis that we may be dealing here with artisans catering to the specific needs of their patrons (in this particular case unquestionably belonging to a fairly well identifiable elite segment of the local community). It is already evident, however, that even a rather preliminary reading of the episodes of Greek myth identified on the large figured vases from Tomb 19, indicates the particular relevance of this context for various observations

---

25 I am indebted to F.-H. Massa Pairault for advice on the reading of the scene in the upper register.
26 Pontrandolfo 1995a.
27 Rouveret 1997.
28 In a lucid formulation of the problem of the relationship between workshops and clients, J. de La Genière (2006, 15) discusses a number of specific cases which imply '…une participation active des acheteurs'.
29 Denoyelle et al. 2005, 222. In the course of the same discussion, M. Schmidt aptly underlines that 'Il repertorio tematico appare quindi troppo diversificato per rendere verosimile la riduzione ad un unico scopo come quello dell'autorappresentazione dei clienti……*anche se non dobbiamo trascurare l'importanza di questo motivo*:' (ibid. – italics are mine!).
30 See Fracchia in this volume.
31 This particular aspect has been dealt with in detail by H. Fracchia in Fracchia & Gualtieri 2004. See also the argument in Gualtieri 2003, 151-152.
32 Fracchia 1984; 1987. See also *LIMC* 6/1, s.v. Niobe.
33 supra n.18.
34 Such a hypothesis had already been proposed in a previous, preliminary analysis of the Roccagloriosa context based on observations made during restoration of the vases: Gualtieri 2007, 264-266. On the general problem see the fundamental observations by M. Schmidt (2002, 262). Ibid., n.32 more specifically on the relevance of the evidence from Roccagloriosa.
35 Morel 2009, 248.
36 On this fundamental issue see the most recent comments (formulated with specific reference to the Roccagloriosa contexts) by J. de La Genière (2009, 241) and J.-M. Moret (2009, 392).

regarding the relationship between the producers of the vases and those who bought them.[36] The mythological representations on the oinochoe and the loutrophoros from Tomb 19, considered in parallel with the depiction of the Tantalidae on the amphora from Tomb 24, seem without doubt to correspond to the specific requests of a highly qualified clientele, of whom we are able to reconstruct both status and role within the local community. Thus, the overall available evidence from the necropolis, as well as from the settlement, concerning the cultural milieu and social standing of the buyers of these large figured vases in the Lucanian community at Roccagloriosa, is apt to provide many elements that shed new light on the diverse function of the Greek figurative tradition and on the phenomenon of its re-interpretation in relation to the status and role of the individual and family groups who used these vases.[37]

All told, the analyzed context of Tomb 19 provides fundamental evidence in support of the reasonable hypothesis that, at least in a number of instances in the Italic milieu, such mythological representations were used in a conscious and coherent manner in order to satisfy a desire for self-representation by the buyers and to express the identity of the emerging Italic aristocracies, within the complex and fast-changing cultural milieus of Magna Graecia during the second half of the fourth century BC.

---

37 Pontrandolfo 1995a; Rouveret (1997, 388) effectively underlines a trend to operate '… aggiramenti della tradizione epica… destinati ad esaltare i valori propri delle aristocrazie locali', among the leading vase-painters of the late Apulian ornate style. Relevant comments on this particular aspect have also been recently formulated by T.H. Carpenter (2003, 19-20). See, above all, the lucid remarks by I. Baldassarre (1998, 33-34), with specific reference to the more recent documentation from the Daunian area (Arpi in particular) and to Mazzei's pioneer work aimed at re-contextualizing late-Apulian red-figure vases from the Canosa-Arpi region.

Changing Contexts and Intent: The Mourning Niobe Motif from Lucania to Daunia

BY HELENA FRACCHIA

Changing Contexts and Intent: The Mourning Niobe Motif from Lucania to Daunia

BY HELENA FRACCHIA

In recent decades, iconographers and archaeologists have underlined that the mythological scenes found on South Italian funerary vases followed, on the one hand, Greek traditions, but, on the other hand, reflected the mental and cultural processes as well as the values of the indigenous society that used the vases.[1] Although the actual myths depicted on the South Italian vases can be identified as Greek myths, both the representational system and the figurative code used by the Italiote painters are recognizably different from those used on Attic vases for the same myths.[2] On occasion, when the entire individual funerary context is known, additional information leading to a more accurate interpretation of the specific mythological depictions can be gleaned. There is even greater potential when an entire necropolis in which mythological scenes have been found is excavated.[3] Thus, the images used by the South Italian vase painters can offer an autonomous interpretation of ancient society, with variable validity depending upon what is also known about the vase context and taking into consideration the actual form and use of the vase on which the mythological scenes were depicted.[4]

It is now widely agreed that many of the heroic themes found in indigenous tombs were used as elements of self representation and eulogy by the aristocratic segments of society, and were therefore chosen by the deceased or the family of the deceased to express aspects or associations of particular importance to the individual and/or his society.[5] If we consider that the corpus of mythological themes that appear on imported Attic vases found in Italy between 470 BC and the early fourth century BC are not the same as those found on the Italiote red-figure production, it is clear that there is no direct transmission of iconographic models and that both the artistic language and the content of the scenes found in Southern Italy must be an independent, and conscious, expression of contemporary society.[6] Furthermore, the recurrent use of similar themes also indicates that the myths were used to characterize either ethnic or ethical aspects or religious or social status.[7] A. Pontrandolfo has also suggested that both the choice of myth and in particular the representational system of the chosen myth was also used, with appropriate 'remodelling', to legitimize the political structure of the Italic populations.[8]

Ancient society, however, was not static and, thus, neither should the elements of self representation, immortality or expressions of political legitimacy be static. F. Colivicchi has recently suggested that the substitution of strigils for weaponry in tombs reflects the progressive development of a 'citizen' mentality tied to the greater political complexities that emerged in the course of fourth century BC Magna Graecia, in particular amongst some of the indigenous tribes.[9] Similarly, the symbolic language or figurative codes that are employed on vases when heroic myths were chosen for inclusion in indigenous tombs should change depending upon the contemporary social and historical circumstances, since those same scenes provide a narrative element about the life of the deceased and therefore reflect contemporary Italic society in all its complexity and its variability across the peninsula.[10]

This suggestion is strengthened by the fact that certain myths were remodelled and used selectively across Southern Italy. For example, the depictions of Cadmus, the founder of Thebes, emphasize the events following the slaying of the dragon. The Cadmus myth is found exclusively on the Tyrrhenian side of Italy, while the saga of Jason and the Argonauts was used on both the Tyrrhenian and Adriatic sides of Italy.[11]

THE MOURNING NIOBE MOTIF IN SOUTHERN ITALY

The Mourning Niobe motif was one of the most popular heroic myths used by several of the indigenous cultures of Southern Italy throughout the fourth century BC.[12] Attic vases of the fifth century BC, found in Greece and Italy, represent the punishment of Niobe and the slaughter of the Niobids.[13] In Southern Italy, however, the actual petrification of Niobe in perpetual mourning is emphasized and established a difference between the Attic and South Italian representational systems, just as the serpent, a secondary figure in fifth century Attic vases, becomes the central element in the fourth century BC South Italian remodelling of the Cadmus myth. The Mourning Niobe myth was first used on a neck amphora of 390-380 BC on the Tyrrhenian side of Italy, at the Western Lucanian site of Roccagloriosa, a vase apparently of local manufacture.[14] From the Adriatic side of Italy, nine Apulian vases have been found with depictions of the same mythological scene. Five of these Apulian vases are without a more precise context, while the other four vases were found in ancient Daunia and Peucetia, at the sites of Canosa, Ruvo and Arpi: all are dated to between 340-320 BC and were produced near their find spots.[15] Some years ago, Marina Mazzei, who studied the Apulian vases, suggested that the use of the Mourning Niobe scene, and subsequently other aspects of the myth, reflected a precise religious belief tied to immortality, and that this interpretation also extended to the Roccagloriosa example.[16]

Proceeding in chronological order, and placing the vases in their appropriate funerary and cultural contexts when possible, I would like to examine both the evolution of the representational system and the figurative codes of the six vases with known provenience from the two areas of Italy, one from Lucania in the west and five from Daunia and Peucetia in the east, to determine if the Mourning Niobe myth can be seen to reflect, as M. Mazzei suggested, a) a shared religious belief, b) an ideological evolution expressed by changes in the representational system and the figurative codes, or c) the historical circumstances of these two areas during the fourth century BC.

THE LUCANIAN REPRESENTATION

The early fourth century BC was a period of increasing complexity for several of the indigenous tribes, a time when they began not only to develop their traditional social and political structures, but also, in the most advanced areas like the Tyrrhenian coast, to adopt distinctive features of an urban society and complex forms of community organization.[17] The later fourth - early third century BC was characterized by the presence of Alexander the Molossion and Pyrrhus of Epirus on the Adriatic side of Italy, the Samnite Wars in Central and Tyrrhenian Italy, and in general by an increasing Roman presence that would culminate in the foundation of numerous Roman colonies in Southern Italy between the late fourth century BC and the fall of Taranto in 272 BC.

On the western coast of Italy, the Lucanian site of Roccagloriosa was a fortified, well-structured settlement of the early fourth century BC where elite houses and an elite cemetery have been extensively excavated. The cemetery at Roccagloriosa offers a clear reading of familial tomb groups, thus providing evidence about the socio-political organization of the community in the fourth century BC, a period of critical development of the Lucanian *ethnos* and, concomitantly, of a complex political organisation

---

1 The bibliography on the subject is now vast: Mazzei 1999; Denoyelle *et al.* 2005; Gualtieri 2006; Pouzadoux 2008; Massa Pairault 2008 with references to preceding bibliography.
2 Pontrandolfo 1995a.
3 In most cases, however, neither the individual context nor the wider necropolis is known, thereby limiting the certainty of the interpretations. It is probably this lack of context that originally caused the South Italian use of either obscure Greek myths or marginal episodes of Greek myths to be interpreted as 'theatrical scenes' in an attempt to provide some meaning to the vases. The fact that the figures in the mythological representations often wear elaborate dress does not mean that the dress is 'theatrical'. Thus, the use of elaborate material can simply mean an elevated social status, as in fact is evident in the painted tombs from Paestum. The 'phlyax' vases represent theatrical scenes, but either the stage set is evident and/or the padded actors or actors' costumes. But it should be noted that not even on these vases, most of which certainly represent a theatrical scene or a stage performance, is the dress 'elaborate' or theatrical cf. Trendall 1967: Cf. Giuliani 1996; Mugione 2000, 147-148; Schmidt 2005; Carpenter *forthcoming*, all with earlier bibliography.
4 Pontrandolfo 1995a, 269.
5 Cf. n. 1 supra.
6 Mugione 2000, 147. The reason why often obscure aspects of myths were chosen is not known. On this issue see Giuliani 1996 and Schmidt 2005.
7 Massa Pairault 2008, 198.
8 Pontrandolfo 1995a, 221.
9 Colivicchi 2009.
10 Pouzadoux 2008, 205.
11 Pontrandolfo 1995a, 219; Mugione 2000.
12 Mazzei 1999.
13 Mugione 2000, 62, tabella 14 and 63.
14 Fracchia & Gualtieri 2010. The notion of local manufacture is based on the clay type, the fact that that same clay is used for the majority of vases with mythological scenes found at Roccagloriosa, and the observation that most of the vases with mythological scenes at Roccagloriosa are misfired.
15 *LIMC* VI, s.v. 'Niobe' 908-914. See also *RVAp* I, 337ff and *RVAp* II, 588; *RVAp* Ist Suppl; Trendall 1972, 309-316; Trendall 1985, 138; Schmidt, Trendall and Cambitoglou 1976. More recently, after more study in terms of attributions, Mazzei 2005, 18 and nn. 25-26 notes that the Varrese Painter vase was from Canosa, a vase by the Baltimore Painter can be located at Ruvo, a vase by the Arpi Painter was found at Arpi, and a painter associated with the Arpi Painter produced a Niobe vase found at Canosa.
16 Mazzei 2005, 18.
17 Gualtieri & Fracchia 1990; Gualtieri & Fracchia 2001; Fracchia & Gualtieri 2009; Gualtieri 2009.

Fig. 1. Amphora from Tomb 24, Roccagloriosa, ca. 390-380 BC.

that accompanied an distinct Italic form of urbanization.[18] By the mid fourth century BC, low walls monumentalized the two cemetery extremities which correspond to the burial areas of two major aristocratic families found at the Roccagloriosa site between ca. 400 to 290 BC. The osteological analysis of the tombs in the northern sector establishes the ages and sexes of the deceased.[19] In brief, a woman older than 40 was buried in the centrally positioned chamber Tomb 24, while Tomb 23 is the cremation burial of a mature man over 40 years old. The two burials can be interpreted as the heads of the gens. The other five tombs contained young adult males between 20 and 40 years old.

The mature female in Tomb 24 was laid out on a high stone bed. At her feet, the most important position for tomb goods,[20] were placed a red-figure lebes gamikos, a red-figure neck amphora decorated with the Niobe myth (Fig. 1), a miniature coarse ware olla, a bronze phiale and an iron knife. Niobe is depicted as she turns to stone, standing on a base decorated with the three Fates, and surrounded by family members; Apollo and Artemis, the vestiges of the representational system and theme emphasized on Attic vases,[21] are shown above. As the granddaughter of the heroic Giant Atlas, as the daughter of the Lydian king Tantalus, as the sister of Pelops, the king of Elis, and as the wife of Amphion, ruling beside him as the queen of Thebes, Niobe was by marriage part of the powerful dynasty of Thebes, and by birth the daughter and sister of kings.

Despite the reliance on Greek myth, the vase represents Italic values, and in this instance both the immediate and wider contexts have been well delineated and studied. At the most obvious level, the story of Niobe is probably a statement of lasting fame and a representation of her aristocratic lineage: given the family tree evident in the cemetery, the myth probably also symbolizes the *pathos* of her life. As C. Pouzadoux has recently suggested, the fact that the vases with mythological scenes are found in tombs does not necessarily mean that their use was exclusively funerary. Even representations, such as the Mourning Niobe scenes, which have an eschatological significance can also provide a discourse about life.[22] The Niobe vase is several decades older than other objects in the tomb, and thus is an heirloom, a theme possibly chosen in life by the deceased to characterize herself, her society, her social standing. The mythological scene can be considered a kind of rhetorical device,[23] providing a eulogy, and serving as a *sema* to the woman, to her life, to her lineage, and to her status.[24] The

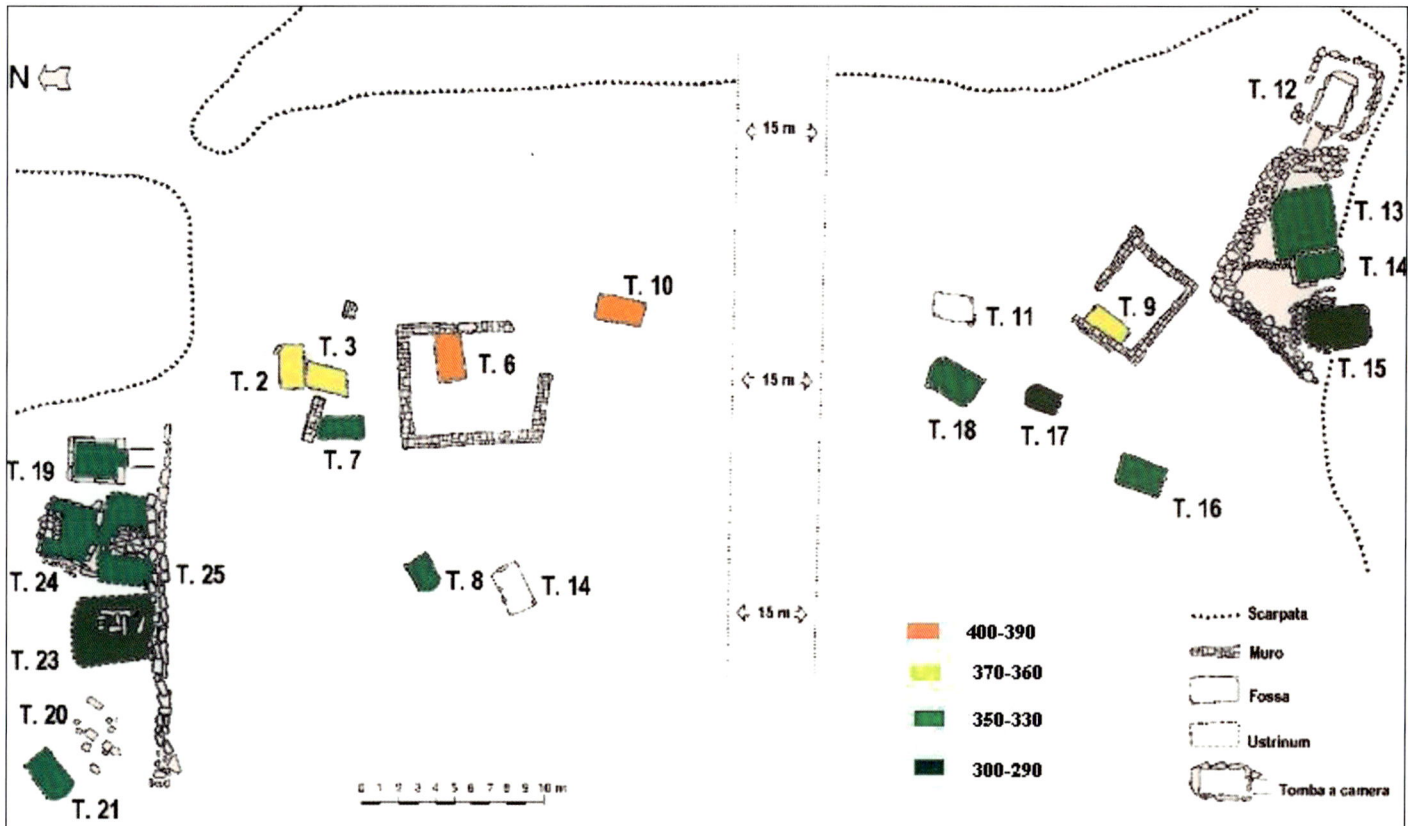

Fig. 2. Plan of the Roccagloriosa Necropolis.

fact that the tomb is the most prominent in the enclosure emphasizes her importance within the family group as the figure of Niobe is emphasized on the vase (Fig. 2). Taking into account the ages of the other burials around Tomb 24, we can suppose that the reference to Niobe's children is not casual. Given the regal standing of Niobe, it is possible that this myth was intentionally chosen to underline the distinguished lineage and important social status of this Italic aristocratic woman. The miniature two-handled olla, the bronze phiale and the iron knife, placed beside the Niobe vase, most probably refer to the role of the deceased within Lucanian Roccagloriosa and provide another element of eulogy.[25] These objects distinguish Tomb 24 from all the other female burials in the cemetery and indicate a qualitative difference in the status and social role of the deceased.[26] It hardly seems coincidental that in all the fourth century cult places in aristocratic houses found at Roccagloriosa, miniature ollae and sacrificial remains are

18 See n. 16 supra.
19 Gualtieri & Jackes 1993, 164-185.
20 Pontrandolfo 1995b.
21 Mugione 2000, 62-63.
22 Pouzadoux 2008, 206, who cites the example of Plato Gorgias 523-525 using the underworld to illustrate earthly justice.
23 Pouzadoux 2008, 206.
24 On the use of mythological scenes as sema, see Lippolis 1994 and Mazzei 1992a.
25 The role of the deceased female in Tomb 24 is discussed in Fracchia & Gualtieri 2004; Fracchia 2011.
26 As early as ca. 900-830 BC in Latium at Osteria dell'Osa, two exceptionally rich female tombs each contained a codolo knife: the females were identified as priestesses by the excavator. The knife and bronze phiale association is rare in Lucanian burials. The codolo knife pertains to the indigenous Italic tradition, and was used exclusively in the religious rituals of archaic Rome.

Fig. 3. Amphora (Taranto, National Archaeological Museum 8935), attributed to the Varrese Painter, ca. 340 BC (Photo: After LIMC vol. 6/1, pl. 610, no. 10).

present. Thus, the female buried in Tomb 24 can reasonably be linked to the type of religious ritual documented in the votive shrines found within the aristocratic houses at the site. Just as the vase representation seems to speak to an aristocratic standing and the importance of a familial lineage through time, the fuller tomb context appears to refer to her religious role in the community, a role probably shared with other aristocratic indigenous women.[27] The fact that the Niobe myth was portrayed on a neck amphora is not coincidental, and nor is the position of the vase amongst the grave goods. In Lucania, including Paestum, the amphora was used in both male and female burials until ca. 350 BC, after which time it was used exclusively in male burials.

But why was the House of Thebes chosen as the mythological heroic model? And why this particular episode? Aside from the particular vicissitudes of her individual life and the regal lineage of Niobe, the myth also tacitly refers to the act of establishing the city of Thebes, and to the fortification walls that Cadmus' son Amphion built, playing his lyre as the walls were erected. In terms of the changes noted in the South Italian use of the myth, Pontrandolfo noted that the myth, particularly on the Tyrrhenian side of Italy, was systematically adopted and remodelled to legitimize the political statutes of the Italic communities, emphasizing the birth of the city and the constitution of the civic body.[28] In the first half of the fourth century BC at Roccagloriosa the fortification walls, towers and the first identifiably aristocratic houses were built, including the house that contained what can be considered a prototype *lararium*.[29] Recently, an inscribed bronze tablet was found at the site.[30] The text, dated by Poccetti to the last quarter of the fourth century BC,[31] constitutes the juridical and administrative structure of the site naming magistrates, an assembly and a kind of senate. Obviously, these developments were carried out under aristocratic control. Beyond the site itself in the rest of ancient Lucania, between 360-350 BC, the first use of the word *Leukanoi* is documented by the ancient sources[32], and the first dedication at the 'federal' sanctuary at Rossano di Vaglio mentioning the magistracy of a certain Nymmelos took place.[33] All of these events or activities are statements of a clear ethnic perception and an evident sophisticated socio-political structure of the Lucanians.[34] Furthermore, the earliest tomb at Roccagloriosa, dated to ca. 400 BC, contained armour and a strigil that suggests the movement towards the 'citizen mentality'.[35]

The mythological model of the House of Thebes was probably chosen as an element of self representation by this woman's aristocratic family/lineage[36] because of its dynastic role in the foundation and subsequent administration of the site recalling Amphion, Niobe's husband, who founded the city of Thebes, and built the walls[37] as well as her own role in that foundation and administration. The theme can be interpreted as a reference to the origins and identity (*aition*) of the Lucanian settlement at Roccagloriosa.

THE DAUNIAN AND PEUCETIAN REPRESENTATIONS

How does this early representation of role and lineage compare with the better known Adriatic Daunian and Peucetian examples found at Canosa, Ruvo and Arpi, all of which are of local manufacture and dated to between ca. 340-320 BC, approximately 50-60 years after the Roccagloriosa example? The Roccagloriosa Niobe vase has a more complete archaeological context than the other vases, to be sure. Nonetheless, all the depictions share major elements of the same representational system. Niobe is shown as she turns to stone, surrounded by other members of the Royal House of Thebes. Variables include the number and identity of family members, the type of structure on which Niobe stands, and the vase shape on which the scene is painted. Do all depictions of Mourning Niobe represent the same thing despite differences in date, in places of manufacture, and historical circumstances?

Originally the sudden surge in Mourning Niobe scenes was connected with the appearance in Italy of Alexander the Molossian in 334 BC, but the Roccagloriosa Niobe predates significantly that event.[38] All the Adriatic examples were found in the geographical area of southern Daunia and northern Peucetia, but we do not know the entire contexts of the large hypogean tombs in which they were found.[39] The Varrese Tomb at Canosa which contained a Mourning Niobe representation has been reconstituted materially, but the tomb had many chambers, and we have no idea what was found with what or how many burials were contained in the tomb.[40] Nonetheless, the size and wealth of the Canosa Varrese Tomb testifies to the importance of the family buried there and the significance of its continuity. The tomb contained nearly 400 vases

---

27 In all probability, the actual votive deposit, fully published in Fracchia 1993, can be considered a type of commemorative ceremony as well as an element of cultural memory, cf. Assmann 1997. The presence of female priestesses in Archaic Rome is well documented and, by analogy, it would be reasonable to assume the same social role for women amongst the other indigenous communities as is certainly indicated by the *defixio* found at Marcellina, see Greco & Guzzo 1992.
28 Pontrandolfo 1995a, 221.
29 An early house with architectural terracottas and a votive statuette was found directly underneath the later house that contained another large votive deposit: the architectural elaboration of the earlier house led Massimo Osanna, in a personal communication, to suggest that the house may have been a regia. The supra-imposition of the two houses and two votive deposits, the largest found at the site, suggest that this was the lodging of the founders of the site.
30 Gualtieri 2009 with preceding bibliography.
31 Musti 2005, 319-320 dates the text to ca. 350 B.C.
32 Musti 2005, 261,269, 271, 273 with reference to Isocrates and Ps. Scilace, 276.
33 Musti 2005, 319-320.
34 A general trend towards more clear ethnic perceptions is found throughout Central-Southern Italy at this time: perhaps not coincidentally, the word Rome first appears in this same time period on the Ficoroni cist.
35 Fracchia & Gualtieri 2009; Gualtieri 2009: Tomb 6, dated to 400-390 BC contained a knife, a lance point and a strigil. Some of the bronze objects that referred to the symposium were heirlooms as well, dating to the last third of the fifth century BC. Tomb 10, also dated to 400-490 BC, similarly contained a bronze strigil and an iron knife. Other tombs contained iron knives, but without any bronze armour, with the exception of large bronze belts which should be considered ceremonial: see Gualtieri 1990. The iron knives may also be ceremonial as they are found in both male and female aristocratic tombs, cf. Fracchia & Gualtieri 2004. The occurrence of 'heirlooms' in the two oldest tombs at the site is curious but could refer to their hereditary role in the establishment of the site.
36 Pontrandolfo 2005a; Gualtieri 2006.
37 Perhaps not coincidentally, in Argos, Niobe was considered to be the original mother of mankind, a particularly appealing connection with the foundation of a site and, seemingly, a dynasty, see Kerényi 1974, 223.
38 This is a long-standing tradition: Livy VIII, 24; Mazzei 2003, 243-261 and the entire volume itself, dedicated to Alexander the Molossian in Southern Italy.
39 Andreassi 1992, 238-336.
40 Andreassi 1992, 238-336 provides full publication of the tomb.

Fig. 4. Amphora (Bonn, Akademische Kunstmuseum 99), attributed to the Varrese Painter, ca. 340 BC (Photo courtesy: Akademische Kunstmuseum, Bonn).

Fig. 5. Loutrophoros (Naples National Archaeological Museum 82267 (H3246)), attributed to the Varrese Painter, ca. 340 BC (Photo: after LIMC vol. 6/1 pl. 610, 12).

as well as armour and weaponry all dated to 340-330 BC. The inclusion of the armour and weaponry documents the conservative political and social structure of the area in the second half of the fourth century BC, in contrast to Tyrrhenian Western Lucania[41], where this practice was abandoned much earlier when more complex forms of settlement and governance were developed. In fact, the armour in the fourth century BC hypogean tombs at Canosa is a tradition documented in the earliest 'princely' or aristocratic tombs of the seventh century BC.[42]

Another element of interest is the change in the vase shape on which the scene was habitually depicted. The Varrese Painter depicts Niobe twice on amphorae and once on a loutrophoros (Figs. 3, 4, 5).[43] In addition to the vase shape, several other structural similarities link the Daunian and Peucetian examples to the Roccagloriosa Niobe, but the differences in the figurative code are more significant than the similarities. In the second half of the fourth century BC, on vases included in aristocratic or elite burials in Daunia and Peucetia, Niobe began to be shown on a monumental structure with columns, interpreted generally as a tomb. The tomb and Niobe share the spotlight. Between the columns of the tomb, an open jewellery box and a patera are displayed. The patera may be a generalized reference to a religious activity, either by Niobe herself or in reference to the community, as libation was considered to be a communal activity. On the other hand, the jewellery box is exclusively an element that pertains to the female world. Niobe was shown flanked by loutrophoroi within the tomb (Figs. 3, 4), and often a kalathos stands outside of it or nearby (Figs. 3, 5). The loutrophoroi are marriage references, and the kalathos refers to the fertility of the earth as well as to the female role in providing sustenance, in this case fruit. Niobe was also accompanied by several other women variously carrying an open jewellery chest, a fan, a wreath, a patera, or a lyre (Figs. 3, 4, 5). The lyre in this instance, in light of the various marriage symbols, is certainly a reference to Amphion, who played his lyre as the walls of Thebes were built. Tantalos and the old nurse are also often depicted (Figs. 3, 5). Another patera, a mirror, another quintessential reference to the female world, and discs (although not visible in these figures) are frequently depicted in the field (Figs. 3, 4, 5). Amongst the 392 objects without precise provenience, two clay patera were found in the Varrese tomb, apparently a residual reference to the religious role held by elite women in indigenous society, including Daunia and Peucetia.[44] The representational system, in its emphasis on the tomb context and figurative code and with its emphasis on the female world, as well as the vase shapes included as part of the whole scene, establishes that the use of the mourning Niobe myth is no longer exclusively tied to dynastic self representation but has been remodelled to emphasise a different aspect of the Italic world of the second half of the fourth century BC. On the one hand, the expression of memory or the use of the vase as a sema has become more important, and this would accord with the suggestion of Marina Mazzei:[45] on the other hand, the baxes, kalathoi and loutrophoroi shown in the field are more generic symbols of the female role in society. The dynastic context is certainly underlined by Tantalos and the lyre, a reference to Amphion, but the women and what they carry – jewellery boxes and fans – or are accompanied by – loutrophoroi and kalathoi, as well as the Eros – provide Niobe's generic context and are certainly parallel to her familial context. This emphasis is particularly evident on the reverse of a second Niobe scene on an amphora also by the Varrese Painter where a loutrophoros, typically associated with marriage, replaces a human figure (e.g. fig. 6).[46] The language of the Varrese Painter's vases is very different, although the complete archaeological context is missing. Nonetheless, the figurative code of mythological heroic model seems now to serve as a generic reference to the role of women, and the representational system has acquired a greater eschatological emphasis across time.

The other Apulian representations of Niobe are similar, but the emphasis on the traditional role of women is even clearer. The scene is now usually depicted on hydriae, loutrophoroi and lekythoi, shapes traditionally associated with women and their role in society. The same shapes were then shown or repeated in the actual painted scene. A similar 'change of status' can be seen in the religious elements within some of the actual burials, as in fact was the case in the Canosa tomb.[47]

The other later fourth century BC examples of the Niobe scene from Daunia and Peucetia confirm this trend

---

41 On the precocity of the Tyrrhenian side of Southern Italy and in particular the area between the Gulf of Policastro and the Savuto river, see Gualtieri 2009; Mollo 2009; La Torre 2009; La Torre & Mollo 2006.
42 Pouzadoux 2008, 211 with previous bibliography.
43 Loutrophoros, Naples Museo Archeologico Nazionale 82267 (H 3246) with no provenience; see also *RVAp*, 341, 22; Amphora, Bonn Akademische Kunstmuseum 99, with no provenience; *RVAp*, 314-315, pl. 4, Trendall 2, pl. 5; Amphora Taranto, Museo Archeologico Nazionale 8935, from Canosa; *RVAp*, 926-97, pl. 363, 1. The amphora from Canosa is fully published by Cassano 1992, 261, no. 1.
44 De Palma 1992.
45 Mazzei 2005, 18.
46 The same use of a loutrophoros in place of an actual person can be seen on the reverse of Fig. 6.
47 Andreassi, 1992; De Palma 1992, 307 no. 26, 308 no. 27. Ceramic phialai are also amply documented in the mid fourth century tombs at Paestum, Agropoli and Laos on the Tyrhennian coast as well as in Daunia, see Fracchia & Gualtieri 2004. In fact, in the later fourth century BC miniature knives and phiale are commonly found in tombs without armour. The knife and phiale found in Daunian tombs of the later fourth century are usually miniaturized indicating a symbolic rather than real value.

Fig. 6. Loutrophoros (Malibu, Getty Museum 82.AE.16), attributed to the Painter of Louvre MNB 1148, ca. 330 BC. Side A and B (Photo courtesy: The Getty Museum, Malibu).

(Fig. 6): an architecturally monumental naiskos with Niobe inside flanked by loutrophoroi, a kalathoi with Orphic eggs, a breastplate, paterae with Orphic eggs, a lyre referring to Amphion, family members, this time Pelops and Hippodameia in a chariot in a lower register, and other unidentified women around the tomb. Thus, changes can be seen in both the representational system, including the actual vase shape on which the scene is painted, and in the figurative code of the Mourning Niobe scenes. What starts in the early fourth century BC on the Tyrrhenian coast as self representation and a personal eulogy, a statement of status and role within familial, community and ethnic groups, seems to have evolved into a more generic eschatological use of the Mourning Niobe myth by ca. 340 BC. Within the light of the evolution outlined above, Mazzei's suggestion that there was a shared religious belief inherent in the repeated use of the Niobe scenes can certainly be accepted. But perhaps that is not the entire story. Can Niobe (and other female heroines such as Andromeda)[48] also be considered as a symbol of the original social role of aristocratic females and as a prototype of behaviour for elite females who shared or held fundamental roles in their respective settlements, interpreting the Mourning Niobe myth as a paradigm? The Apulian vases still refer to fame and memory but make equal reference to the traditional female role as it is transmitted to us by the Roman ancient sources.[49] The same critical elements – aristocratic lineage, family, matrimony, suffering, piety, religion – are found but the emphasis is different, especially in the repeated appearance of women with jewellery chests, the use of the naiskos, the appearance in the scene of vases tied to marriage (loutrophoroi) and to the role of women such as hydriae, and the actual vase shape, e.g., loutrophoroi, hydriae, lekythoi, on which the scene is painted. On the other hand, the sequential aspect of the use of myths dealing with the House of Thebes at Roccagloriosa itself[50] might suggest a gentilician connection in the origin of the families using the myths of the House of Thebes.

THE EVOLUTION OF THE MOURNING NIOBE MOTIF

But what causes the differences in the representational system and in the figurative codes between the Tyrrhenian and Adriatic coasts, between Lucanians and Daunians or Peucetians? What we see in the Niobe vases from Canosa, Ruvo and Arpi may well be part of a local conservatism documented in the archaic social and political structures of the area, where until the last decades of the fourth century BC the local aristocracies had absolute control over their fortified centres and still displayed armour and weaponry in their tombs.[51] But those local aristocracies maintained their control as well as their conservative political and social structure longer than was the case elsewhere only because they had previously joined with Rome. In this case, the Niobe myth could still be used as self representation by the elite females; but the figurative code that emphasizes funerary practice, marriage and women's role in the later vases affirms not so much a female pertinence to a dynastic centrality and importance, but rather the pertinence to the female world. Is this a selective adjustment in the presentation of the Niobe myth, an adjustment that responds better to the Roman system?[52] Certainly it has been suggested that some of the Daunian painters were amongst the most 'political' vase painters, so that a pictorial echo of or resonance with the Roman political support that the conservative Daunian aristocracy enjoyed would not be anomalous.[53] In the course of the fourth century BC Daunia underwent several important changes in funerary ideology which signal a break with what could previously have been considered a Daunian practice.[54] Could this postulated mythological adjustment or remodelling of the Niobe myth also be connected to the fact that the Mourning Niobe motif is not used in any artistic medium again after ca. 320 BC? After 320 BC, the slaughter of the Niobids becomes popular in the vase paintings of the local Arpi Painter and his circle as well as in terracotta tomb offerings in Daunia and Peucetia, reflecting, perhaps, the Roman takeover at Arpi in 326, the bloody defeat of Canosa in 318 BC,[55] the foundation of a Latin colony at Lucera in 315 BC, and the Daunian participation as allies of the Romans against Pyrrhus in the 290's.[56]

The idea that there is an element of immortality in the use of the myth through time is quite plausible, but it would be reductive to consider all these changes either as the product of a stylistic evolution or only as the expression of immortality, particularly in the light of the disappearance of the Mourning Niobe motif in ca. 320 BC and its substitution with the slaughter of the Niobids in the artistic production of Canosa. The change to an emphasis on the slaughter of the Niobids is eloquent if considered within its historical context.

The use of the Niobid motif in South Italian art is by no means linear or one dimensional. The length of time that the myth was used, the geographical distances between its production sites, the way in which the representational system and the figurative code of the myth developed across time, can and should certainly speak to the cultural reality and memory, individual as well as socio-political, of the indigenous world from ca. 400 BC until the second century BC.

---

48 Depictions of Andromeda follow the same evolution as those outlined for Niobe. From an emphasis on her being bound in Attic vases, in South Italian vases she is shown being freed by Perseus instead. The depictions of Andromeda also become more eschatological in time. She is often shown in a naiskos like Niobe, a clear reference to funerary symbolism, see Mugione 2000, 95.
49 The role of women in ancient Lucania has not been well studied.
50 Gualtieri in this same volume; Gualtieri 2006.
51 Colivicchi 2009 and Pouzadoux 2008, 211. Livy (8,25,3:27,2) refers to a Roman alliance with the 'Apuli' in 326 BC.
52 In this same light, the appearance in the second half of the fourth century of elements referring to Rome (e.g. bucrania) in the works of the most intellectual of the Apulian vase painters, the Darius Painter, is not coincidental, see Massa Pairault on the Darius Painter 2008, 203 and 1996, 2356-262. For the Roman influence in the large hypogean tombs, see Torelli, 1992.
53 Massa Pairault 2008, 202: The Arpi Painter often included references to Rome in his vase paintings, and he also had a predilection for unhappy mothers.
54 Mazzei 1992b, 585-586.
55 Not coincidentally, evidently Canosa had earlier sided with the Samnites against the Romans (Pani 1979, 86-90), although Canosa had previously been allied with the Romans since the end of the fourth century BC. On terracotta offerings of the slaughter of the Niobids, see Mazzei 2005.
56 Dionysius of Halicarnassus 20, 3, 2.

ACKNOWLEDGEMENTS

A special thank should be given to Jacklyn Burns (The J. Paul Getty Museum) and Martin Bentz (Akademische Kunstmuseum, Bonn) for providing photos of vases in their collections.

Boeotian Red-figured Vases: Observations on their Contexts and Settings

BY VICTORIA SABETAI

Boeotian Red-figured Vases: Observations on their Contexts and Settings

BY VICTORIA SABETAI

Contextualizing the study of fifth century BC Boeotian red-figured vases involves consideration of various factors, such as ways and means of artistic transmission, workshop realities and findspots. First, since Boeotian red-figure is dependent on Attic models and receptive of Attic trends, influences stemming primarily from Athens should be analyzed. It is, however, equally important to grasp the degree of the local painters' role in selecting, adapting and inventing iconographical schemata for their own needs. Second, workshop realities should be studied, for some Boeotian red-figure painters were affiliated with local black-figure workshops, such as those manufacturing floral and Kabiric ware. Third, the role of red-figure in various social contexts, sacred as well as profane, should be examined through findspots and diffusion. One should keep in mind that the circumstances of preservation may yield a biased picture, as the greater part of the material is preserved in graves, less in sanctuaries and almost none in habitation areas. The latter have been archaeologically unrecoverable in Boeotia, but the analysis of grave material may on occasion point towards life-use for some items. For example, chronological discrepancies among items in a grave and ancient repairs may indicate life-use or heirlooms. The qualifying parameter of quantity is important when trying to assess the social identity of red-figure in Boeotia, for both Attic and Boeotian red-figured vases occur in small numbers and in only a few graves, usually combined with a plethora of late black-figured Haimoneian vases, Boeotian floral ware and black-glazed pots.[1]

So far, the general picture of the Boeotian red-figure pottery appears incohesive, because each painter appears to constitute a separate case,[2] with distinctive imagery that they paint on a limited range of shapes. This is the reason why Boeotian red-figure production has been referred to as having an 'episodic character',[3] with red-figure painters being members of workshops that were located in major urban centres (e.g. Thebes, Tanagra, Thespiai) and traded all over Boeotia and Lokris.[4] The small, yet regular, production of Boeotian red-figure spans the second half of the fifth century BC and continues well into the fourth. The upper chronological limits of Boeotian red-figure production are unknown, while the lower ones may reach the mid fourth century BC.[5] In the limited range of this paper I trace the contexts and settings that are essential in understanding fifth century BC Boeotian red-figure as outlined above.

Fig. 1. Boeotian red-figure lekythos, Thebes Museum, inv. no. Th.P. 697 (Photo courtesy: Thebes Museum).

Fig. 2. Boeotian red-figure lekythos, Thebes Museum inv. no. Th.P. 698 (Photo courtesy: Thebes Museum).

ATTIC IMPORTS AND BOEOTIAN ATTICIZING IMITATIONS

In general, Attic red-figure imports occur in smaller quantities than the black-figure ones that prevailed in the sixth and in the first half of the fifth century BC. Medium and small forms predominate and the overall quality is lower than the elaborate red-figured vessels that were exported from Athens to Etruria.[6] Based on Beazley's lists in the second edition of *The Attic Red-Figure Vase-Painters* [1963], the imported shapes in the fifth century BC comprised mainly drinking and unguent vessels, such as skyphoi, cups, oinochoai, head-kantharoi, lekythoi, pyxides and alabastra; larger shapes such as hydriai, pelikai and kraters are infrequent, although the last became popular in the fourth century BC.[7] In the first decades of the fifth century BC cups predominate, but from the middle of the century skyphoi become more popular. The lekythoi and the alabastra, both popular shapes in Boeotia already from Archaic times, occur mainly in the first half of this century. The subjects depicted on imported Attic red-figure are mostly generic, as is common in the Classical period: youths and women in agonistic, cultic, sympotic, domestic, nuptial and Dionysiac settings. Single gods are not frequent and mythological themes are rather rare.[8] Although the Attic imports cover the basic spectrum of vase shapes, the Boeotian red-figured repertory is much more limited and favours mainly small and often lidded kraters, skyphoi, kantharoi, dishes, lekanai and pyxides.[9] The subject matter of the Boeotian repertory is mainly generic and thus corresponds to the themes decorating the imported Attic

Fig. 3. Boeotian red-figure lekythos, Thebes Museum inv. no. Th.P. 699 (Photo courtesy: Thebes Museum).

---

1 Further study of the Haimoneian vases found in Boeotia is needed in order to determine what is Attic and what is a local copy. The black-glazed vases are mostly, if not all, Boeotian.

2 For a recent systematic monograph focusing on the Argos Painter, see Avronidaki 2007.

3 Pelagatti 1970, 146. For the lack of uniformity in the Boeotian black-figure production see also Kilinski 1990, 59-60.

4 For fifth century BC finds from Athens, Lokris and the West see Avronidaki 2007, 44, no. 15; 47, no. 22; 141-142; see also *CVA* Berlin 11, text for pl. 71 (allegedly from Attica).

5 For the upper limits see Avronidaki 2007, 31 (perhaps ca. 470 BC; one example). If vases listed by Beazley as Attic are reattributed to Boeotia, the lower limits may reach the mid fourth century BC: see *CVA* Thebes 1, text for pls. 86 and 88; *CVA* Benaki 1, text for pls. 45-46 and 51-52 (with amended archaeometric analysis in *CVA* Berlin 11, 83-90, esp. 87 and 89-90 [H. Mommsen-A. Schöne-Denkinger]).

6 For statistics of Attic red-figured imports based on Beazley's lists see Avronidaki 2007, 36, n. 148. ARV^2 contains 81 red-figured vases dated from 510/500 to 400 BC with various Boeotian provenances. These numbers are subject to change after the discovery of a necropolis at Thebes. Several unprovenanced vases listed as 'from Greece' may have come from Boeotia. In the fourth century BC Attic imports seem copious, but this impression will change if some groups that are probably Boeotian and not Attic are taken out of Beazley's lists (see previous note). The distribution of Attic pottery within the Greek mainland and in particular Boeotia is a poorly studied field: see Paleothodoros 2007, 168.

7 For an overview of vase painters/potters and shapes found in Boeotia see Appendix. A small number of large shapes, such as pelikai, are reported from Phokis and Lokris: ARV^2 285, 3; 586, 52 (Early Mannerist); 1104, 11 (Orpheus Painter); 1117, 3 (manner of Hephaistos Painter). From these areas are also reported a few small shapes such as a cup (ARV^2 76, 74), oinochoai (ARV^2 540, 5), head vases (ARV^2 1534, 17), alabastra (ARV^2 100, 26; 1560), skyphoi (ARV^2 973, 12; 1302, 4) and lekythoi (ARV^2 713, 137 [?]).

8 Mythological themes on fifth century BC Attic vases found in Boeotia: Herakles and Bousiris, divine pursuits (Eos and Tithonos; Zeus and Ganymede; Boreas and Oreithyia), Gigantomachy (the last occurs at the end of the fifth century). Gods and mythological figures: Apollo, Athena, Artemis, Leto, Hermes, Zeus, Nike, Eros, winged goddess in chariot, Menelaos and Helen (wedding), Perseus and Medusa, maenad, satyr, centaur, sphinx, anodos of a goddess.

9 The kantharoi, the lekanai and the dishes have a long tradition in Boeotian black-figure vase-painting.

Fig. 4. Boeotian red-figure krater by the Painter of the Dancing Pan. Athens, National Archaeological Museum inv. no. 1367 (Photo courtesy: National Archaeological Museum at Athens, Ministry of Culture/TAP).

Fig. 5. Boeotian red-figure krater. Athens, National Archaeological Museum inv. no. 12683 (Photo courtesy: National Archaeological Museum at Athens, Ministry of Culture/TAP).

vases. Mythological themes are rare and include scenes of Hermes killing Argos, the delivery of Dionysos to the nymphs, Phineus fighting a Harpy, the Judgment of Paris, the departure of Triptolemos, Boreas and Oreithyia, Danae receiving Zeus in the form of rain and the Delian Triad. The number of depicted gods and legendary figures outside a mythological narrative is limited: Artemis, Athena, Apollo, Dionysos, Herakles, Zeus, Pan, Nike, Iris, Selene, Skylla, the amazon and the siren are all represented, though mostly only by isolated examples.[10]

The few more or less exact Boeotian copies of Attic red-figured vases currently known indicate that the latter were so desirable that they were deemed worth imitating faithfully.[11] The findspots of both Attic and Boeotian red-figured vases in a few, on occasion significant, graves may further indicate that they were cherished possessions reserved for a deceased person of special status or social standing. Among the Atticizing pieces found in context are those unearthed in the Thespian Polyandrion, the massive burial of the fallen soldiers at the battle of Delion in 424 BC. A handful of vases that are close copies of Attic models were unearthed there together with a wealth of grave gifts consisting of black-glazed vases, especially kantharoi, figurines and metal objects, such as strigils.[12] Had it not been for their findspot and the buff clay, these red-figured vases might easily have been mistaken for Attic products. Three lekythoi were made by a Boeotian copyist of the Achilles Painter, which indicates that certain themes must have passed into the Boeotian repertoire through specific Attic painters. These lekythoi depict a divine pursuit (Zeus and woman), a libation performed by Athena and Herakles and a female pyrrhic dance (Figs. 1-3); one further pyrrhicist is depicted in a symposium scene on a bell-krater that follows closely the Polygnotan Group and, in particular, the Kassel Painter.[13] The selection of Zeus, Athena and Herakles by the Atticizing painters does not seem fortuitous: the former two were the Boeotian ethnic gods par excellence, and Athena is recurrent in the

Fig. 6. Boeotian red-figure pyxis. Thebes Museum inv. no. 31923 (Photo courtesy: Thebes Museum).

Boeotian red-figured repertory in general. Her favourite hero Herakles, a native of Thebes, is an important figure in Boeotian cult and art. After 447/6 BC, he became the representative of oligarchic Thebes on an unusually pictorial coinage that depicts him in various age-classes and which has some correspondences with Boeotian red-figured scenes, as on a kantharos in Athens.[14] The emphasis on Herakles as a youth and mature hero manifests the most important phases in the life of a Boeotian elite citizen and makes the hero a patron of youths and a model of ephebic transition and heroic accomplishment. Pursuits, libations and symposia, the three types of scenes occurring in the Thespian Polyandrion, were common in the Attic repertory[15] and were taken over by Boeotians,[16] but exotic dances such as the pyrrhic and the oklasma were not and it is notable that the pyrrhic dance recurs twice in the handful of the Polyandrion red-figured vases. It occurs again on a krater by the Painter of the Dancing Pan, where the pyrrhicist is juxtaposed with a bridal female next to a louterion (Fig. 4), while another Atticizing krater features the oklasma as its main theme (Fig. 5).[17] The formula of the female pyrrhic has been recently considered as a humorous theme that expresses inversion, i.e. the cultural norm reversed, and was thus semantically connected with the sphere of prenuptial transition. Themes related to this realm were popular in Athens, especially in the second part of the fifth century BC, and were also diffused in Boeotia, where a heightened interest in ephebic themes is attested.[18] An Atticizing pyxis from a grave at Kanapitsa (Thebes) further documents the Boeotian painters' interest in nuptial scenes (Fig. 6).[19] Dated to 430-425 BC, this vase

---

10 For mythological themes and legendary figures on fifth century BC Boeotian vases see Lullies 1940, pls. 8-13; 23, 1; 28, 2; Avronidaki 2007, pls. 4; 8-9; 11-12; 14, 1; 16; 22; 26-27; 30-31. Most of the above mythological themes occur once, while single divine figures are more frequent and also occur in various combinations; recurrent are scenes of the Judgment of Paris, Athena on her quadriga, Danae, Skylla and a few gods. Divinities were rare subjects also in Boeotian black-figure: Kilinski 1990, 45-47.

11 For the various terms used to describe imitation in vase painting and for eclecticism in regional fabrics, see Coulié 2002, 170; 176-182.

12 For the Thespian Polyandrion, see Schilardi 1977.

13 *CVA* Thebes 1, pls. 16-20.

14 For Zeus and Athena in Boeotia see Schachter 1994. For Athena in the Boeotian red-figure repertory see *LIMC* 2009sup, s.v. Athena, 111, no. add. 23; *CVA* Berlin 11, pl. 71. For Herakles on the Theban coinage of the latter part of the fifth century BC see Ritter 2002, 102-120. For the Boeotian kantharos depicting Herakles see Avronidaki 2007, pl. 11 and note 58, below. For Attic vases depicting the hero and found in Boeotia see *CVA* Thebes 1, pls. 84-85.

15 For Attic vases with divine pursuits found in Boeotia see *ARV²* 519, 17; 381, 182; *Para* 383, 67. The erotic pursuit is a formula that connotes the impending wedding; in Attic art it is popular in the first half of the fifth century BC. Libations: *ARV²* 424, 131; 1155, 41; 1392, 18; Symposion: *ARV²* 140, 29; 176, 1.

16 For Boeotian red-figured vases with these themes see: Pursuit: Argos Painter (Avronidaki 2007, pl. 22). Libation: Imitator of the Painter of the Louvre Centauromachy, Painter of the Judgment of Paris and Argos Painter (*ibidem* pl. 2, 1; 4, 1; 14, 1; 16; 23 c; 29; 45); Maffre 1975, fig. 55; *CVA* Benaki 1, pl. 67.

17 Pyrrhicist: Painter of the Dancing Pan; Avronidaki 2008, pl. 3, 1. Atticizing painter: *eadem* 2007, pl. 3.

18 *CVA* Thebes 1, text for pls. 16 and 18.

19 *CVA* Thebes 1, pls. 21-22; for another, badly preserved pyxis from the Thespian Polyandrion see Sabetai 1998, pl. 64, c-d.

Fig. 7. Boeotian red-figure krater, Athens, Benaki Museum inv. no. 38554. Sides A and B (Photo courtesy: Benaki Museum).

is an interesting pastiche of a hybrid type A pyxis of local inspiration. The shape is reminiscent of floral pyxides by the Boeotian Van Branteghem Workshop, while the scene is informed by Attic wedding imagery. The Boeotian artist conflated here two Attic nuptial themes, namely the loutrophoria procession and the procession to the bride's new home. In an *interpretatio beotica*, the Attic loutrophoros is rendered as an amphora, presumably because that shape was unknown in Boeotia. This could imply that the painter was not an Athenian immigrant, but a local painter who copied from various Attic examples. The tone of the scene is more jovial than its Attic counterparts, which are characterized by a calm ethos. Instead of leading his bride solemnly to their new home, or gazing at her while holding her by the wrist, the Boeotian groom has taken hold of her arm and the couple amusingly rushes along. The vase is over-filled with *kalos/kale* inscriptions in the Ionic rather than the Boeotian alphabet and a red wash was applied to make the local clay look as Attic as possible.

Generic themes decorate also a few other Atticizing vases that are unprovenanced. A sacrifice scene on a krater by a copyist of the Kadmos and the Dinos Painters, as well as a Dionysiac (Fig. 7) and a libation scene (Fig. 8) on two others by an imitator of the Painter of the Louvre Centauromachy attest to the interest of Boeotian painters in this sort of standard-type repertory that features the citizen, especially the ephebe, in highly valued cult activities of the Greek polis. In addition to the known examples by the latter imitator, three more kraters, about to be published, depicting a Dionysiac scene, a sacrifice and an athletic scene, may be added. The total of five vases makes this imitator the most prolific Boeotian Atticizing painter known so far; furthermore, it highlights the importance of the Painter of the Louvre Centauromachy as a model for Boeotian painters.[20] The youth in the transient state from ephebe to citizen-hoplite also becomes the quintessential emblematic figure in the oeuvre of other indigenous painters, such as the Argos Painter; he is further raised to heroic status on late monumental kantharoi by the Painter of the Great Athenian Kantharos, where he is depicted as a victorious warrior and cavalryman (e.g. Fig. 15).[21]

BOEOTIAN RED-FIGURE AND ITS LINKS TO INDIGENOUS BLACK-FIGURE WORKSHOPS

Once local red-figure becomes established after the mid fifth century BC, it co-exists with three main categories

Fig. 8. Boeotian red-figure krater. Athens, National Archaeological Museum inv. no. 12600. Sides A and B (Photo courtesy: National Archaeological Museum at Athens, Ministry of Culture/TAP).

of black-figure: cup-skyphoi in a crude Haimoneian style, floral ware, and Kabiric vases. The upper chronological limit of the Kabiric ware and the floral ware production is unknown, but may be postulated as some time in the third quarter of the fifth century BC, the *terminus ante quem* being the date of the Thespian Polyandrion, 424 BC, where early specimens of these ceramic categories were found.[22] The category of the Haimoneian cup-skyphoi comprises Attic as well as local copies and dies out sometime in the last quarter of the fifth century BC, whereas the floral and Kabiric wares, both indigenous, continue into the fourth.[23] All three categories in the outdated black-figure technique outnumber greatly the red-figure production with which they co-exist,[24] a situation that is also attested in the archaeological record of sanctuaries and graves. Besides co-existing, black and red-figure productions in Boeotia are also variously interconnected. Affiliations may be at the level of collaborations between a black and a red-figure painter, as in the case of the red-figure collaboration-skyphos, whose side A is by a painter of Kabiric ware from the Thetis/Mystai Painter's[25] Workshop, and whose side B is by the Boeotian Argos Painter (Fig. 11).[26] Alternatively, a Kabiric-ware painter may on occasion use the red-figure

20 Avronidaki 2007, pls. 1-2; *CVA* Benaki 1, pl. 64. The three new kraters by an imitator of the Painter of the Louvre Centauromachy will be published by the present author.
21 Lullies 1940, 18-21; Sabetai 2012, 129-131.
22 For a bibliography on Kabiric and floral ware see *CVA* Thebes 1, text for pls. 12 and 13.
23 For late black-figured Boeotian copies of Haimoneian and other vases see Kilinski 2004, 58-59; Kathariou 2007b; *CVA* Athens, Museum of Cycladic Art 1, pls. 44-49. Attic Haimoneian cup-skyphoi are often found together with red-figured vases dated in the third quarter of the fifth century BC. See Fig. 13 and discussion below.
24 More than 300 Kabiric vases are currently known.
25 Named Thetis Painter by Ure; Mystai Painter by Bruns: see Ure 1958, 391, n. 12. I prefer the former and use it hereafter, for the latter implies that Kabiric-ware imagery realistically depicted scenes of a mystery cult, whereas, in fact, it parodied Attic and Boeotian iconographic schemes. For a critique on the 'mysterious mystery' cult at the Kabirion as a modern misleading concept and for the view that the Kabiric-ware parodies should be seen in the frame of a religious carnival see Mitchell 2009, 248-279. For Kabiric-ware imagery in the frame of ritual mockery see further Thompson 2006.
26 Avronidaki 2007, 43-44; 118-120; pls. 27; 75-76. See also the following paragraphs.

Fig. 9. Boeotian red-figure krater by the Painter of the Judgment of Paris. Athens, National Archaeological Museum inv. no. 1383 (Photo courtesy: National Archaeological Museum at Athens, Ministry of Culture/TAP).

Fig. 10. Boeotian red-figure lekane. Athens, National Archaeological Museum inv. no. 12881 (Photo courtesy: National Archaeological Museum at Athens, Ministry of Culture/TAP).

style in order to depict formal scenes related to cult, as is the case with the Thetis Painter, from whom we know a single, late fifth century BC red-figured krater depicting a symposiast with a snake drinking from his kantharos on side A, usually named Asklepios or Trophonios, and a worshipper bringing offerings to a healing goddess on side B.[27] Conversely, a red-figure painter may decorate in this technique a ritual shape that is normally painted in black-figure, as attested on three red-figured and notably non-grotesque Kabiric skyphoi, two of which come from the Kabirion.[28] What is more, a Kabiric-ware painter may still use black-figure, though in non-grotesque mode, when decorating a shape other than a Kabiric skyphos.[29] In addition to noting affinities between Boeotian red-figure and Kabiric-ware painters, we may further observe here that the Kabiric-ware parodies are closely linked to black-figure, while red-figure was not deemed suitable for grotesques, even when it decorated the Kabiric shape par excellence. Thus, red-figure in Boeotia is tuned in a different mode and speaks a visual language of a more elevated tone. It is expressed rather seriously in scenes emphasizing citizen values, such as those appearing on skyphoi and kantharoi, but is also jovial and celebratory on certain other ones, as on the pyxis previously discussed.

Besides Kabiric ware, Boeotian red-figure is also affiliated with workshops producing floral vases in a limited range of shapes (cups, pyxides, lekanai and other composite vessels). This is a particularly ornamental ware that should be understood primarily in a festive frame.[30] Red-figured scenes complemented by black florals are attested in various combinations and on a variety of examples. A red-figure vase may have a floral lid, as on a krater by the Painter of the Judgment of Paris, the lid of which is by the Van Branteghem Workshop (Fig. 9); or black florals and red-figured figures may co-exist on the same vase, as on bilingual Boeotian cups and lekanai (Fig. 10).[31]

All the above suggests that at least some Boeotian red-figure painters worked in the frame of established local black-figure workshops that were thriving in the latter part of the fifth century BC, and that some painters were even competent in both techniques. It also suggests that although black-figure was deemed old-fashioned in Athens after the mid fifth century BC, this was not so in Boeotia, where the Kabiric and the floral wares are both new series of products in an old style. Finally, the visual language of red-figure imagery should be understood in a formal and elevated discursive context in the Boeotian cultural milieu.[32] This does not mean that all Boeotian red-figured scenes are serious in tone; underlying humorous currents intended to evoke pleasure in a festive context may be detected on some of them.

The joint-piece mentioned above by the Argos Painter and another Kabiric-ware craftsman, although a rarity, is worth examining more closely, as it lies at the intersection between red-figure and Kabiric-ware iconography (Fig. 11).[33] The vase is a big red-figured skyphos of the same dimensions as the usually small Boeotian kraters.[34] It is unprovenanced and dates from the end of the fifth and the beginning of the fourth century BC. Its good state of preservation without any missing sherds may point to a funerary findspot, rather than a cultic setting. The subject matter of this monumental skyphos is overtly nuptial: all of side B, by the Argos Painter, is covered by a magnificent Eros, a figure that also appears on side A by the Kabiric-ware painter, here on a reduced scale and as part of a larger composition, holding a wreath above a louterion while looking at an elaborately adorned seated bride who gazes in a mirror while performing the *anakalypsis* gesture. The bride's crown is comparable to the one worn by Hera (identified by an inscription) on a Kabiric skyphos that depicts the Judgment of Paris in caricature, thus the Kabiric-ware painter here uses artistic vocabulary familiar to him from elsewhere, presumably to ascribe elevated status to the figure. Boeotian red-figure bridal figures do not usually feature any crown at all, but goddesses such as Hera and Demeter do.[35] The bride is placed in a Dionysiac context among ugly satyrs, one of whom performs the gesture of *aposkopein*, indicative of the arrival of Dionysos, while another, half-hidden behind the hill-line, gazes frontally and a third raises his hand in respectful salute

---

27 Lullies 1940, pl. 26; Avronidaki 2007, pls. 77b; 9b (note the black floral).
28 Avronidaki 2007, 45-46; 75-77; pls. 23 c; 30 (Argos Painter); CVA Bruxelles 3, III G, pl. 4, 9.
29 For a stamnoid pyxis depicting the Nereids carrying the arms of Achilles, see Barringer 1995, 180, no. 38, pls. 40-44. For a krater and an almond-shaped amphoriskos, see Ure & Ure 1933, 25-26, figs. 25-26; Wolters & Bruns 1940, pls. 26, 9-10; 36, 3-4.
30 For examples from sanctuaries, see Wolters & Bruns 1940, pls. 60, 1-5; 8 and 61, 1-3; 9; Zampiti & Vassilopoulou 2008, figs. 8-11.
31 For the cooperation between red-figure painters and black-figure workshops in Boeotia, see Avronidaki 2007, 32-35; 95-97; pls. 6-10. For florals on Kabiric skyphoi, see Braun & Haevernick 1981, pl. 9, 3.
32 See Sabetai 2012.
33 Athens, NM 1406: Avronidaki 2007, 43-44; 118-120; pls. 27; 75-76.
34 Height: 20 cm. The monumentality of this skyphos aligns it with contemporary oversize kantharoi, such as those by the Painter of the Great Athenian Kantharos.
35 For the Kabiric Hera, see Wolters & Bruns 1940, pl. 37, 2. For goddesses with crowns, see Lullies 1940, pls. 10, 2; 11, 1 (Demeter; Hera). For other Boeotian brides in red-figure, see e.g. Danae: Lullies 1940, pl. 23, 1 (no veil); Oreithyia: Avronidaki 2007, pl. 22 (plain veil). For a fragment with an unidentified seated woman wearing a high crown cf. further Avronidaki 2007, pl. 40 b. However, a high, polos-like crown of a different sort is a typical feature of contemporary bridal females in terracotta. For the association of the polos with maidenal deities and mortals in Boeotia, see also Simon 1972.

Fig. 11. Boeotian red-figure skyphos by the Argos Painter and a Kabiric-ware painter. Athens, National Archaeological Museum no. 1406 (Photo courtesy: National Archaeological Museum at Athens, Ministry of Culture/TAP).

or awe. The female was interpreted as Aphrodite by Ure, who considered Eros an attribute of the goddess, despite the fact that in the latter half of the fifth century BC he is an independent figure in women's scenes.[36] Avronidaki aptly identified the female with a bride, but explained the scene as referring to the initiation of a mortal into the Bacchic mysteries, an interpretation conditioned by her overall approach to the Argos Painter as an iconographer of ephebic initiation in the frame of the Kabiric cult.[37] While it is true that this painter was connected to Kabiric-ware workshops and some of his vases were found at the Kabirion, his imagery should be contextualized also in the frame of contemporary Attic imports, many of which focus on images of youth. His depictions of young men and women in various normative gendered roles, some of which emblematize the transitional status of the ephebe, may also reflect an emphasis on civic values and heroic ideals that imbues Boeotian art in the latter part of the fifth century BC. An alternative to considering this scene the visual record of cultic realities might be to understand it on the level of paradigmatic myth and name the bridal figure Ariadne. In this case, the winged god is Dionysos' special agent and personifies the god's love for her, as well as the upcoming change in status of the heroine. In fact,

Eros of side B, the biggest figure ever painted by the Argos Painter, is directed toward the female and his festive band is meant for her upcoming wedding, as any spectator would have realized when turning the vase around. A double, joyful, play of emphasis through the repetition of Eros may be at work here. Ariadne is more easily identifiable when she appears next to Dionysos, yet the arrival of the god is here anticipated by the gesturing satyrs, while the painter places the emphasis on the bride, not her consort. Such an omission of elements germane to the narrative, as may be the case here, is a characteristic of contemporary and earlier Boeotian art. In Attic imagery Ariadne is also a rather generic bridal figure and hard to recognize without an inscription until the fifth century BC, when her iconography becomes more fixed. Polygnotan painters often depict her waiting for Dionysos in the presence of Eros, but the god is normally present in the Attic scenes. The Attic schemata do not depict the louterion, which, however, becomes part of the iconography of legendary heroines in scenes with nuptial content, such as Helen, in Attic scenes that are contemporary with the skyphos under discussion here and occur on vases found in the region.[38] The Kabiric-ware painter places Ariadne at the louterion, an allusion to the ritual prenuptial bath and the beautification of the bride, in order to express her transient status which will end with her marriage to Dionysos. The louterion also features in other Boeotian scenes with bridal females.[39] Although Attic brides often appear gracefully naked at the louterion, Boeotian painters prefer to depict them demurely dressed; Ariadne's elaborate attire here stresses her high status and may suggest that this exceptionally large skyphos was intended for a formal occasion. The emphasis on Eros, and the fact that Ariadne was an archetypical bridal figure that exemplified eternal bliss as the outcome of a happy marriage between a god and a mortal, would make this monumental vase appropriate as a display piece at social events such as wedding banquets and, secondarily, funerals; it could also serve as a votive on a happy occasion perhaps related to coming of age or marriage, as it would propose a euphemistic comparison between the legendary heroine and the owner of the vase.

FINDSPOTS AND SETTINGS: SANCTUARIES AND GRAVES

The majority of Attic and Boeotian red-figured vases are found in graves, and the good state of preservation of pieces from Boeotia should normally be considered as implying funerary findspots.[40] A few, mostly fragmentary, red-figured pieces dating from the late Archaic to the fourth century BC were unearthed in two Boeotian sanctuaries, namely the Kabirion (Attic and Boeotian) and the grotto of the Nymphs at Helicon (Attic).[41]

The iconographic repertory of the fifth century BC vases from the Kabirion comprises youths, warriors, women, pursuits, sacrifices, banquets (?), gods (?), satyrs, centaurs, Dionysiac themes, Nikai, Eros, children, heads and animals. The shapes comprise cups, oinochoai 8A (mugs), skyphoi, lekythoi, head-vases, rhyta, a chous and a hydria.[42] The percentage of the red-figured vases is small by comparison to other classes of pottery in this sanctuary, and most are not of first-rate quality. Nevertheless, despite their limited numbers, the material from the Kabirion constitutes the richest assemblage of Attic and local red-figure from any sanctuary in the region known so far.

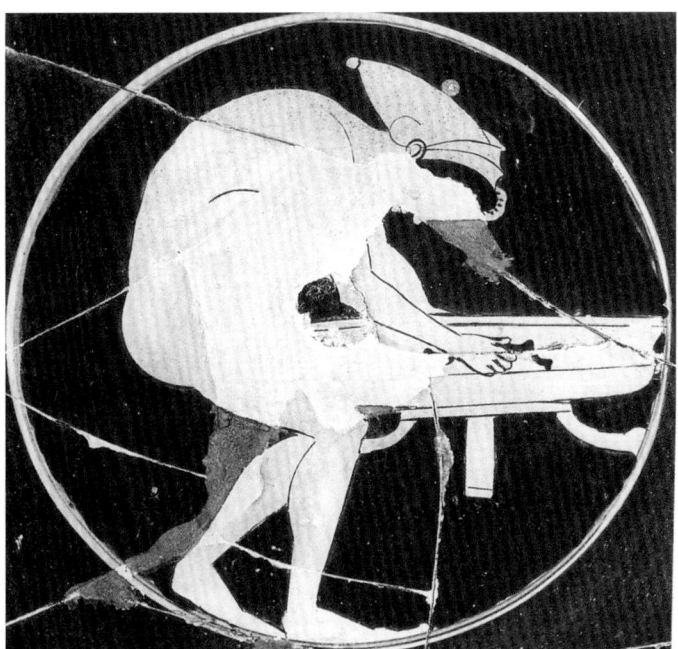

Fig. 12. Attic red-figure cup. Thebes Museum 23425 (R.18.255) (Photo courtesy: Thebes Museum).

36 Ure 1958, 390.
37 Avronidaki 2007, 118-120 with previous discussion and further, 98-118. For the question of mysteries at the Kabirion and their alleged influence on art, see most recently Mitchell 2009, op. cit. above, n. 25.
38 For Ariadne waiting for Dionysos in the presence of Eros, see Diez del Corral Corredoira 2007, 161-244, esp. 181, pl. 97; 187, pl. 100. For the theme on fourth century BC kraters from Boeotia, see Sabetai 2011, 155-157. For a louterion featuring in a scene of Helen's abduction which decorates an Attic hydria found in the region (Lokrian Halai) see *CVA* Thebes 1, pl. 76, 2. For the omission of elements germane to the narrative in archaic Boeotian art, see Kilinski 2004, 61.
39 See Avronidaki 2008, pl. 3, 1; eadem 2007, pl. 5; *CVA* Louvre 17, pl. 45, 2. It is possible that it was these louterion scenes depicting a woman with cupped palms, as if holding water in them, that made Ure wonder whether the females were engaged in mantic activity: see Nelson & Todd 2000, esp. 405-408.
40 Although there are some reports publishing finds from graves, comprehensive publications of Boeotian necropoleis and grave groups are lacking. This is partly due to the plethora of objects with which Boeotians buried their dead in the sixth and fifth centuries BC: see e.g. Sparkes 1967, 128 (Rhitsona grave 49, which contained 447 items).
41 Wolters & Bruns 1940, 84-89; Braun & Haevernick 1981, 77-83; Zampiti & Vassilopoulou 2008. For red-figure sherds found in Thebes and tentatively associated with the sanctuary of Demeter Kadmeia see Sabetai & Karakitsou *forthcoming*.
42 Wolters & Bruns 1940, 84-89; Braun & Haevernick 1981, 77-83: Schöne-Denkinger 2012. A total of 55 mostly fragmentary vases dating from 510/500 to the mid fourth century BC are listed in these publications; Attic outnumbers Boeotian in a ratio of ca. 3:2. A few big shapes occur only in the fourth century BC, but a fragment of a hydria by the Orchard Painter depicting a divine pursuit is also associated with this sanctuary: *Para* 383, 67; *Add.* 254.

Fig. 13. Boeotian red-figure skyphos by the Lewis Painter (inv. no. 41823) in the context of its grave-group (Pyre 46: vases and a figurine) Thebes Museum. Excavation material under publication by the author (Photo: Victoria Sabetai).

In the cave of the Nymphs at Helicon there were less than a dozen red-figured pieces, among many second-rate black-figured, black-glazed and floral vases. An exquisite late-Archaic Attic cup bearing the dipinto *Epilykos epoesen*, as well as a Boeotian graffito mentioning that this vase was offered to the nymphs as an *agalma*,[43] an object of pleasure and delight, was an exceptional offering. Such votives indicate that good-quality red-figured vases, even if not as elaborate as those exported to Etruria, did exist in Boeotia and were acknowledged as such by their owners, but were either rare or never hit the archaeological record in any number.

This dearth of red-figured pottery is also attested in the funerary record, for red-figured vases, both Attic and Boeotian, do not occur in everyman's grave and were only placed in limited numbers even in rich burials. The situation of scarcity is best exemplified in the rich Rhitsona grave no. 18 comprising 270 objects, among which there are several black-figured and splendid black-glazed pieces made in Attica, Boeotia and Euboea, but only one Attic red-figured cup of average quality that depicts a naked woman by a wash-basin (Fig. 12).[44] The grave dates back to the first decades of the fifth century BC and the cup is notably among the earliest of its contents.[45] By the mid fifth century BC a sharp contrast exists between the quantities of Haimoneian cup-skyphoi and the small number of red-figured vases in the graves, as can be seen in mid fifth century BC grave-groups at Akraiphia. An Attic red-figured skyphos by the Lewis Painter depicting youths in an athletic setting was the only red-figured vase that was given to a cremated adult together with 10 Haimoneian cup-skyphoi and four other black-glazed pots (Fig. 13).[46] A roughly contemporary grave from the same necropolis contained three red-figured skyphoi in a total of 22 vases, of which 9 are cup-skyphoi and one a floral pyxis.[47] A later Akraiphian grave assemblage of ca. 430-420 BC combines a Boeotian red-figure skyphos by the Argos Painter depicting *hoplitodromoi* together with Boeotian floral cups.[48] A similar situation is attested in Tanagra, although only a few clusters of graves have been excavated there and the general picture remains lacunose. Only two graves, an elaborate monolithic sarcophagus and a pit grave, contained a single red-figured vase each. The former contained at least one Attic squat lekythos depicting an Eros among Haimoneian cup-skyphoi and floral cups, and the latter a Corinthian krater with a Dionysiac scene among figurines of various types.[49] Thus, there seems to exist a pattern, at least in the grave record of the latter half of the fifth century BC, whereby Attic, Boeotian and, on occasion, Corinthian red-figure is scarce, usually ranging from one to three red-figured vases that were deposited together with several black-figured Haimoneian, or floral vases and black-glazed pots.

In Thebes, the Kanapitsa grave with the Atticizing pyxis discussed above, also contained a floral cup, a plain type C pyxis, two band-lekythoi, two bronze mirrors and a kore figurine with a high-polos, a common Boeotian type representing the bride.[50] The items of the grave point to a woman's burial and the combination of vessels for cosmetics and unguents may point to a bridal vessel-set (Fig. 14). The concentration of objects that are rarely found in fifth century BC tombs, such as the bronze mirrors, and their combination with the red-figured pyxis accentuates the social status[51] of

---

43 Zampiti & Vassilopoulou 2008, 453-456, figs. 30-31. For this cave, see also Trantalidou & Kavoura 2006/2007, 459, n. 6. It is worth noting that the digs are still going on.
44 *CVA* Thebes 1, pl. 73. The black-figured and black-glazed vases of the grave are amphorae, skyphoi, kantharoi, cups and lekythoi: see Burrows & Ure 1907/1908, 294-295, pl. XIII a; Sparkes 1967, 129; for the incomplete grave no. 22 that contained a red-figured skyphos by the Brygos Painter and a cup by the Pithos Painter see Burrows & Ure 1907/1908, 301-304, pl. XIII b-XIV; Sparkes 1967, 130; *CVA* Thebes 1, p. 98-99; Ure 1959, 4, n. 9 notes that while 300 black-figured vases were unearthed at Rhitsona, only three red-figured ones were found.
45 *CVA* Thebes 1, p. 98-99. The date range of this tomb's figured vases is ca. 20-30 years. By traditional chronology the red-figured cup is the earliest item of its group, which may mean that it had a use-life before being buried.
46 Such as a kantharos, a mug and skyphoi. The grave-group (pyre no. 46) also comprised one female figurine and is under publication by the author. For its associated cluster of graves see Sabetai 1995.
47 Andreioménou 1994, 107, n. 29; 109, fig. 8 (one skyphos is illustrated).
48 Avronidaki 2007, 41-42, pl. 23 a; Andreioménou 1985, 149, n. 17; pl. 47 c (floral cups).
49 Sarcophagus: Andreioménou 2007, 223-224 (grave T/8), pls. 105, 7-8; 151, 1; it was found partially robbed. Pit-grave: ibidem, 240-241 (grave T/1), pl. 130. Both date back to the last quarter of the fifth century BC. The publication includes finds from a total of 680 graves of all periods, several of which were found robbed, thus no statistics can be extracted with reference to the frequency of red-figured pottery in Tanagran tombs.
50 Philippaki, Symeonoglou & Pharaklas 1967, 234, pl. 164, 2; 4-6.
51 For a different but relevant discussion of gender as an indicator not only of social status but also of social standing and for the visibility of gender roles in death as expressed by gender-specific grave-goods, see Riva 2010, 72-107.

Fig. 14. The Kanapitsa Grave Group. Vases, figurine and mirror (Photo: after Philippaki, Symeonoglou & Pharaklas 1967, pl. 164).

a

Fig. 15a-c. Boeotian red-figure kantharos by the Painter of the Great Athenian Kantharos. Side A; detail of side A and side B. Athens, National Archaeological Museum inv. no. 12486 (Photo courtesy: National Archaeological Museum at Athens, Ministry of Culture/TAP).

the dead woman by defining her as a bride, a valorized role for a citizen woman and often especially highlighted in the instance of untimely death. The theory that red-figured vases in Boeotia must have been special items often connected with special status is further supported by their rarity in child burials, which, however, are rich in plain or glazed vases and figurines. A distinction should be made here with reference to the size of the red-figured vases, as small squat lekythoi are on rare occasions found in child burials, but medium or large vase-forms are not.[52]

The gender-specific grave-goods and vase-imagery of the Kanapitsa tomb may express a wish to portray the deceased in the normative role most appropriate to citizen women, and the deceased individual may have been someone who missed the socially sanctioned role of bride and wife. The presence of floral cups in this burial indicates that banquet vases were not thought inappropriate for female burials, and this accords with a mid fourth century BC grave of an adolescent girl at Thebes that contained two small red-figured kraters by the L.C. Group with Dionysiac themes, together with other objects referring to her missed bridal status.[53] The floral cups of the Akraiphia and the Kanapitsa tombs were produced by workshops that also manufactured floral pyxides of various types; the presence of floral ware in the grotto of the Heliconeian nymphs, deities particularly associated with women and brides, shows that they were made for use in life and that they featured in festive and votive contexts, some of which were particularly associated

b

c

with the female sphere. Thus, we can assume that the occurrence of floral ware and red-figure pottery in tombs is secondary and both could have been originally combined to form vase-sets for special, formal and celebratory occasions such as banquets and weddings.[54]

However, there are also a few cases indicating that a specific category of Boeotian red-figured vases was manufactured primarily for the tomb. Although it is unprovenanced, in this category belongs the kantharos by the Argos Painter depicting a woman visiting a warrior's tomb in a scheme that is borrowed from the repertory of the Attic white lekythos.[55] Here belong also the huge kantharoi by the Painter of the Great Athenian Kantharos (end of the fifth century BC) that heroize and emblematize the Boeotian dead by casting them in the type of the heroic soldier, cavalryman and symposiast (Fig. 15-16).[56] They are in an almost intact state of preservation and thus may be safely assumed to derive from the interior of cist tombs, which were the most elaborate grave-types of all and must have belonged to the elite. This category of monumental vase is particularly affiliated with contemporary, engraved Boeotian grave stelai that depict the dead in a heroized

---

52 For child burials in Boeotia, see Sabetai 2000.
53 Bonanno-Aravantinos *forthcoming*.
54 The view that floral vases must have been popular in symposia and at wedding banquets, or may have belonged to bridal dowries, is corroborated by the existence of floral cups depicting red-figured bridal heads in their interior: see, e.g., Avronidaki 2007, pl. 7; this does not exclude their secondary use in burials. For the rich burial of a woman of status that contained floral cups among other objects that exemplified her as a married woman, such as generic female protomes, see Aravantinos 1994, 281, pl. 87c; for floral cups in the pyre of a presumably young woman that also contained female protomes see Sabetai, *forthcoming*. For floral ware from sanctuaries, see above note 30.
55 Avronidaki 2007, 50, no. 28; 139-140; pls. 40, 1; 41.
56 Lullies 1940, 19-20. Cf. further *CVA* Tübingen 1, pl. 49 (white-ground).

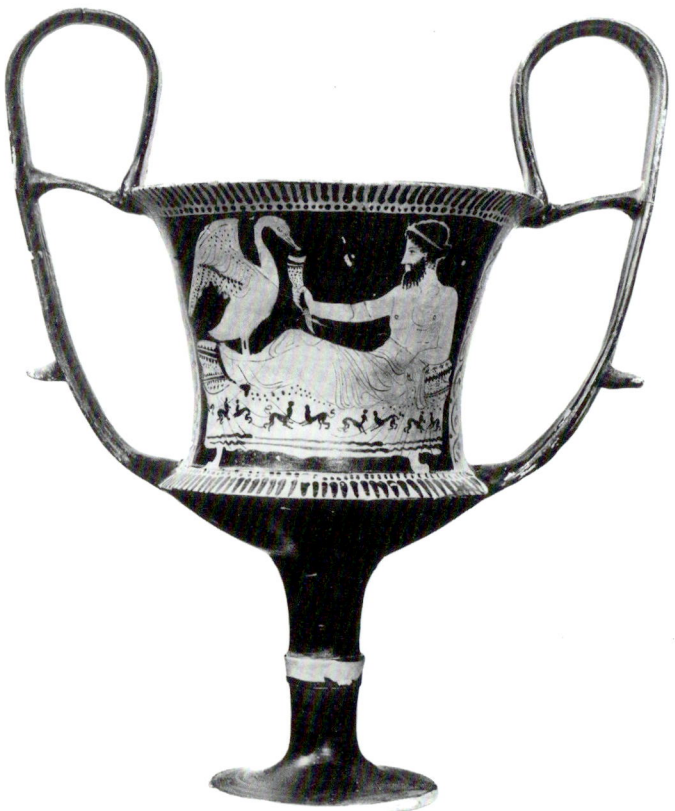

Fig. 16. Boeotian red-figure kantharos by the Painter of the Great Athenian Kantharos. Athens, National Archaeological Museum inv. no. 12487 (Photo courtesy: National Archaeological Museum at Athens, Ministry of Culture/TAP).

Fig. 17. Boeotian engraved stele of Mnason. Thebes Museum no. 54 (Photo: after Demakopoulou & Konsola 1981, pl. 39).

manner (Fig. 17).[57] The choice of the kantharos as the ceramic base of such images should not be taken to refer only to Dionysos, for this ritual shape also had heroic connotations in Boeotia, where it was connected with Herakles, the Kabiros (who is cast as a Dionysiac male) and the heroized male on the so-called Asclepios or Trophonios krater.[58] The depiction of females on kantharoi also probably set these figures in an elevated context.[59] The extreme rarity of monumental kantharoi depicting warriors may suggest memorialisation of the heroized dead in a frame of conspicuous consumption and a praise of the arête of the members of the elite families. It is possible that such ceramic images played a significant role in the funerary ceremony and were then buried with the deceased as personal items, while their counterparts in stone functioned as public markers of permanent commemoration.

When we assess Boeotian red-figured vase-imagery, we should keep in mind that the regular production of Boeotian red-figured pottery coincides chronologically with the formation or re-organization of the Boeotian *Koinon* in which Theban aristocratic groups held key roles. This organization of the federation was recently argued to have occurred after the battle of Koroneia (447/6 BC) and may have affected the construction of a new civic and regional identity. There may be correspondences between the new self-image of the Boeotian and especially Theban elites in the second half of the fifth century BC and the heroic iconography of the funerary kantharoi. The consumption of Attic red-figured pottery and the production of indigenous imitations and other creations influenced by Attic art occurs during an era of conflict between Athens and Boeotia. During the Peloponnesian War Boeotia was allied with Sparta against Athens and some fierce battles took place on Boeotian soil. *Poleis* such as Thebes, Tanagra and Thespiai were anti-democratic and anti-Athenian city-states, but they were also active receptors of Attic artistic trends. Set against this complex background of social and political differences, the consistent and conscious adoption of Attic iconographic themes and their adaptation to suit the Boeotian interest in civic, family and heroic ideals may reveal deeper affiliations on the cultural level and is resonant with the cultural ideologies of the symposion, the marriage, the athletic competition and the performance of rituals in the historical frame of the latter part of the fifth century BC. This field should receive further scholarly comment in the future.[60]

CONCLUSIONS

Boeotian red-figure co-exists with Attic red-figured imports and is influenced by them in various degrees regarding style and iconography, but less so in terms of shape.[61] The role of Attic red-figured imports in moulding local tastes is pivotal, for Attic imagery provides the basic pictorial language that the Boeotians emulate and integrate creatively into their own visual culture despite their anti-Athenian ideology. Boeotian red-figure of the latter part of the fifth century BC develops in the framework of local black-figure workshops, such as those manufacturing the floral and the Kabiric wares.

Attic and Boeotian red-figured vases occur in shrines and graves in small numbers, medium forms and average quality; large shapes and good-quality pieces are infrequent. When placed in tombs, red-figured vases are a small minority among several imported and indigenous Haimoneian cup-skyphoi, black-glazed pots (mainly skyphoi and kantharoi) and other objects. Although publications of entire grave-groups are scarce, there are indications that fifth century BC red-figured vases may have been associated with burials of special status that contained a wealth of pottery types (e.g. soldiers fallen in war, women defined as brides/matrons). Although Boeotian red-figured pottery was used in various 'functional' contexts, some vases were intended specifically for the tomb: elaborate examples, such as the late monumental kantharoi, are objects of distinction employing a visual language of heroic praise, are emulative of the grave stelai, and must have accompanied graves of the elite.

Boeotian visual imagery in red-figure belongs to a formal genre that builds on gendered roles and promotes civic and family ideals. It depicts the male citizen as a virtuous ephebe in transition to adulthood, heroic soldier/rider and symposiast, and the female as nubile maiden and matron. Thus, it highlights normative civic roles that are pictorially thematised in emblematic images, such as scenes of libations, athletics, sacrifices, departing from the home (and the family), music (educational/agonistic ideal) and partaking of the Dionysiac sphere; the female realm is thematised with wedding preparations and pursuits, while visual metaphors such as the female pyrrhic may also belong here. A few mythological figures are cast as heroes or ideal brides.[62] The tone of the scenes may be serious, but also jovial, as would have been expected for vases on display and use in celebrations such as symposia and weddings; such vases may also have been used in graves secondarily. The limited number of Boeotian vase-painters, their small production and the unique pieces lead to the hypothesis that they worked under the auspices of patrons

---

57 Lullies 1940, 19-20; Schild-Xenidou 2008, pls. 10, Kat. 28; 20-26. As Lullies notes, the phenomenon may have some analogy with the huge late fifth century BC loutrophoroi and lekythoi in Athens, which are later replaced by their equivalent in marble. For interconnectedness between reliefs and vase-imagery in Attic art see Shapiro 2009a.
58 For Herakles as a mature seated figure on one side and a standing, fillet-offering ephebe (the hero himself or Iolaos) on the other on a red-figured Boeotian kantharos see Avronidaki 2007, pl. 11. For youths in heroic or ritual nudity on kantharoi by the Argos Painter see ibidem pls. 33-39; 41-42. For the kantharos in the hands of a female deity see Wolters & Bruns 1940, pl. 36, 3-4. For banqueters with kantharoi in terracotta see Schmaltz 1974, 170, no. 233, pl. 19. For the heroic connotations of the motif of the snake that drinks from a kantharos and its applications in heroic imagery beyond Laconia, where it was originally created, see Salapata 2006, esp. 555-558. Black-glazed kantharoi are ubiquitous in Boeotian graves.
59 Maffre 1975, 513-516. See further Tomei 2008 for a recent synthesis on the imagery of the kantharos.
60 On the history of Boeotia see most recently Rhodes 2010, 279-292 (with previous bibliography). For the long-lived oligarchic regime that prevailed at Thebes in the fifth century BC, see Kurke 2007, 68-69. For the organization of the Boeotian federation after the battle of Koroneia see Larson 2007. For the notion of 'Boeotia' and the Boeotian identity in the fifth century BC as attested in choral song, see Kowalzig 2007, esp. 352-391,
61 The kantharos, the dish, the lekane and the kalathos-like pyxis are shapes that are firmly anchored in the Boeotian ceramic tradition.
62 For example Phineus, Oreithyia (Avronidaki 2007, 131-133, pl. 26; 41, 134-136, pl. 22) and, if the interpretation advocated above for the jointly made skyphos is accepted, Ariadne.

and may have created commissioned vases for special circumstances.

The impression of a dearth of red-figured vases in Boeotia is compatible with a similar general picture for central Greece. The phenomenon may be related to issues of trade, tastes or mentalities.[63] Its relatively limited availability may have rendered red-figured pottery in Boeotia a cherished commodity. When found in graves, red-figured vases seem associated with deceased individuals of special status or social standing. The lack of excavated domestic contexts precludes us from assessing the role of red-figured pottery as household ware as well. The presence of vases which have been repaired in tombs suggests that they were household equipment originally.[64] It is possible that such vases were kept at home more often than is usually assumed, and may have originally formed part of bridal trousseaus. The evidence from the sanctuaries is lacunose and cannot, at present, fully document the patterns of dedication of red-figured vases. It is hoped that the circumstances of use of Attic and Boeotian red-figured pottery in Boeotia will be clarified with further study in the future.[65]

APPENDIX

1. Attic painters/potters whose drinking and pouring vessels were found in Boeotia:

Skyphoi: Brygos Painter, Painter of Louvre CA 1694 (follower of Douris), Tarquinia Painter (Group of the Pistoxenos Painter), Group of Ferrara T.981, Painter of Louvre CA 1849, Akridion Painter (the last three are classified in the manner of the Lewis Painter); Penelope Painter. **Cups:** Phintias (potter), Epiktetos (?), Skythes, Pedieus Painter, Pamphaios (potter), Pithos Painter, Chairias Painter, Onesimos, Penthesilea Painter, workshop of the Splanchnopt Painter, Submeidian: Painter of London E 106. **Oinochoai:** Painter of Berlin 2268 (Coarser Wing), Group of Athens 10452 (shape 8A: mugs); Shuvalov Painter (shape 4). **Head-vases:** Syriskos Painter, Sotades Painter, workshop of the Phiale Painter. **Rhytons:** Manner of the Sotades Painter. **Kantharos:** Brygos Painter. **Skyphoid or kantharoid vase:** Painter of Athens 10464 (manner of the Lewis Painter).

2. Attic painters whose unguent and cosmetics vessels were found in Boeotia:

Lekythoi of various types: Painter of Würzburg 517, Painter of the Paris Gigantomachy (circle of the Brygos Painter), workshop of the Villa Giulia Painter, Providence Painter, Mys, Zannoni Painter, CL Class, Bowdoin Painter, Icarus Painter, Angers Painter, Aischines Painter, Painter of London E 673 (following of the Seireniske Painter), Beth Pelet Painter, Carlsruhe Painter, Painter of Athens 1344 (manner of the Carlsruhe Painter), Utrecht Painter. **Alabastra:** Group of the Paidikos Alabastra, Group of the Negro Alabastra, Painter of Munich 2676 (circle of the Brygos Painter), manner of the Foundry Painter, Aischines Painter, Painter of Copenhagen 3830. **Pyxis:** Montlaurès Painter.

3. Attic painters whose hydriai, pelikai and kraters were found in Boeotia:

Hydriai: Orchard Painter, Kassel Painter, Naples Painter. **Pelikai:** Pan Painter, Agrigento Painter, Methyse Painter (perhaps), Nausicaa Painter, Dinos Painter, near the Pronomos Painter. **Kraters:** Syracuse Painter, manner of the Dinos Painter, Painter of the Athens Wedding, Suessula Painter. **Amphora:** Syracuse Painter.

---

63 This issue requires further study. Although we know that red-figured pottery was less copious in Boeotia than in Etruria, it is not yet known whether it was more or less plentiful than in other regions of Greece. Paleothodoros 2007 argues that the pattern of distribution of Attic vases in Greece depended on the existence of commercial networks that met their clients' demands.

64 It is worth noting that an elaborate krater by the Niobid Painter depicting the Theoxenia and repaired in Antiquity was found in a building at Achaia Phthiotis (unpublished; Lamia Museum): see Stamoudi 2006, esp. 140-142; Dakoronia and Bouyia 2002, 37-40; figs. 45 and 48. For more fifth century BC kraters from non-funerary contexts at Pella in Macedonia see Akamatis 2008, 6-8.

65 The Athenian evidence indicates that figured pottery was especially linked to the Acropolis and the Agora, while the graves were frugal (except for the Mesogheia). For the dearth of red-figured pottery in the Peloponnese see further Hannestad 1991; Pemberton 2003, esp. 172-174 (Corinth); Bentz 2009 (Olympia).

ACKNOWLEDGEMENTS

I thank B. Bundgaard Rasmussen and S. Schierup for their invitation to the workshop in Copenhagen, E. Langridge for editing my text, the National Archaeological Museum at Athens (N. Kaltsas, C. Avronidaki), the Benaki Museum (E. Papageorgiou) and the Thebes Ephoreia (V. Aravantinos) for study amenities and photographs.

Elean Red-figure Pottery from Olympia

BY MARTIN BENTZ

Elean Red-figure Pottery from Olympia

BY MARTIN BENTZ

During the Peloponnesian War, a period of economic crisis, some potters and painters left Athens and established workshops which produced red-figure pottery in several parts of the Greek World. Some of them, like the Boeotian, Corinthian, Laconian, Northern Greek and Northwestern Greek workshops have been studied recently, but there is no comprehensive analytical study of this phenomenon.[1] A particular case is that of the South Italian workshops which developed something approaching mass production until about the end of the fourth century BC, whereas the others produced on a moderate scale just for a local public and mostly until the first half of the fourth century.

In this brief survey a general idea of the character of the Elean red-figure material from the excavations of Olympia will be given. In Olympia different kinds of red-figure pottery have been found – mainly Attic and local Elean, but also a few examples of South Italian, Corinthian and Northwestern Greek.

Since the beginning of excavations at Olympia the study of pottery has played an insignificant role compared to the bronzes, which were found in great quantities. However, with the recent publication of the Laconian, Corinthian and Attic black-figure sherds from excavations in Olympia this tradition has changed. Elean black-gloss has been studied in detail by Jürgen Schilbach, and a preliminary survey of the Attic red-figure has been offered.[2]

Elean red-figure pottery has been published [mainly] in articles by Ian McPhee presenting among others about 30 mostly small fragments from the Austrian excavations of Ancient Elis, by John E. Coleman presenting sherds from the excavations of Pylos in Elis, and by Wolfgang Schiering and Jürgen Schilbach presenting single pieces from Olympia.[3] There are very few Elean red-figure vases in museums outside Greece.[4]

The Olympic material is not very numerous; it consists of about 100 pieces from complete vases to small fragments. When the other known examples are added, it becomes clear that Elean red-figure was never produced in large quantities, as is equally true for other local red-figure fabrics.

CHRONOLOGY

As with other local red-figure workshops, the Elean production starts during the period of the Peloponnesian War and was presumably founded by emigrated Athenian potters and painters. From about 430/20 BC we find the first clearly local vases made with the typical pale clay of the region. The first potters may even have arrived with Phidias and his workmen, who made the cult statue of Zeus. In the homogeneous and well dated Classical debris of the Phidias workshop, several fragments were found together with Attic vases by the Kleophon Painter and others.[5] From the last quarter of the fifth century BC we have about 20 Elean vases. The main bulk, however, comes from the first half of the fourth century, although exact dating within this period is not always easy. The production seems to decrease quickly just before the middle of the fourth century. Altogether we can define three generations of painters who worked in groups of two or three.

SHAPE

As has already been observed for the Attic vases from Olympia, there is not a wide range of shapes (Fig. 1). Of the total 78% are bell- and calyx-kraters – in the case of small fragments it is not always possible to distinguish between these two shapes. There are a few examples with a rim diameter of 21 cm, but the bulk of the material is about 35 to 40 cm and the largest 52 cm. The ornaments below the pictorial zones consist mainly of meanders and more rarely of egg-patterns or wave-patterns, with only a few examples of a combination of two decorative elements. The rims develop characteristic forms of their own in the fourth century BC and are decorated with wreaths that might only be half-wreaths.

From the fourth century 5% of the material consists of pelikai. Two fully preserved examples are known from collections in Liverpool and London.[6] In addition, 5% of the vases are lekythoi: only one shoulder lekythos and a few squat lekythoi.

The rest (8%) consist of some fifth century plates[7], two or three oinochoai, and shapes that cannot be defined with certainty.

IMAGES

The subject of the images can be identified in about 40-45 of the 100 pieces that have been analysed, of which a great number are, of course, rim or foot fragments or mantle

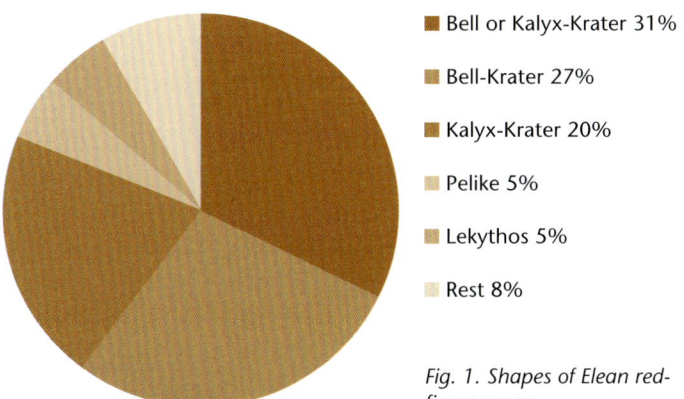

Fig. 1. Shapes of Elean red-figure vases.

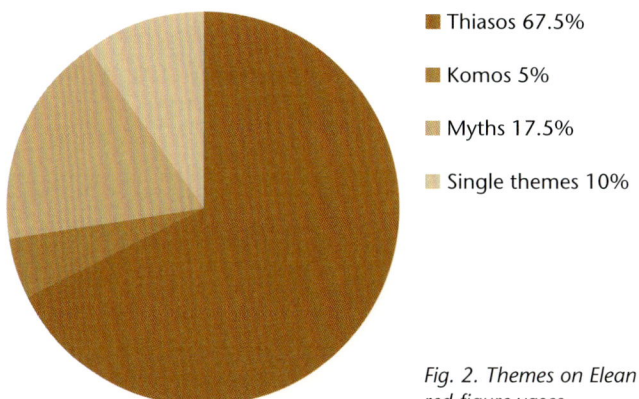

Fig. 2. Themes on Elean red-figure vases.

figures from the reverse of the vessel (Fig. 2).

Of the identified iconographic themes 67.5% show variations on the thiasos and 5% a komos: this means that three quarters show Dionysiac themes. The thiasos images are quite repetitive: they show the well established motif of maenad and satyr to which a third person such as Dionysos, another figure of the thiasos, or a herm can be added.

There are several interesting mythological depictions together with single themes or undefinable subjects. As has been observed of the Attic red-figure, there are no images linked to the sanctuary, no images of Zeus, of Hera or Pelops, and there is not one athletic scene which could be related to the Olympic Games. In the following, I will present some of the more interesting vases in a chronological order.

Six fragments come from a bell-krater with two Nereids riding on dolphins and carrying the weapons of Achilles (Fig. 3). They belong to the first generation of Elean workshops still in the Classical style with simple drapery without the later Rich Style elements. For the rendering of the head we may compare heads of figures by the Phiale Painter or the Polygnotan Group, which gives an idea of the period when they were made.[8]

The iconographical theme appears around the middle of the fifth century BC and is frequent in the second half of the fifth century in all parts of Greece. It is also known from Apulian red-figure in the fourth century, but the style is different. Here the erotic element becomes more and more evident, as Judith Barringer has pointed out.[9]

A plate (Fig. 4) also belongs to the early phase, in the last quarter of the fifth century BC. It shows Perseus (with inscription) in chlamys and petasos with the head of Gorgo in the outstretched right hand. This particular gesture appears in Classical times in Athens and continues in South Italy. Some scholars think it derives from a statue by Myron or a painting on the Acropolis described by Pausanias.[10]

---

1 Exhaustive references cannot be given here, see in general MacDonald 1981; Williams 1999, 96-111; on Boeotian, see Victoria Sabetai in this volume; on Corinthian Herbert 1977; McPhee 1983; on Laconian, most recently Stroszeck 2006; on the Agrinion Group, Papadopoulos 2009; on Euboean, Gex & McPhee 1995; on Northern Greek, McPhee 1981.
2 Schilbach 1995; Burow *et al.* 2000; Bentz 2009.
3 Schiering 1964; Coleman 1986; McPhee 1990; Schilbach 1999.
4 Trendall & McPhee 1982; Trendall & McPhee 1986; Williams 1999, 97, fig. 70c.
5 Schiering 1964.
6 Trendall & McPhee 1982; Williams 1999, 97, Fig. 70c.
7 Schiering 1964, 259, no. 12; *ibidem* 215, fig. 62,8.
8 Oakley 1990, for example pl. 13B, 28B and 57E.
9 On Nereids, see Barringer 1995; *LIMC* VI, s.v. Nereides, 785-824; compare a relief frieze from a louterion in Copenhagen from Agrigento of about 450 BC, *ibidem* no. 355 pl. 499; an amphora by the Achilles Painter in St. Petersburg, *ibidem* no. 371 pl. 501; and a Boeotian vase of 425-400 in Paris, *ibidem* no. 339 pl. 495; see the later Apulian dinos from Ruvo, *ibidem* no. 344 pl. 498.
10 The vase has already been published by Schiering (Schiering 1964, 259-261 pl. 88), who refers to the literature on the Myron theory. On Perseus, see Schauenburg 1960; *LIMC* VII, s.v. Perseus, 332-348 (L.J. Roccos). Cf. from the fifth century BC a calyx-krater in Catania: Libertini 1930, pl. 74, 697 by the Mykonos painter, a bell-krater by the Polydektes Painter: Schauenburg 1960 pl. 37,2; from South Italy see a krater in St. Petersburg by the Dechter Group: *ibidem* pl. 32,1. And the volute-krater by the Karneia Painter in Taranto: *LIMC* VII, s.v. Perseus, no. 32 pl. 276.

Fig. 3. Bell-krater with Nereids. Inv. K 10255 (Photo: J. Schubert).

A well preserved calyx-krater of the second generation in the first quarter of the fourth century BC shows a detailed scene with a seated couple: a young naked man and a young woman under trees, playing morra flanked by a seated satyr on the right and a standing and a seated maenad with a torch on the left (Fig. 5).[11] Details of the heads show that the style of rendering the hair by delining every detail resembles the way Attic painters painted in the last quarter of the fifth and first quarter of the fourth century BC.

The game of morra is depicted several times in South Italian vase painting, but not in Attic.[12] The idea of the game is to guess the number of fingers that the other player holds up quickly, going from zero (fist) to five (all fingers). They hold a stick with marks and if one of them guesses correctly he/she moves to the next mark. The game is often played by women or a boy and a girl and alludes to sexual attraction and luck in love affairs. The earliest example is the famous volute-krater by the early Apulian Sisyphos Painter with two Erotes playing morra on the neck of the vessel. Beside this scene, on the right side, Aphrodite is depicted, and on the body of the vase there is a mythological wedding scene.[13] So the whole scene clearly alludes to marriage. There are two more late fourth century Apulian vases – the first in Naples, the second in Bari – with young couples playing the game.[14]

The next vase is a bell-krater (Fig. 6) of the third generation of Elean red-figure painters from the second quarter of the fourth century BC. Two travelling youths with chlamys, petasos and spears move to the right towards a female figure seated on an altar and holding a key. Undoubtedly the scene should be interpreted as Orestes and Pylades arriving at the sanctuary of Artemis, where the priestess was Iphigenia.

Fig. 4. Plate with Perseus. Inv. K 3891 (Photo: Martin Bentz).

This iconographical theme appears in different variations on Apulian vases around the middle of the fourth century BC.[15] A krater formerly in New York shows Orestes in exactly the same manner.[16] Iphigenia usually[17] stands upright and it is Artemis who is occasionally sitting on her altar as on a krater in Moscow.[18] On the basis of this scene, the Olympia krater may also have shown four figures – the hand with the key belonging to the standing Iphigenia (which would suit the high position of the arm) with Artemis seated. The long drapery, however, would be unusual for Artemis, who is commonly depicted in a short chiton.

Another bell-krater (Fig. 7) of the same period shows a very typical thiasos scene with satyr and maenad moving to the left, the satyr holding a torch, the maenad a phiale and a tympanon. The krater can be compared well with Apulian vases, thus suggesting that its images derive from Apulian

---

11 Kunze 1964, 173, pl. 175c.
12 Pfisterer-Haas 2004; Schauenburg 1976.
13 Pfisterer-Haas 2004, 376, fig. 36.8.
14 Naples H 2574 by the Iliouspersis painter and Bari, Cotecchia coll., Schauenburg 1976, 45, fig. 10-11.
15 *LIMC* V, s.v. Iphigeneia, 706-718.
16 *ibidem*, no. 21, pl. 469.
17 There is one exception with a seated Iphigeneia: Neapel SA 24, *ibidem* no. 15.
18 *ibidem* no. 22, pl. 470.

Fig. 5. Calyx-krater with young couple playing morra. Inv. K 1305 (Photo: J. Schubert).

prototypes by followers of the Tarporley Painter in the first half of the fourth century BC.[19] Note the typical Elean badly painted egg-pattern below the figures and the half wreath under the rim.

This short stylistic analysis of these selected pieces makes it clear that the first generation of Elean red-figure painters were strongly influenced by Attic style and iconography, and perhaps they were even immigrant Attic painters. The later generations, by contrast, are very near to South Italian vase painting in terms of style and iconography, and I would go as far as to postulate that they were made by South Italian painters who had settled in Olympia.

The drapery of a female figure depicted on an Elean bell-

Fig. 6. Bell-krater with Orestes and Pylades. Inv. K 10274 (Photo: J. Schubert).

krater (Fig. 8) seems to support this theory. On the border of the drapery little black lines can be seen, a feature which appears on several other Elean vases and which otherwise only has parallels in South Italian vase-painting.[20]

FUNCTION

The findspots in the sanctuary only provide us with sparse evidence for the function of the red-figure vessels (Fig. 9). As observed for the Attic red-figure material, no fragments of Elean red-figure ware have been found within the temenos wall, i.e. the inner sanctuary.[21] A dozen of the fragments came to light in the workshop of Phidias. They were found in the chronologically homogeneous layer of the workshop debris together with the moulds used for the work on the statue of Zeus, so it is quite probable that the material was used here for profane purposes by the Athenian workmen.

Another dozen fragments were found in fillings from the slopes and pits of the stadium. Nothing can be said about their original context and use.

Most of the red-figure sherds were found in the southern and eastern part of Olympia; a dozen from the south stoa and the majority from the east baths and the so-called south-east zone. In connection with the building activities and reorganization of the sanctuary in the Classical and

---

19 Compare bell-kraters in Paris (Cab. Méd. 930): *RVAp* 226.2, pl. 70,3-4 and Naples (2187, inv. 81446): *ibidem* 136.2, pl. 44,1.
20 A calyx-krater (inv. K 10283) with such a garment decoration comes from a pit which gives a *terminus post quem* date of 362 BC: Schiering 1964, 265, no. 17, pl. 91. In Paestan and Campanian workshop this decoration is very frequent, Trendall 1987 *passim*; it also occurs more rarely on Lucanian and Apulian vases, compare a vase by the Lycurgos Painter, *RVAp* I pl. 149.
21 Bentz 2009.

Fig. 7. Bell-krater with satyr and maenad. Inv. K 2501 (Photo: J. Schubert).

late Classical period, the whole area was levelled and filled with earth, stones and debris. Of course we have no idea from where exactly the fill was brought. But since we have several examples of nearly complete vessels whose fragments were found together, it cannot have come from too far away. One hypothesis is that the Greek remains under the so-called House of Nero might have been a kind of public dining place like the later Leonidaion in the west, where several bell-kraters were found. This would explain well the concentration of pottery here.[22]

Only one example of an undisturbed ritual context with red-figure pottery has been found. Near the altar of Artemis just south of the Roman baths, three bell-krater fragments were found in a black ash layer. They must have been used during religious ceremonies.

Olympia differs from, for example, urban sanctuaries as

Fig. 8. Bell-krater, detail of a maenad. Inv. K 10242 (Photo: J. Schubert).

CONCLUSIONS

To conclude, we can state that Elean red-figure seems not to have been produced in very high numbers. It occurs mainly in the three generations from 425 to 350 BC. The findspots give few hints as to the use of the vases, and there are only very few ritual contexts. The images show no particular relation to the sanctuary and its cults; Dionysiac images dominate. The heroic images of Theseus, Perseus and the weapons of Achilles also fit the context of the male symposion. The main shape is the krater and not one drinking or storage vessel has been found. Furthermore, there are no votive inscriptions and there are none of the under- or oversize vessels that are often connected with a ritual context.

In my opinion all the observations made up to now lead to the conclusion that most of the Elean vases, like the Attic figured material from Olympia, were not votive offerings.

Painted pottery seems never to have played a significant role in Olympia, and seems mostly to have been used for profane and not for ritual or votive purposes. The Elean workshops were founded at Olympia (and probably not at ancient Elis) to provide the visitors staying for a longer time near the sanctuary with decorated vases for their symposia and/or daily use. The iconography fits this purpose well and seems not to be related to the rituals executed in the sanctuary. Thus, Elean red-figure is not a particular sanctuary-ware as produced for other places.[25] And there is no particular Elean iconography that is distinct from that of other regions. The finds in the town of ancient Elis show, too, that it was a form of pottery that was used in daily life.

The daily use is stressed by the observation that where the bottoms of the kraters are preserved they show traces of consumption – the typical scratches caused by bronze ladles.

the numerous foreign visitors came for a longer stay during the Olympic Games and had to live nearby – mostly to the south towards the Alpheios – in tents or other temporary dwellings. When the religious and athletic programme ended in the evening, profane celebrations started outside the sanctuary. There were modest private meals, official banquets and enormous mass-celebrations. So maybe it is not by chance that most of the pottery was found to the south and south-east of the *altis* and not inside.

The findspots analysed here together with the fact that the main shape found is the krater shape[23] seems to indicate that the primary function of the red-figure pottery in Olympia has to do with dining. A similar range of shapes can be seen for the Attic pottery from Olympia which consists of about 50% kraters.[24]

---

22 Leypold 2008, 110-114.
23 Usually there is a broader range of shapes of painted pottery in sanctuaries, cups dominate other forms; there is no in-depth study of ceramics in sanctuaries, see latest Fortunelli & Masseria 2009.
24 There is not very much Attic red-figure in Olympia, we have fragments of about 120 vases, see Bentz 2009.
25 In several sanctuaries we find images related to the cult, like the many Athenas on vases from the Acropolis of Athens or many scenes related to Demeter and Kore and their cult from Eleusis, see e.g. Roscino 2009, 163-187; Tiverios 2009, 280-290.

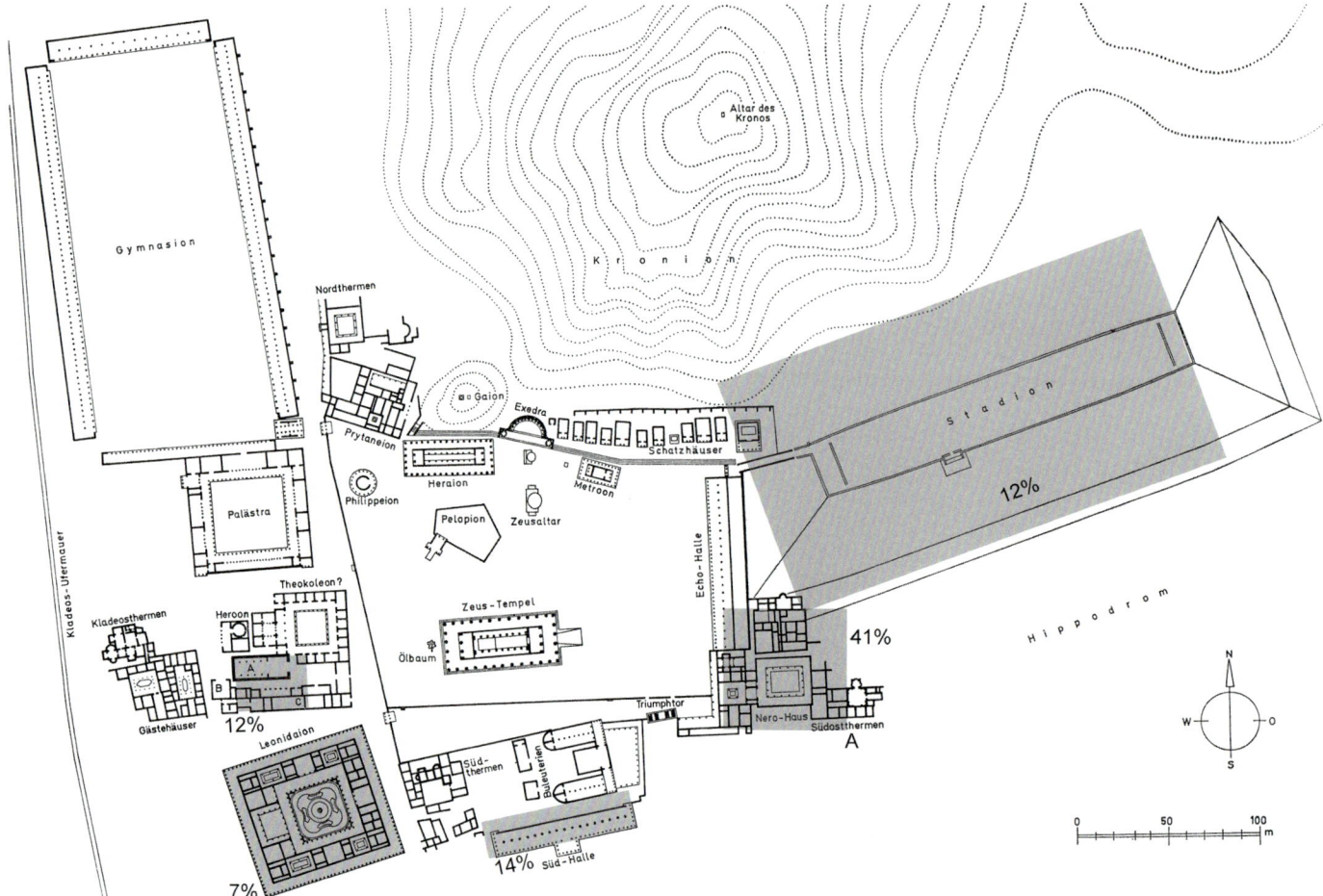

Fig. 9. Distribution of Elean red-figure pottery in Olympia.

ACKNOWLEDGEMENTS

I owe particular thanks to the former and the current directors of the German excavations at Olympia, Helmut Kyrieleis and Reinhard Senff, for the kind invitation to publish the red-figured pottery from Olympia, a project which was started in 2006. Friedrich-Wilhelm Hamdorf generously gave me information on his previous research on part of the material. Jürgen Schilbach kindly shared his knowledge on Olympia and its finds with me, and Susanne Bocher and Kathrin Fuchs provided me with much information and help during my stays in the German excavation house.

An Overview of Athenian Figure-decorated Pottery in Southern Italy and Sicily

BY THOMAS MANNACK

An Overview of Athenian Figure-decorated Pottery in Southern Italy and Sicily

BY THOMAS MANNACK

In Athens and most of mainland Greece, there is little doubt about the use of pottery: figure-decorated vases were dedicated in sanctuaries, placed in graves, and used in public and private buildings for dining purposes.[1]

In Italy, Attic figure-decorated pottery was imported from the last quarter of the seventh century BC, first by the Etruscans in the north, and a little later by Greeks and natives in the south and Sicily. In both regions, Athenian pottery competed with and – around 550 BC – replaced Corinthian vessels. By then, Athenian vases reached most parts of the ancient world. Greek pottery appears to have been a status symbol; its use often followed local customs.[2] The earliest South Italian potteries were founded by Athenian emigrant craftsmen around 440 BC in Lucania. Their workshops supplied Greeks and natives with red-figure pottery which appears to have been made specifically for use in graves, initially in competition with products from Athens, which they replaced entirely after a short period of time. Only very few South Italian vases were found in settlements.[3] This raises the questions of whether Greeks and natives imported Attic pottery mainly for the grave, for use in symposia, or whether there was a change of offering practices in the later fifth century, and whether potter-painters in Athens were aware of the use of their containers. It is feasible that Athenian imports served a multitude of purposes and were used in daily life and funerals for their exotic or even luxury appeal. It is also possible that the function of Athenian imports changed with time.

The investigation of the use of pottery is somewhat impeded by archaeological tastes and the iniquitous art market. The art market serves collectors, and tomb robbers procured first Attic and then South Italian pottery following the tastes and purses of their customers. Archaeologists preferred to excavate sanctuaries and cemeteries, because they bestowed prestige and supplied higher quality or complete objects. Settlements, on the other hand, are often buried under modern cities, and the finds are so unprepossessing that they are rarely illustrated. As a result, the use of Athenian vases in Italian graves is relatively well documented; but settlements – at present only Vaste[4], Monte Iato[5] and Monte Maranfusa[6] have yielded useful numbers of Athenian vases – have been somewhat neglected.

However, we have some evidence and it may be possible to attempt some observations with the help of recent publications, Beazley's vase lists and the Beazley Archive's pottery database. The following will give an overview of Athenian figured pottery found in Southern Italy and Sicily:

LUCANIA

In Lucania Attic vases were used in burials until they were replaced by South Italian vases, and graves provide the richest evidence. Burials in and near Metaponto contained a number of Athenian figure-decorated vases, including a tomb from the site of Montescaglioso which housed two successive inhumations and was equipped with a range of locally made vases and 'Athenian type black-glaze' vases.[7] An Athenian red-figure column-krater is the only figure-decorated vase (Fig. 1). Its obverse shows three women. One holds an alabastron, a perfume flask used by women, and two naked women are freshening up at a laver. Since it was found in a grave, one could insist on a funerary interpretation and see nymphs or similar creatures in the scene, and propose that the deceased was a woman (the human remains have not been clearly gendered), or perhaps that the deceased liked women. But it is also possible that the family required a krater, that is the shape, and figure-decoration, but that the theme of the pictures was not important.

The tomb contained two successive inhumations. The red-figure column-krater takes pride of place in the earlier of two sets of symposium wares, which are mostly composed of local pots. The double grave confirms the impression of a relative paucity of Athenian figure-decorated vases in the south. We have two burials, probably of the same family with a liking for Attic pottery, and there is only one rather humble krater.

A poorly equipped tomb with an undecorated neck-amphora[8] and the grave of a woman[9] contained the most common offering in and around Metaponto, namely lekythoi. Of the 138 Attic vases found in Metaponto, 91 are lekythoi.

Fig. 1. Montescaglioso, tomb 1, with Attic column-krater (Photo: after NSc 42/43, figs. 32-33).

Some of the Attic vases exported to Poseidonia in Lucania are rather better than those from Metaponto. Among the early Attic products is a black-figure lekythos[10] from the grave of a child, which also received a curious black-figure amphora of uncertain provenience, a locally made stamnos, and a figure vase in the shape of a sandaled foot. Normally one would dismiss the black-figure lekythos as one of an unappealing multitude, but here the lekythos is decorated with a small horseman between large youths. It is therefore not entirely impossible that the parents picked the vase as a suitable last gift for their child.

There are apparently no sets of Athenian symposium vases; and given the very large number of known Athenian red-figure cups, their absence from Lucanian and other southern graves is surprising. Cups were certainly used in symposia if the wall paintings in Paestan graves are reliable representations of real feasts. In the famous native tomb known as the 'Tomb of the Diver'[11] the drinking cups are black, but we cannot say whether the painter was sparing with detail or wanted to represent black glaze or metal cups. The garlanded krater depicted on the east side of the tomb is definitely not Athenian, but looks like a narrow necked version of the so-called Chalcidian krater.[12]

Regrettably, the pictures on Athenian vases do not help to determine their use or the nature of their buyers. One suspects that the black-figure lekythoi were not desirable oil flasks for domestic use, but there is no absolute certainty.

---

1 Rotroff & Oakley 1992.
2 Cook 1959.
3 Plat Taylor *et al.* 1977
4 Mannino 2005, 183, fig. 225.
5 For a summary, see *JdI* 124 (2009) 148-201.
6 *Kokalos* 39-40 (1993/94). For Maranfusa and Monte Iato see also Spatafora & Vassallo 2002.
7 *NSc* 42/43 (1988/89), 330-331, figs. 32.3, 33.
8 Carter *et al.* 1998, 384, T 312.
9 *Ibidem* 372, T 336. The picture on the red-figure oil flask is eminently suitable for a female: it shows a single woman at home.
10 Paestum, Museo Archeologico Nazionale, 48484: Cipriani, Longo & Viscione 1996, 33, fig. 7.2.
11 Robinson 2011.
12 Pontrandolfo & Rouveret 1992, 15-16, figs. 4-7.

Fig. 2a-d. Volute-krater from Silbion, Tomb 3. 460/450 BC (Photo: after Ciancio 1997, figs. 104-107).

Some examples are white-ground – not yet a technique exclusively destined for the grave, but easily damaged. The scenes, gods, Athena in a chariot, and Dionysos are exceedingly common on black-figure lekythoi and one can at least be certain that they were not special commissions, but could have been packed aboard any trader going west.

APULIA

Taranto in Apulia is chosen here because the finds are relatively well published and because the city was praised for retaining her Greek character by Strabo and Aristoxenos.[13] The inhabitants of sixth century Taranto seem to have equipped their dead with vases which archaeologists like to call symposium ware. To date, 540 black-figure vases have been excavated there – the numbers are taken from the Beazley Archive's pottery database.[14] Of these, 307 are cups, 83 lekythoi, and 32 amphorae. Attic black-figure cups were imported from the first quarter of the sixth century onwards, and among the many drinking vessels are numerous Siana Cups. A typical grave of the Archaic period contained a large vase, normally an amphora, and several cups and cup skyphoi.[15]

In the fifth century, a significant change in the number of imported vases can be seen. Only 119 red-figure vases have been excavated in and around Taranto: of these there are 12 cups, 3 amphorae, 35 lekythoi and 27 kraters of all types. This may indicate a change in burial practices or fashion. Taranto was involved in a disastrous war with

c

d

the native inhabitants in the first quarter of the fifth century BC, which led to the establishment of a democratic constitution. Athenian figure-decorated cups may have been replaced by Attic or local black-glaze wares in this period.

Almost all the vases from Taranto were found in graves, but there is at least one Attic find from a sanctuary; a black-figure band-cup decorated with a horseman and an incised dedicatory inscription on the handle.[16]

Attic pottery was bought not only by Greeks settling in Apulia, but also by the native inhabitants, the Daunians, Peucetians, and Messapians, who are collectively known as Iapygians. Finds from near Rutigliano[17] in Peucetia are similar to those from Taranto. Tomb 55[18] contained at least two sets of symposium vases deposited in the grave itself and in an adjoining storage chamber. However, only one contains an Attic figure-decorated vase assigned to a Later

---

13 Strabo, *Geography*, VI.1.2; Athenaeus, *Deipnosophists*, XIV.632.
14 www.beazley.ox.ac.uk
15 *AttiMemMagnaGr*, NS 8 (1967). See e.g. tombale da Lizzano 6: *NSc* 13-14 (2002-2003) 480-482, figs. 19-21.
16 Taranto, Museo Archeologico Nazionale: Lippolis *et al.* 1995, pl. 64.1.
17 *AttiTaranto* 16 (1976).
18 *AttiTaranto* 17 (1977), pl. 60.1; *AttiTaranto* 18 (1978), pl. 24.1.

Mannerist.[19] The scene on the vase shows a divine pursuit[20]: Eos, the winged personification of the morning sky, pursues the young huntsman Kephalos. The krater can be dated around 440 or 430 BC. By then, divine pursuits had gone out of fashion, and the Late Mannerists belong to the few workshops which continued to produce such scenes. The subject may have held a special appeal for buyers in Southern Italy and Sicily, where kraters were popular grave offerings, but there are only very few kraters with such pictures, and the scenes on most mixing vessels do not easily lend themselves to funerary interpretations.

The offerings in tomb 27 include a South Italian lekythos with net decoration, a red-figure lekanis, and a symposium set which includes a locally made column-krater, a black-glaze skyphos and an Athenian red-figure oinochoe. The figure on the oinochoe, a woman holding a sash and an alabastron, appears to be a gift more suited to a woman, at least to a modern viewer.

The inhabitants – both Greeks and natives – around Gravina in Apulia shared the taste for splendid funerals with complete symposia sets as we know them from Spina and Etruria graves.[21] Tomb 3 from Silbion contained a proper symposium set: an Attic volute-krater, Athenian red-figure and black-glaze cups, a black-glaze oinochoe and a proto-Italiote amphora of Panathenaic shape. Most are dated around 440/430 BC[22], but the volute-krater (Figs. 2 a-d) appears to be earlier and was probably made around 460/450 BC. It may therefore be a treasured possession of the deceased that was placed in the tomb after 20 years of use. Whether it was acquired for feasting is uncertain. The shape and decoration suggest that the vase may have been bought for use in a funeral. Graves in nearby Ruvo in Apulia contained exceptionally fine volute-kraters.[23] In the fourth century, the natives of the region were exceedingly fond of the large Apulian volute-kraters with mythological scenes and a multitude of figures. Earlier, around 400 BC, they had imported the finest Athenian examples: the famous Pronomos krater with a complex theatrical scene and Greek inscriptions,[24] and the Talos Painter's name vase showing Castor and Polydeukes killing the bronze giant Talos in the presence of Medea and Poseidon.[25] The concentration of such fine kraters decorated with added colours, of a size which made them difficult to handle, and in a region where volute-kraters would be the favourite grave offering, permits the conjecture that Athenian potters and painters made such vases with Italian customers in mind. This does not mean that the vases were special commissions (although in the case of the Pronomos-krater this idea is tempting), because the experience that particularly splendid vases sold well in Italy would have been sufficient.

The scenes on the krater from Silbion can also be connected with funeral use, because they show divine and heroic pursuits which are regarded as euphemisms for death:[26] Boreas and Oreithyia on the neck on the obverse, Theseus and an unnamed woman on the neck of the B side, and a bearded hero on the body on the reverse. The main picture on the obverse is rather enigmatic: a young man in heroic attire attacks a young woman on an altar, an older comrade tries to restrain him, while a king and a mourning woman are looking on. The scene has been interpreted as the sacrifice of Iphigenia,[27] an eminently suitable subject for a funerary vase, since Iphigenia was replaced by a deer at the last minute and whisked away to safety. However, the identification is not certain. There are no close parallels to this scene. The young hero could be Theseus, who is shown attacking Aithra on a cup attributed to Makron in a similar manner;[28] both figures are named with inscriptions. Theseus is also shown on a cup in Bologna attacking a woman who has sought refuge on an altar[29]. An altar and a man with a sceptre are present in a more conventional pursuit scene on a kalyx-krater in Batumi attributed to the Niobid Painter's workshop,[30] but the vase could also represent Alkmaion and Eriphyle.[31]

Among the very few excavated settlements containing Attic pottery is Vaste in southern Apulia. There, archaeologists excavated the fragment of a black-figure krater of fairly low quality in a late sixth/early fifth century house.[32]

SICILY

Finds of Athenian pottery in Sicily share most of the characteristics of those in Southern Italy, but there are striking regional differences. The pottery sets are smaller and frequent offerings of bronze strigils appear to stress the athletic prowess of the deceased. Among the imported containers, lekythoi are most numerous: more than half of about 2300 recorded Athenian vessels are lekythoi. There are black- and red-figure, and patterned examples, some of them white-ground, or plain.

The inhabitants of Agrigento placed a variety of shapes in graves, some of them of exceptional quality. There are several types of burial. Some, for example tomb 842 of the Pezzino necropolis[33], contained a krater, a cup and two or three oinochoai. In others, such as tomb 315,[34] the place of the krater was taken by an amphora, and a lekythos was added to the ensemble. The sympotic vases were perhaps only a symbolic reference to the Greek culture of the deceased, because the amphora is frequently the only wine-related shape in a tomb (albeit not usually shown in representations of mortal symposia); tomb 551[35] contained a neck-amphora with a satyr capering at a kantharos, the tip of a spear or spit, a bronze strigil, and four black-figure lekythoi.

Agrigento provides firm evidence that Athenian pottery was dedicated in local sanctuaries. While the inhabitants of Messapia used the same shapes for burials, domestic use, and dedications in sanctuaries, we can discern a slight preference for cups: in the Asklepieion[36] and the temple of Zeus in Agrigento, most date from the sixth century.[37] Two lekythoi[38] are from graves in the so-called 'chthonic' area of the Zeus sanctuary. However, the published plates show almost all the figure-decorated pottery recovered in the sanctuaries, which illustrates the extremely small number of Attic vases used in this fashion.

The necropolis of Vassallaggi[39] in Sicily was excavated in 1956 and 1961. According to the excavators, the inhabitants were natives, but they appear to have embraced Greek culture wholeheartedly. The graves of men, mostly inhumations, for example Tomb 41,[40] were normally equipped with a krater, Attic in richer tombs, often a second Attic vase, normally an amphora or pelike, and figure-decorated and/or black glaze lekythoi. The wealthier male graves also contained bronze strigils. It is perhaps noteworthy that there are no symposium sets, since drinking vessels such as cups and skyphoi are usually missing. The squat lekythoi could – like the strigil – indicate that the deceased had leisure to visit the palaistra, but it is more likely that they were part of the funerary rites, since such lekythoi were also part of the inventory of the graves of women. The pictures on these oil flasks in the graves of men cannot easily be connected with a deceased male: they are decorated with women on their own or even engaged in domestic pursuits such as holding a mirror and standing at a kalathos.

The recently catalogued finds from Gela[41] conform to the established pattern: the site contained numerous black-figure lekythoi, which are decorated with the whole range of stock-images typical of these vases: Dionysos and his companions, warriors departing, goddesses mounting chariots, horsemen and many more. There is a very small number of early red-figure cups,[42] and even Athenian white-ground lekythoi. Many show domestic themes.[43] In Athens, these lekythoi would have been made as grave offerings. Their find place shows that they were used in burials in Agrigento too. Some are decorated with funerary scenes, which indicate that they were bought as grave offerings and not for use at home.[44] Classical funerary lekythoi

---

19 Taranto, Museo Archeologico Nazionale, 150292: *BAPD* Vase 32030.
20 Kaempf-Dimitriadou 1979; Stewart 1995; Sourvinou-Inwood 1979; Mannack 2012.
21 Reusser 2002.
22 Ciancio 1997, 79, 81-86, figs. 103-111, 216, no. 266.
23 Burn 2010.
24 Naples, Museo Archeologico Nazionale, 81673: *FR* III, 147, fig. 65, pls. 143-145; Junker 2003, pls. 74-75; *ARV*² 1336.1, 1704; *BAPD* Vase 217500.
25 Ruvo, Museo Jatta, 36933: *ARV*² 1338.1.; *FR* I, 196-203, pls. 38-39; *BAPD* Vase 217518.
26 Kaempf-Dimitriadou 1979.
27 Ciancio 1997, 79, 81-86.
28 St. Petersburg, State Hermitage Museum, B1543: *BAPD* Vase 204694. See also Naples, Astarita, I: *LIMC* I, s.v. Aithra I 38, pl. 330; *CAVI* 7537.
29 Bologna, Museo Civico Archeologico, 423: *CVA* Bologna 5, 133.3-4; *ARV*² 1398.8; *BAPD* Vase 250123.
30 Georgia (S. Russia), State Museum: Prange 1989, N33, pls. 34-35; *BAPD* Vase 3004.
31 Cf. London, British Museum, E 120, *LIMC* I, pl. 411, Alkmaion 13.
32 Lecce, Mus. Prov. Sigismaondo Castromediano: Mastronuzzi 2005, 132, figs. 45-46.
33 Braccesi *et al.* 1988, 360-361.
34 *Ibidem*, 362.
35 *Ibidem*, 364.
36 Miro 2003, pl. 91.1-8.
37 Miro 2000, pls. 122-129.
38 *Ibidem*, pls. 125.4, 126.
39 *NSc* 9-10 (1998-1999); *NSc* 1971, Suppl.; Giudice 2007.
40 *NSc* 25 (1971) 75-76, figs. 111-112.
41 Panvini & Giudice 2003; Panvini 2004; Panvini 2005.
42 Panvini & Giudice 2003, 276-277, E 7-E 9, E 12; 314, G 50, G51.
43 Panvini & Giudice 2003, 384-385, L 9-12.
44 London, British Museum, D 63: *ARV*² 1378.34. Christchurch (N.Z.), University of Canterbury, J.Logie Mem.Coll., 16.56: Panvini & Giudice 2003, 211, figs. 6-7; *ARV*² 849.239. Syracuse, Museo Arch. Regionale Paolo Orsi: *ARV*² 760.33. London, British Museum 1928.2-13.1: *ARV*² 746.4; Panvini & Giudice 2003, 210, fig. 5.

were also excavated in Selinus.[45] Whether these vases were ordered for Athenians who had emigrated to Sicily, or whether Athenian potters sold surplus burial vases because they knew that their wares were often destined for tombs overseas, is unclear.

Graves in the island of Lipari off the west coast of Sicily contained a variety of often small or miniature and carelessly decorated Athenian vases which cannot be assembled into symposium sets. While some high-quality vases reached the island, for example a column-krater attributed to the Pan Painter,[46] most are hastily painted lekythoi and some are decorated in the white-ground technique, which is impractical for vases used frequently or over a longer period.[47]

CONCLUSIONS

A variety of Athenian vases reached Greek cities and native inhabitants in Southern Italy in fairly large numbers, and they were widely distributed. Black- and red-figure Athenian lekythoi were probably bought almost exclusively for use in funerals, although some have been found in domestic contexts[48] There would have been no need for commissions or even a special knowledge of the market, because Greek ceramics appear to have sold everywhere, and taking them aboard a trading ship must have been a safe investment. Larger shapes such as amphorae and kraters, and a smaller number of hydriai and pelikai, were also often destined for graves, since only very small numbers were found in domestic contexts and sanctuaries, and because the finds do not reveal the existence of sympotic assemblages in the region. Only in northern Apulia were graves equipped with complete sets of symposium vases. Moreover, Attic figure-decorated vases were combined with Italiote red-figure vessels, which – as far as we know – were used only in funerals. The intended use of pottery overseas would not necessarily have been of importance to Athenian potters and painters, because their choice of images suited a range of uses: pictures of the symposium on kraters were appropriate for use in feasts and in funerals, since pictures of symposia were regarded as fitting decoration of the walls of Etruscan and Paestan graves. Many mythological scenes were open to different readings, either as conversation pieces or as a source of comfort in burial ceremonies.

Outside Etruria and northern Apulia, there do not appear to have been any attempts to acquire whole sets of Attic figure-decorated pottery. It is not possible to determine whether overseas buyers wanted to assemble a set, could not afford one, used local or black glaze pottery in daily life, or were not able to procure one. What is certain is that even small and carelessly painted products of the Kerameikos found willing buyers overseas.

---

45 Palermo, Mormino Collection, 3398: Giudice *et al.* 1992, II, 173, E 65. Palermo, Mus. Arch. Regionale, T 12: Adriani *et al.* 1971, pl. XVII. Palermo, Mus. Arch. Regionale, T 3: Giudice 2007, 234, fig. 227; Adriani *et al.* 1971, pl. XVIb. Palermo, Mormino Collection, 3200: Giudice *et al.* 1992), II, 191, E 126; Adriani *et al.* 1971, pl. 17.
46 Lipari, Museo Eoliano, 2073: Bernabó-Brea, Cavalier & Spigo 1995, 73, figs. 50-51.
47 Lipari, Museo Eoliano, T 1059: Bernabó-Brea *et al.* 2001, pl. 176.7. Lipari, Museo Eoliano, T 1056: Bernabó-Brea *et al.* 2001, pl. 176.1.1. Lipari, Museo Eoliano, T 1013: Bernabó-Brea *et al.* 2001, pl. 175.3.6, 4.
48 Spatafora & Vassallo 2002, 85 (Monte Iato).

ACKNOWLEDGEMENTS

I am most grateful to Bodil Bundgaard Rasmussen and Stine Schierup for the invitation to take part in the Copenhagen conference. I am hugely grateful to Stine for her hard work on my paper. I am indebted to Thomas Carpenter, Ted Robinson and Guy Hedreen for valuable help and suggestions.

A Heroic Emblem:
The Cultural Transformation of the Panathenaic Amphora in Southern Italy

BY STINE SCHIERUP

A Heroic Emblem: The Cultural Transformation of the Panathenaic Amphora in Southern Italy

BY STINE SCHIERUP

In a tomb at the Italic site of Pisticci (Casinello, tomb 1) a Panathenaic amphora (Fig. 1) was found together with a lekythos and a bronze strigil.[1] The amphora is smaller than the traditional Attic prize vessels (40 cm), but it is decorated in the canonical black figure style with the athletic discipline on one side, in this case running athletes, and the armed Pallas Athena on the other side. However it lacks the obligatory inscription, 'ΤΟΝΑΘΕΝΕΘΕΝΑΘΛΟΝ', and Martine Denoyelle's attribution of the amphora to the Pisticci Painter emphasizes that the vessel was produced in Southern Italy without any reference to the original cultural context of use as a prize vessel in the Panathenaic games.[2] However, some reference to an athletic sphere seems to be indicated by the simple focus of the grave goods, the lekythos and the bronze strigil, that accompanied the amphora in the tomb.

A close parallel to this pseudo-Panathenaic amphora from Pisticci can be found in the fragment of an early Italiote amphora now in the National Museum of Denmark (Fig. 2).[3] Together these two examples reveal a special interest in the Panathenaic amphora shape from the beginning of the Italiote production of figured Greek pottery, an interest which is further emphasized by the fact that it is the only amphora shape that survives into the repertoire of the South Italian painters to any significant degree.[4]

The aim of this article is to analyze the social and cultural transformation that the Panathenaic amphora as an emblematic vessel underwent: from being an Attic prize vessel secondarily imported and used in the aristocratic tombs of Taranto and Ruvo, to being an essential part of the funerary vessels in the repertoire of the local red-figure production. Despite the significant position of the amphora in the South Italian production, the transformation process of the shape and the reasons for its popularity have so far only been treated summarily. For example Jenifer

a

Fig. 1a-b. Pseudo-Panathenaic amphora attributed to the Pisticci Painter. Tomb 1, Casinello, Pisticci (Photo courtesy: Metaponto, Museo Archeologico Nazionale/Soprintendenza per i Beni Archeologici della Basilicata).

Neils states that the shape in Southern Italy "functioned for men (and women) much as the loutrophoros did for the young women in Athens, as a funerary symbol, and possibly as a sign that they died young".[5] In this way she contradicted the observations made by Hans Lohmann in his monograph on *Grabmäler auf Unteritalischen Vasen*, that the amphoras should merely be considered containers of wine without any reference to their original context of use, since they were usually found side by side with other types of banquet equipment such as kraters and drinking cups.[6]

b

Fig. 2. Fragment of a pseudo-Panathenaic amphora produced in southern Italy. Copenhagen, National Museum, inv. ChrVIII757 (Photo courtesy: The National Museum of Denmark).

THE ANCESTORS OF THE ITALIOTE PANATHENAIC AMPHORA

In order to understand the transformation process of the Panathenaic amphora in Southern Italy, we need first of all to dwell briefly on the history and characteristics of its ancestors. As a result of Martin Bentz's comprehensive monograph and catalogue on the prize vessels, our knowledge of their development and the distribution of the shape is profound, and the Panathenaic amphoras hold an important position in the research into Greek painted pottery.[7] Three important characteristics differentiate the vessels from other types of ancient pottery. First of all, no

1 Metaponto, Museo Archaeologico Nazionale, inv. 310.897: Denoyelle 1997, fig. 11-12, n. 38.
2 Denoyelle 1997, 402-403.
3 Copenhagen, National Museum, inv. ChrVIII757: *CVA* Copenhagen 8, pl. 318.2. The fragment was identified as an Italiote pseudo-Panathenaic amphora by Dr. Dyfri Williams, who kindly informed me of his observations. The fragment was acquired in Naples in 1821 by the Danish Prince Christian Frederik (later King Christian VIII), the provenance is unknown.
4 Only a few painters have been connected with other types of amphora shapes, see e.g.: the neck amphora by the Painter of Vienna 1091 (*LCS* no. 415, 80) and the neck amphora by the Painter of the Berlin Dancing Girl (*RVAp* I, no. 13, 7 and Mannino 2005, fig. 12).
5 Neils 2001, 130.
6 Lohmann 1979, 145-147.

major changes were made in their shape and decoration from about 530 BC, when they reached their canonical form in the black figure technique, until the second century when the production ends.[8] Secondly, they were a specific order by the Athenian state and produced in great numbers for more than four centuries. And thirdly, they are one of the few types of vessels that bear inscriptions that are directly relevant to their specific context of use in the Panathenaic games. These characteristics emphasize the strong emblematic nature of the vessels; and in addition to being emblems of the achievements of heroic athletes, the strong and healthy young men, they should be considered emblems of the Greek city state of Athens. The connection between the popularity of athletics and Athenian democracy has been stressed by Stephen G. Miller, among others. The theory is partly based on the fact that representations of Greek athletes on figured pottery seem to be particularly popular from around 520/10 to 460 BC (contemporary with the rise and fall of Athenian democracy) and partly on the ideology that the *gymnikos agon* was for every man.[9] Even though Panathenaic amphoras do seem to have flourished contemporarily with Athenian democracy, the canonical archaic manner of production continues into the next centuries, emphasizing that images of the athlete and Pallas Athena were still very closely connected to the self-representation of the Athenian state as projected in the Panathenaic games. This is emphasized by the fact that the amphoras are depicted on other state controlled objects, such as official weights and coins.[10]

In the wake of these canonical prize vessels, a range of so-called pseudo-Panathenaic amphoras was produced. As a common feature they all reproduce the original shape, but not necessarily the black-figure technique and the iconographic themes. The first group discussed here reproduces the black-figure technique and to some extent the decoration. According to Martin Bentz, this group of vessels was mainly produced in Athens within the period 550-475 BC.[11] Three such imported Archaic examples are known from rich tombs in Taranto,[12] but only the two examples of pseudo-Panathenaic amphoras described above (Figs. 1-2), belong to the Classical period and are connected to the production of South Italian painters. Furthermore, the Pisticci Painter's amphora belongs to the group closest to the original prize vessels, which follows the canonical scheme omitting only the inscription. These examples seem to indicate that there was a market for Panathenaics without any direct connection to the games, and thus that the demand for this type of vessel was too great to be satisfied by the prize vessels sold or redistributed by their winners. Miniature vessels made in the Panathenaic shape and usually decorated with Athena in black-figure are also known, and served most probably the function of perfume vessels.[13]

Another variant of the Attic Panathenaic amphora is characterized by the use of the red-figure technique. The iconographic themes of this group are usually mythological and rarely carry any direct references to the games by depicting Athena and/or athletes. However, H. Alan Shapiro has argued comprehensively in his article on the iconography of this group that even the mythological themes on these vessels should be considered a reference to the changing ideology of the festival, and he emphasizes that this aspect of the vessels should always be taken into consideration in any analysis.[14] A total of about 100 examples of Attic pseudo-Panathenaic amphoras in the red-figure style are known from the beginning of the fifth century and until the beginning of the fourth century BC, after which they completely disappear.[15] Within this period they seem primarily to be connected to early fifth century painters who were at the same time significant suppliers of prize vessels, such as the Kleophrades Painter and especially the Berlin Painter.[16] From Southern Italy two examples of Attic red-figure Panathenaic amphoras are known: one is the Talos Painter's well-known amphora depicting the apotheosis of Herakles from a tomb in Taranto.[17] The other is an amphora attributed to the Group of Naples 3235 which was found in Ruvo.[18]

THE PSEUDO-PANATHENAIC AMPHORAS OF LUCANIAN AND APULIAN PRODUCTION

To this group of pseudo-Panathenaic amphoras in the red-figure technique a second group, the Lucanian and Apulian production, can be added. As stated earlier, the shape is the only type of amphora that survives into the repertoire of the South Italian red-figure painters.[19] This is interesting, for in the preceding phase with Attic import various other types of amphora shapes have been documented in tomb contexts.[20] Thus, they must reflect a very specific preference or demand for this type of vessel not paralleled in Greek contexts, a preference which may be explained by the special status of its ancestors. After the rise of the local

Italiote production, the import of original prize vessels ceases completely, possibly due to the fact that the demand was now met by the locally produced vessels.

In the early generation of Lucanian vase-painters the shape seems to become increasingly popular by the time of the Amykos Painter: indeed, 19 vases have been attributed to the Amykos Painter,[21] only two examples have so far been attributed to the Pisticci Painter,[22] and one to the Cyclops Painter.[23] To these should be added the two examples of early Italiote Panathenaic amphoras in black-figure technique (Figs. 1-2).

The following generations of Lucanian vase-painters all produced amphoras, though always in moderate numbers.[24] A rise in the production can, however, be observed from around the middle of the fourth century BC with the production of the Choephoroi Painter, the Roccanova Painter, the Painter of Naples 1959 and finally the Primato Group.[25] A similar pattern is observable in the Apulian production with a more moderate number of amphoras known from the early Apulian painters and a significant rise in the production around the middle of the fourth century BC.

What distinguishes the South Italian production of pseudo-Panathenaic amphoras from all other types of pseudo-Panathenaic amphoras is both the sheer number of vessels produced for more than a century and the transformation of this strongly emblematic vessel outside its original context of use in the Panathenaic games. In order to increase our understanding of the use and symbolic meaning of these vessels, the following sections are dedicated first to an analysis of the archaeological context of the imported and locally produced amphoras of Panathenaic shape from the period predating the local

---

7 For contributions concerning the Panathenaic prize vessels, see Neils 1992; Bentz 1998; additional aspects of the vessels including their reception history have been dealt with at a conference in 1998 and subsequently published by Bentz & Eschbach (2001).

8 The amphoras are considered to be the outcome of a long lasting tradition of using ceramic vessels as prizes. The earliest known vessel serving this purpose is an oinochoe dating from the middle of the eighth century BC, which carries the inscription "Whoever of all the dancers dances most spiritedly, let him receive this" (London, British Museum, B 130: *ABV* 98.1).

9 Miller 2004, 233-34.

10 Neils 1992, cat.no. 70 and cat.nos. 67-69.

11 For a complete catalogue of the pseudo-Panathenaic amphoras in black-figure style, see Appendix 1, in Bentz 2001.

12 Taranto, Museo Archeologico Nazionale, 4319: Lippolis 1994, no. 34.1; Bentz 2001, Appendix 1, no. 310. Taranto, Museo Archeologico Nazionale, 4320: Lippolis 1994, no. 34.2. Taranto, Museo Archeologico Nazionale, 50290: Lippolis 1994, no. 55.1; Bentz 2001, Appendix 1, no. 311.

13 Bentz 2001, 117, Appendix 2.

14 Shapiro 2001.

15 See Neils *et al.* 2001 for a list of known Attic red-figured amphoras of Panathenaic shape.

16 For examples of the production of the Berlin Painter, see Neils et al. 2001, nos. 7-24, and for the Kleophrades Painter, *see ibidem*, nos. 3-6.

17 Taranto, Museo Archeologico Nazionale, inv. 143544: *BAPD* Vase 41697; Lippolis 1994, 347-350, fig. 124.1.

18 Naples, Museo Archeologico Nazionale, inv. 81401: *BAPD* Vase 220519; ARV^2 1316.1; *Addenda* 362.

19 See n. 4 for a couple of examples of other types of amphoras known from the Lucanian and Apulian workshops.

20 For example the following neck amphoras: a) Metaponto, Museo Civico, inv. 20113: *BAPD* Vase 6555, from Pisticci (Basilicata) attributed to the Achilles Painters; Taranto, Museo Archeologico Nazionale, inv. 54384: *BAPD* vase 206310, from Novoli (Messapia), attributed to the Pan Painter; Taranto, Museo Archeologico Nazionale, inv. 4546: *BAPD* Vase 202717, from Taranto, attributed to the Flying Angel Painter.

21 *LCS* no. 184, 41 (from Ruvo); *LCS* no. 218, 44 (from Ruvo); *LCS* no. 218a, 45 (from Policoro); *LCS* no. 246, 48 (from Ruvo); *LCS* no. 247, 48 (no context); *LCS* no. 248, 48 (from Ceglie del Campo); *LCS* no. 249, 49 (from Ruvo); *LCS* no. 250, 49 (no context); *LCS* no. 183a, 698 (no context); *LCS* 219b, 698 (from Nocera); *LCS* 1st supplement, nos. 218b and 219a, 8 (no context); *LCS* 2nd supplement no. 247a, 157 (from Apollonia); *LCS* 3rd supplement, no. 184b, 15 (from Metaponto); *LCS* 3rd supplement, no. 219c, 17 (no context); *LCS* 3rd supplement, no. 219d, 17 (no context); *LCS* 3rd supplement, no. 252a, 18 (no context); Krannart Art Museum inv. 70.7.3: *CVA* Illinois, I, pl. 56f (no context); Crucinia, Metaponto, tomb 390 (on exhibition in Metaponto, Museo Archeologico Nazionale).

22 Metaponto, Museo Archeologico Nazionale, inv. 310.897: Denoyelle 1997, 402-402, n. 38; Taranto, Museo Archeologico Nazionale, inv. I.G. 8001: *NSc* 1902, 313, fig. 1.

23 *LCS* 1st supplement, no. 100b, 6 (from Pisticci, Sta. Maria del Casale, tomb 1) The amphora have earlier been associated with the Amykos Painter and the Lycurgus Painter.

24 From the intermediate group the following amphoras can be identified: one example from The Via Dante Group (*LCS* no. 334, 67); one example by the Hamburg Painter (*LCS* no. 369, 72); five examples to the workshop of the Creusa and Dolon Painters (*LCS* no. 422, 83; nos. 458-459, 91; nos. 536-537, 103); and five examples to the Brooklyn-Budapest Painter (*LCS* no. 572, 110; nos. 590-592, 114; no. 597, 115).

25 From the late Lucanian production the following amphoras can be identified: 10 examples by the Choephoroi Painter (*LCS* nos. 615-623, 121-22; no. 643, 125); seven by the Roccanova Painter (*LCS* nos. 726-731, 136; no. 778, 140); 11 by the Painter of Naples 1959 and his followers (*LCS* nos. 811-815, 146-47; nos. 862-864, 151; nos. 876-877, 153; no. 891, 155) and finally 21 by the Primato Group and related painters (*LCS* nos. 919-920, 165; nos. 944-957, 168-70; no. 1084, 180; nos. 1094-1096, 182).

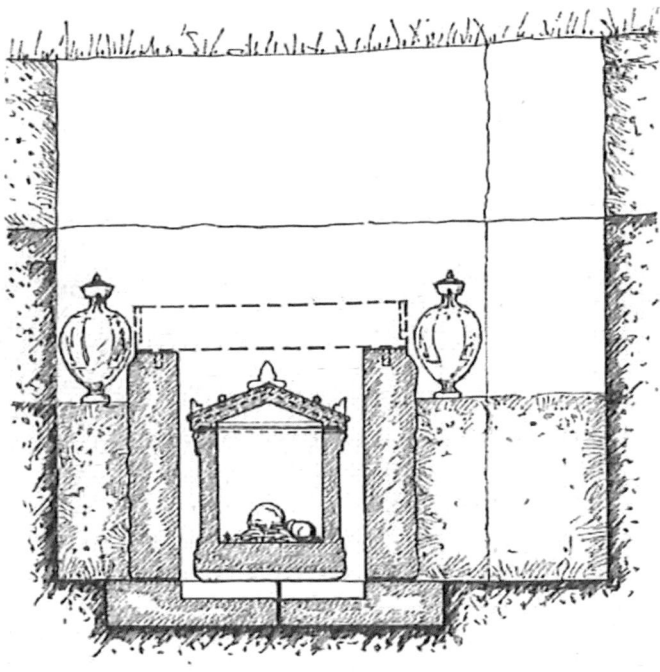

Fig. 3. Reconstruction of tomb C, via Genova 35, Taranto (Drawing: after Lo Porto 1967, figs. 4-5).

production and until the beginning of the fourth century BC, and then to an analysis of the iconographical evidence reflecting their context of use.

The Archaeological Contexts

Of the 26 examples of imported Attic Panathenaic amphoras recorded from Apulia, 20 have been found in Taranto,[26] two are from the extramural sanctuary of Saturo,[27] two are from Ruvo (although the provenance of one of them is tentative)[28] and two are from undocumented sites in Apulia.[29] Of the 20 Panathenaic amphoras found in Taranto, all with a documented context can be connected to tombs within the time frame of c. 550 to 430 BC.[30] To my knowledge, no Panathenaic prize vessels have been documented from Metaponto or Herakleia or their hinterland.

While the context of the Panathenaic amphoras from Ruvo is undocumented, our knowledge of some of the Tarantine examples and their tomb contexts is very good. Although they cannot be proved to be the actual prize vessels won by the person buried in the tomb, the setting does seem to reflect heroic and athletic values. The tombs were first published by Lo Porto in 1967 under the heading *Tombe di Atleti Tarentini*, being treated as part of a specific athletic funerary ideology. The tombs share common traits in their monumental size and the type of deposited tomb goods, which can be connected to the sphere of symposion (e.g. kraters, kylikes and tomb constructions inspired by the Greek *andron*[31]) and sport, represented by the Panathenaic amphoras, strigils and alabastra. Usually the Panathenaic amphoras are deposited outside the main tomb chamber or sarcophagus, while only single items are found with the deceased, usually strigils and/or alabastra. While early tombs published by Lo Porto contain several burials, the latest of them provide unique evidence for the use of the Panathenaic amphoras in a heroic context.

The amphoras were found in a rectangular fossa tomb cut into the bedrock (3.95 x 1.95m) near the modern Via Genova.[32] The covering of the tomb was lost as it had been partly disturbed due to the modern building activity in the area. However inside the tomb was found an intact sarcophagus with a cover (2.37 x 0.85 cm) oriented in an east-west direction with the head of the deceased towards the east. Outside each corner of the sculptured, temple-like sarcophagus, a Panathenaic amphora had been placed on a high stone bench (Fig. 3). Three of them are intact, but only a small fragment remains of the fourth amphora. An alabastron found inside the sarcophagus was the only additional tomb gift besides the amphoras. The three preserved amphoras are all decorated in the traditional manner of Panathenaic amphoras with an armed Pallas Athena on the main side, the discipline of the games on the other, and an inscription along the column. On the three preserved amphoras three different disciplines can be identified: the pentathlon (with scenes of discus-throwing and long jump), boxing and chariot racing. On the basis of the Panathenaic amphoras the tomb has been dated to c. 480 BC. Since the amphoras are the means by which the tomb has been dated, the duration of time from their production until their deposit in the tomb cannot be determined. But considering the fact that the vessels have all preserved their lids and are in a relatively good condition without any significant marks of use, it is reasonable to suppose that the duration of time between production and final deposition in the tomb was relatively short. Stylistically the vessels are also closely connected, and the shield of Athena is decorated with a pegasos. The pegasos is usually considered the trademark of the Kleophrades Painter's production of Panathenaic amphoras, and he is usually considered the originator of the four amphoras in the tomb.[33]

The fact that these four Panathenaic vessels were found in the same context and probably produced in the same workshop strengthens the assumption that they followed a very similar path of life and entered similar social contexts. The most apparent interpretation of them has been that they were won by the deceased himself in the Panathenaic games, and accordingly Lo Porto defined the deceased as an aristocrat who had sponsored the chariot race, won the pentathlon as a youth and later become a boxing champion.[34] However, this hypothesis has been contradicted by several scholars including Martin Bentz. One of the strong counterarguments is the fact that a commercial mark is found on one of the vessels.[35] In this case they might instead have been ordered directly from the workshop in order to serve the purpose of funeral vessels. At least, this could be implied by the homogeneity of the vessels and their good state of preservation.

Further evidence against the amphoras being actual prize vessels won by the deceased has been provided by the physical anthropological analysis carried out by Baggieri on the skeleton of the 'athlete' buried in the sarcophagos.[36] From the analysis it could be confirmed that the person died young, probably at an age between 27 and 35, and that he seems to have lived on a good and relatively healthy diet consisting mainly of meat but also fish and sea food. There was also some slight evidence indicating that he carried out regular exercise, which might define him as an athlete. But the skeleton did not reveal any fractures or examples of broken bones indicating he had been a boxer or participant in the pankration, and thus it must be doubted whether he won the amphoras himself. But considering the construction of the tomb with the temple-like sarcophagus, and the fact that the deceased was a young and presumably strong and healthy aristocrat, the amphoras were probably

---

26 *BAPD* Vase nos. 8455; 8789; 8791; 8793; 8794; 8795; 8796; 8797; 8803; 8814; 8815; 8816; 13829; 15111; 21760; 44912; 202126; 302108; 9021982; 303039; 13883.
27 A) Taranto, Museo Archaeologico, fragments: *BAPD* Vase 9503; Bentz 1998, cat. no. 6.136; *AttiTaranto* 16, 730, taf. 100. B) Taranto, Museo Archaeologico, fragment: *BAPD* Vase 9016582; Bentz 1998, cat.no. 6.041; *AttiTaranto* 16, 730, taf. 100.
28 A) Naples, Museo Archeologico Nazionale, Santangelo 693: *BAPD* Vase 205703; *CVA* Naples 1 (1950), III.H.G, pl. 3.2.4; 4.3; Bentz 1998, cat.no. 5.090; *ABV* 407. B) Naples, Museo Archeologico Nazionale, inv. 81293, probably from Ruvo: *BAPD* no. 13832; Bentz 1998, cat.no. 5.092; *CVA* Naples 1 (1950), III.H.G, pl. 3.1.3.
29 A) Taranto, Museo Archeologico Nazionale, inv. 4320: *BAPD* Vase nos 310343; *CVA* Naples 1 (1950), III.H.G, pl. 1.3-4. B) Taranto, Museo Archeologico Nazionale: *BAPD* vase 16055.
30 A) Tomb XII, Arsenale Militare, Villa Pepe (ex Capecelatro), date: 550-520BC: Lippolis 1994, cat. no. 34 (includes two Panathenaic amphoras). B) Tomb 9.IV.1934, Carceri Vecchie, date: c. 500 BC: Lippolis 1994, cat. no. 55 (includes one Panathenaic amphora). C) Tomb 9-18.XII.1959, Via Genova, date: c. 480 BC: Lippolis 1994, cat. no. 98 (includes four Panathenaic amphoras); Lo Porto 1967, 69-84 (tomba C). D) Tomb 30.I.1911, Montegranaro (near C. Nitti road and the house of V.Benedetti), date: 440-430 BC: Lippolis 1994, cat.no. 123; Lo Porto 1967, 84. E) Chamber tomb, via G. Oberdan 35, date: 530-480 BC: Lippolis 1994, cat.no. 50 (includes fragments of four Panathenaic amphoras); Lo Porto 1967, 43-44, tav. X.
31 For a description of the Archaic tombs representing an andron, see Lo Porto 1967, 42-68 (Tomb A and B).
32 For a thorough description of the tomb and its contents, see Lo Porto 1967, 69-84; Lippolis 1994, nos. 98-98.4, 314-316, figs. 98.1-98.3.
33 Some stylistic oddities have been noted by Matheson (Matheson 1989, 112) who is critical of Lo Porto's attribution of the vessels to the Kleophrades Painter.
34 Lo Porto 1967.
35 Bentz 1998, 115: of the Panathenaic amphoras found in Southern Italy Bentz only considers the amphoras from the sanctuary of Satura as 'true' prize vessels brought back home by winning athletes.
36 Baggieri 1999.

acquired in order to represent a more general set of athletic or heroic values.

In the case of all of the Tarantine tombs with Panathenaic amphoras, the vessels are placed outside the main chamber or sarcophagus of the tomb. This seems to indicate that the vessels were not considered tomb equipment for use in life after death. They could instead, as Valenza Mele has suggested, be interpreted in relation to a collective ideology, where the individual is seen only as a member of the community and his deeds are seen only in relation to the prestige that they bring to his hometown.[37] An ideology which is usually considered a characteristic feature of the city state of Sparta, the mothercity of Taranto. Thus, the vessels could instead be intended for regular ritual activities outside the tomb or specifically for use in connection with the burial ceremony.

While the imported Attic Panathenaic amphoras can mainly be connected to aristocratic tombs with athletic pretensions in Taranto, the archaeological contexts known from the initial phase of the local red-figure production are different. All the pseudo-Panathenaic amphoras attributed to the Pisticci and Cyclops Painters have been found in the Italic, but strongly Hellenized site of Pisticci, located only about 20 km from the urban centre of Metaponto and on the periphery of the chora.[38] With the Amykos Painter, the distribution of the shape widens, seeming to point towards a predilection for the shape in the two Peucetian sites of Ruvo and Ceglie de Campo. But one example is also known from a tomb context and one from a kiln deposit in Metaponto.[39] More unusual are the isolated examples of the export of the shape outside Lucania and Apulia: a tomb in Nocera (near Salerno) and a tumulus in Apollonia (Albania).[40] The size of the vessels ranges from around only 37 cm to the more monumental size of 66 cm.

Important differences can be seen between the contexts of the amphoras found in Metaponto and Pisticci on the one side of the region and Ruvo and Ceglie de Campo on the other. While the Pisticci Painter's black-figure amphora from Pisticci was found in what was presumably an athletic context with only a few tomb gifts (in this case a strigil and a lekythos), and the amphora from Metaponto (Crucinia necropolis, Tomb 390) was found together with a squat lekythos and a lebes gamikos, the Peucetian contexts with pseudo-Panathenaic amphoras are far richer. The latter contexts are aristocratic tombs, monumental in their size and number of tomb gifts. For example, the large double-

Fig. 4. Pseudo-Panathenaic amphora. Heroic warrior statue placed on a base with an amphora. From Gravina tomb 1/1974 (Photo: after Ciancio 1997, fig. 153).

chambered tomb (Tomb 45) which was excavated in 1924 at the intersection between *Via I Maggio and Corso Antonio Jatta* in Ruvo. One of the chambers in the tomb was empty, but the other one contained an exceptional proto-Lucanian volute-krater by the Karneia Painter, two proto-Lucanian amphoras by the Amykos Painter, a set of drinking cups and askoi as well as a bronze helmet.[41] Both of the amphoras, one with a pursuit scene and the other with a naked athlete, are rather small (37.5 and 39.5 cm), in contrast to the monumental size of the volute krater (86 cm). At Ceglie del Campo another large chamber tomb excavated in 1898 yielded one of the Amykos Painter's amphoras with a warrior theme together with a volute krater by the Karneia Painter,[42] as well as a large hydria, a lekythos and various other fragments.[43] Another important find from Ruvo with amphoras by the Amykos Painter is an outstandingly rich warrior tomb, which besides three Amykos amphoras and a hydria also included an early Apulian volute krater by the

Sisyphus Painter, Attic kantharoi, kylikes, a bell krater, Attic Nolan amphoras, bronze armour and a helmet, together with smaller finds. These contexts clearly indicate that the amphoras seem to have been considered part of the banquet equipment of the aristocratic warrior tombs in this area, a pattern which can also be seen in a group of rich tombs from Gravina including Panathenaic amphoras attributed to the early generation of Apulian painters.[44] So to some extent the assemblages of the Peucetian tombs within the early period of Italiote red-figure production reflect Lohmann's interpretation of the amphoras in a sympotic setting.[45] At the same time, however, there seems to be a different set of values connected to the amphoras in the areas of Greek influence, and the iconographical evidence seems to indicate that the emblematic meaning of the vessels was still in some ways connected to the meaning applied to the vessels in the preceding phase of use in Taranto.

The Iconographical Evidence
The iconographical evidence in general clearly reflects themes relevant to the tomb cult, and in numerous cases the amphoras are depicted in ritual scenes around the tomb. The first tomb scenes on the amphoras can be seen already within the last quarter of the fifth century BC in the workshops of the second generation of Lucanian painters, especially the Brooklyn and Budapest Group. From then on amphoras are at times depicted in the figure scenes and they can be divided into the five overall types of scenes.

Panathenaic amphoras
in front of a statue base
Examples of this type can be found from the end of the fifth century BC, and according to Pontrandolfo et al.'s typology they can be connected to the earliest occurrence of a funerary monument on South Italian red-figure vases.[46] One early example is the Gravina Painter's amphora mentioned above.[47] The Gravina Painter's amphora depicts a naked youth on a statuebase, in front of which is placed a black Panathenaic amphora and a number of what seems to be miniature vessels (Fig. 4). In addition, two skyphoi are shown hanging on the statuebase. The statue represents a heroic youth in accordance with the Greek ideal, and his posture closely reflects some of the Greek athlete statues known from the Classical period. However, this is not an athlete but a warrior, as indicated by the fact that he carries a helmet and a shield and wears a chlamys. Around him worshippers, women and men, can be seen carrying wreaths. One of the women is in the process of crowning the statue; another woman is carrying a small cista.

The amphora was found in a rectangular fossa tomb dated to the last quarter of the fifth century BC containing a great number of figured vessels: a volute krater and two pseudo-Panathenaic amphoras attributed to the Gravina Painter, three pseudo-Panathenaic amphoras attributed to 'near the Tarporly Painter', three Attic red-figure kylikes, one attributed to the Eretria Painter and one to the Penthesilea Painter, an Attic kantharos (also attributed to the Eretria Painter), a lekanis (attributed to the Achilles Painter), three Attic oinochoai, and finally one black gloss oinochoe. This tomb belongs to a group of tombs in the Botromagno/Gravina area that can be dated to the end of the fifth century BC and which are significant because they contained Attic and proto-Italiote pottery found side by side, as well as several examples of pseudo-Panathenaic amphoras.[48]

The rendering of the statue in another example without a known context and now in the Allard Pierson Museum in Amsterdam is not as detailed. But again we see the statue of a naked youth standing on a high base in front of which can be seen two black amphoras of the Panathenaic shape and a suspended kylix (Fig. 5).[49] In this case the

---

37 Valenza Mele 1991, 8-9.
38 See n. 22 and 23 above.
39 Tomb 390 from the Crucinia necropolis in Metaponto (propr. Giacovelli), on exhibition at the Museo Archaeologico Nazionale in Metaponto. The amphora was found together with a squat lekythos and a lebes gamikos. For the kiln deposit, see *Metaponto* I (in *NSc* XXIX, 1975, supplement), 448, no. 413, fig. 78A.
40 Apollonia (Albania), 490, from Tumulus I, tomb 110: *LCS* 2nd suppl. no. 274a, 157. Nocera, tomb 21: *LCS* 698; *ArchReps* 1967, 31.
41 Montanaro 2007, 340-348, no. 45.1-45.10, figs. 217-227.
42 *LCS* no. 280, 55, pl. 24.
43 *NSc* 1900, 506; *LCS* no. 248, 48.
44 Ciancio 1997; for further examples of these contexts, see Lohmann 1979, 146, n. 1226.
45 Lohmann 1979, 145-147.
46 Pontrandolfo et al. 1988, 182.
47 Taranto, Museo Archeologico Nazionale, from Gravina T1/1974: Pontrandolfo et al. 1988, fig.33.1; Ciancio 1997, fig. 153, attributed to the Gravina Painter by Trendall (*RVAp* I, no. 3, 33, pl. 8,4).
48 Ciancio 1997.
49 Amsterdam, Allard Pierson Museum, inv. 3478: Pontrandolfo et al. 1988, fig. 33.2; *RVAp* 9/160, 244, tav. 80,1.

Fig. 5. Apulian pseudo-Panathenaic amphora. Amsterdam, Allard Pierson Museum, inv. 3478 (Photo: after Pontrandolfo et al 1988, fig. 33.2).

Fig. 6. Pseudo-Panathenaic amphora with tomb monument. Schwerin, Staatliche Museen, inv. 703 (Photo: after Pontrandolfo et al. 1988, fig. 42.3).

youth carries a long mantle but no other attributes, and nothing definite can be said about the identity of the statue. Around the statue we find several worshippers, a young man holding a wreath towards the statue, and on the opposite side a naked youth with strigil. Below, two women carry small jugs of the *chous* type to the base of the statue. On a third pseudo-Panathenaic amphora now in Schwerin Staatliche Museum a Panathenaic amphora is again depicted in a heroic setting: in this case a statue of a rider on his horse (Fig. 6).[50] On either side of the statue are two worshippers, a man and a woman.

Panathenaic amphoras
on or near a columnar tomb stele

Several examples of pseudo-Panathenaic amphoras appear in scenes with columnar tomb monuments or stelai.[51] These scenes can in most cases be linked to the representations of Greek tragic plays, like the following two examples, both of which have been attributed to the Lucanian circle of the Brooklyn and the Budapest Painter. The first one was found in the Italic site of Anzi.[52] Because of the inscriptions on the Doric column-shaped stele (ΑΓΑΜΕΜΝΩΝ), and above the seated woman's head (ΗΛΕΚΤΡ[Α]) the scene can be interpreted as the mourning Elektra, accompanied by another woman carrying a cista, sitting by the tomb of Agamemnon. The two naked youths have been identified as Orestes and Pylades, and the scene has been connected to Aeschylus' *Libation Bearers*.[53] The painter has emphasized the tomb monument as that of a heroic warrior by means of the helmet placed on the top of the stele and the black-figured Panathenaic amphoras placed on the base of the tomb monument. On the Panathenaic amphora a naked youth is depicted possibly holding a strigil and the woman in front of him seems to hold a ribbon, as if she is in the process of tying the ribbon around his head and is to be thought of as celebrating him as a victor. The relationship between the heroic tomb and the prominent placement of the Panathenaic amphoras outside the main chamber recall the Tarantine 'athletes' tomb described above.

A similar significance should most probably be ascribed to the two pseudo-Panathenaic amphoras depicted in a tomb scene on an amphora likewise attributed to the Brooklyn and Budapest Painter, now in the Louvre (Fig. 7).[54] Here too, the theme of the scene can be interpreted as the tomb of a tragic hero, in this case Oedipus, who is identified through the inscription on the stele. Again, the scene depicts the cultic activities around the tomb monument of the hero, scenes which most probably have their origin in the actual plays as they were performed at the time of the production of the vessels. Even though the amphoras are usually depicted in tomb scenes on vessels of the amphora shape, there are some exceptions, such as a

Fig. 7. Lucanian pseudo-Panathenaic amphora. Paris, Musèe du Louvre, inv. CA 308 (Photo courtesy: RMN, Musée du Louvre).

50 Schwerin, Staatliche Museum, inv. 703: Pontrandolfo *et al.* 1988, fig. 42.33.
51 For example: A) Napoli, Museo Archaeologico Nazionale, inv. 817544: Pontrandolfo *et al.* 1988, fig. 34.4, Apulian pseudo-Panathenaic amphora. B) Napoli, Museo Archaeologico Nazionale, inv. 82140: Pontrandolfo *et al.* 1988, fig. 36.2, Lucanian pseudo-Panathenaic amphora. C) Bari, Museo Archaeologico, inv. 1394: Pontrandolfo *et al.* 1988, fig. 38.2, Apulian volute krater. D) Paris, Musée du Louvre, inv. CA308: Pontrandolfo *et al.* 1988, fig. 38.4., Lucanian Panathenaic amphora attributed to the Brooklyn-Budapest Painter. E) Brussels, Mus. R. d'Art et d'Historie R407: Schneider-Hermann 1980, fig. 52; *LCS* no. 631, 123. Nestoris attributed to the Lucanian Choephoroi Painter.
52 Naples, Museo Archaeologico Nazionale, inv. 82140: *LCS* no. 597. The amphora is depicted in Hart 2010, no. 21, 64.
53 Taplin 2007, 52-53; Hart 2010, 64.
54 Paris, Musée du Louvre, inv. CA308: Pontrandolfo *et al.* 1988, fig. 38.4., Lucanian Panathenaic amphora attributed to the Brooklyn-Budapest Painter.

Fig. 8. Lucanian nestoris with a columnar tomb monument (Photo courtesy: MRAH, Bruxelles)

nestoris which is now in Brussels (Fig. 8). This nestoris has been attributed to the Choephoroi Painter and thus belongs to the later group of Lucanian painters.[55]

Panathenaic amphoras on a tomb mound
Several examples of tomb mounds are depicted on the red-figure vases, and in a few cases a ceramic vessel has been placed on top of the mound as a *sema*. One example of a Panathenaic amphora from Ruvo illustrates a figure-decorated amphora placed on a tomb mound decorated with *taeniae* and wreaths (Fig. 9).[56] Beside it a woman is standing with a cista and a plate with offerings. Behind her a naked man with stick and himation is sitting, and opposite the mound another naked man stands holding out a wreath.

The amphora has been dated to c. 370-350 BC, and it was found in a rich tomb localized near the Lago Porta Noè (modern Piazza Bovio). According to the description

Fig. 9. Apulian pseudo-Panathenaic amphora. Tomb 159, Ruvo. (Photo: after Montanaro 2007, fig. 619).

Fig. 10: Apulian pseudo-Panathenaic amphora attributed to the Hearst Painter. Oxford, Mississippi, inv. 77.3.134. (Photo: after Neils 2001, tafel 36.4).

of the tomb from the time of excavation (1837), it was found undisturbed. The first finds recorded include a band and floral-decorated askos (*tipo canosino*) and possibly small *unguentari* used for different kinds of scented oils (unidentified). The finds were connected to a double-chambered tomb cut into the bedrock and covered with slabs of tuff stone. In the tomb was also found a three-disc cuirass with relief decoration – an embossed Athena head in the lower disc (Napoli, Museo Archeologico Nazionale 5795). A great number of red-figure fragments from two Apulian pan-Athenaic amphoras and a hydria (Napoli, Museo Archeologico Nazionale 82138 and 81943). Of these the hydria has not so far been identified. The amphoras were both of a considerable height, the one depicting the mound is 67.4 cm and the other with a Dionysiac theme is 97 cm.

Panathenaic amphoras
in a victory scene
While the examples described so far can be closely connected with the activities on or around the tomb, one example by the early Apulian painter of the Sisyphus Group, known as the Hearst Painter, to some extent connects the amphoras to what appears to be a victory scene (Fig. 10).[57] In this scene we see two black-figure amphoras with a victory branch protruding from the rim. The figure scenes on the amphoras are difficult to decipher, but they seem to be groups of two draped youths, scenes which traditionally appear on the B-side of most larger vessels of early Apulian and Lucanian production. Framing a young woman carrying an offering plate on her head are two naked youths carrying fillets. While the youths combined with the amphoras could indicate a victory scene, the woman with the offering basket is a typical motif in scenes relating to tomb cult, and thus the scene should probably be interpreted as funerary.

Panathenaic amphoras
in or near a naiskos
The naiskos scene is one of the most common scenes in fourth century BC South Italian red-figure production.[58] Usually the statue of a hero is depicted in the scenes, and

---

55 Brussels, Mus. R. d'Art et d'Historie R407: Schneider-Hermann 1980, fig. 52; *LCS* no. 631, 123. Nestoris attributed to the Lucanian Choephoroi Painter.
56 Napoli, Museo Archeologico Nazionale, inv. 82138, from Ruvo: Pontrandolfo *et al.* 1988, fig. 40.1-2; Montanaro 2007, tomb 159, 682-690, fig. 619-620.
57 Oxford, Mississippi, inv. 77.3.134: *RVAp* no. 46, 13.
58 Lohmann 1979, 145-147.

Fig. 11: Lucanian pseudo-Panathenaic amphora (Photo: after Pontrandolfo et al. 1988, fig. 42.2).

woman carrying offerings, can be seen. In the background of the scene a naiskos-like building is depicted, a type of tomb construction that has also been documented archaeologically from the excavations in Herakleia.[61] There seems to be a great emphasis on the amphora in the scene because of the way the youth is putting his hands on it as if he is protecting it in some way. Another interesting aspect is the archaeological context of the vessel. It functioned as an urn and was found deposited directly on the ground, where it had only been protected by a terracotta bowl.[62]

Another example included here is a scene depicted on a nestoris attributed to the early Lucanian Brooklyn and Budapest Painter.[63] The scene depicts a monumental naiskos with ionic columns. Inside the naiskos a large amphora decorated with a figurescene has been placed. No human figures are included in the scene, but the motif rendered on the black-figure amphora shows a seated woman who holds out a phiale or bowl to a young man approaching her.

THE ROLE OF THE PANATHENAIC AMPHORA IN HEROIC CULT

From the circumstances of these examples, the following characteristics of the use of pseudo-Panathenaic amphoras can be outlined. They are connected with scenes relating to a heroic cult and they seem to have been closely involved in the cult ritual, probably as containers for oil, wine or other liquids. As noted above, the preserved examples emphasize the heroic connotations of the amphoras. The fact that they never appear in a Dionysiac setting, such as the bell and calyx kraters, emphasizes that they cannot simply be interpreted as symposion ware even though they appear as such in the Peucetian tomb contexts from Ruvo, Ceglie del Campo and Gravina. Furthermore, the iconography emphasizes the assumption indicated by the archaeological evidence that pseudo-Panathenaic amphoras were part of an active tomb cult initially connected to a heroic cult and later on as an essential part of the Italic tomb ritual. According to Hans Lohmann's synthesis on *Grabmäler auf Unteritalischen Vasen*, one-third of all the tomb monuments in South Italian red-figure painting are to be found on amphoras of Panathenaic shape.[64] The use of the amphoras in the tomb cult is further emphasized from around the middle of the fourth century BC, when a production of vessels with a perforated base was begun, apparently for the purpose of using the vessel in a libation ceremony. This production, according to Lohmann, was

around the naiskos male and female worshippers can be seen carrying different types of offerings. Such scenes appear on all larger vessel shapes within this period, and they are also the most common iconographic theme on the pseudo-Panathenaic amphoras from the middle of the fourth century BC until the end of the production. This emphasizes that the pseudo-Panathenaic amphora produced at this time should definitely be considered a shape destined specifically for use in tomb cult and as a tomb offering. Thus, at this point, we could (as concluded by Neils) define it as a funerary object.[59]

During the early phase of the production of Italiote red-figure pottery, a couple of interesting forerunners to these scenes can be seen combined with pseudo-Panathenaic amphoras. One of the earliest has been found in Policoro (Via Avellino, tomb 53) within the territory of the Greek colony of Herakleia (Fig. 11).[60] The amphora can be associated with the first generation of Lucanian painters. On the vessel we see a naked youth leaning on a Panathenaic amphora on which a male figure in black-figure technique can be seen. In front of him another naked youth is depicted with a *taenia*, and behind him a

initiated by the closely related Apulian workshops of the Snub-Nose, Varrese and "H.A." Painters.[65]

The iconographic evidence from the end of the fifth century through the fourth clearly refers to an active use of the Panathenaic amphora in the cult ritual around the tomb monument and both black-glossed versions and figured vessels are represented. Unfortunately the archaeological evidence for the tomb rituals carried on above the tombs is rather limited, which might possibly be explained by the fact that this evidence rarely survives in areas such as Taranto where building activities have been carried out for many centuries, and the fact that pottery deposited in the tomb chamber was usually the only thing to be recorded in excavations carried out in the nineteenth and early part of the twentieth centuries. However, evidence from the Pantanello necropolis at Metaponto has shown that the black gloss variant of the Panathenaic amphora is a rather common find among the ceramic deposits inside and outside tombs. The black gloss Panathenaics have, as a result of the significant number found, been interpreted as a local Metapontine production by Maria Elliott.[66] One such example can be connected with great confidence to tomb 209 in Pantanello, where it accompanied a Lucanian red-figure squat lekythos attributed by Lucilla Burn to the Pisticci-Amykos group and a red-figure pelike attributed to the Pisticci Painter,[67] a context which seems to indicate that it was produced at approximately the same time as the local red-figure production began. Another example from Pantanello (tomb 209) seems to indicate that red-figure vessels of the Panathenaic shape were also used as *semata*.[68] Examples of semata in stone formed as Panathenaic amphoras are likewise known from Athens in the fourth century BC.[69]

CONCLUSION

To sum up, the legacy of the original Panathenaic amphoras to the pseudo-Panathenaic amphoras lies only in their shape. Their decoration as well as the circumstances of their production are different. After an initial step made by the Pisticci Painter to reproduce the original Attic prize vessels, the iconographic themes are chosen freely in accordance with the taste of the individual painter and the consumers of the pottery. Similarities in their meaning and use can however be seen in the way that the imported Panathenaic amphoras were used prior to the establishment of the local red-figure workshops.

In order to emphasize the emblematic meaning of the type of vessel discussed here, I have tried to underline that we need to make a clear distinction between the meaning of the Panathenaic amphoras as prize vessels in their Attic context and their meaning as funerary vessels in the late Archaic and early Classical 'athlete' tombs excavated in Taranto. First of all, no definite argument can be put forward for considering these amphoras as trophies of the individual athletes buried in the tombs. The evidence, on the contrary, is in favour of regarding these amphoras as having been bought second-hand for the use in aristocratic tombs (presumably for individuals of athletic importance or pretension), and therefore they should be considered more as general emblems emphasizing the heroic virtues and arête of the deceased. The pseudo-Panathenaic amphoras found in Pisticci, of which the Pisticci Painter's amphora was found together with a strigil and a lekythos, emphasizes that the Greek athletic ideal influenced directly the burial traditions of an Italic community.

It is commonly known from ancient sources that athletic competitions were of no less importance among the western Greeks than among the Greeks in their homeland.[70] Athletic competitions were especially important in Kroton and in Taranto, and victors from Southern Italy and Sicily are frequently recorded among the winners of the Olympic Games.[71] The sources indicate that the main period of athletic competition in Southern Italy was the late Archaic and early Classical period, contemporary with the Tarentine

---

59 Neils 2001, 130.
60 Policoro, Museo Nazionale della Siritide, Lucanian amphora: Pontrandolfo et al. 1988, fig. 42.2; Pianu 1990, 23-24, tav. VI, 1-2.
61 See e.g. Neutsch 1967, 141, abb. 27.
62 Pontrandolfo et al. 1988, 192, n. 41.
63 Naples, Museo Archaeologico Nazionale, inv. 82125: *LCS* no. 589, 114; Söldner 2007, Abb. 189.
64 Lohmann 1979, 145-147.
65 Lohmann 1982, 215-223, table 3.
66 Elliott 1998, 648.
67 Burn 1998, T209-1 and T209-7, 620.
68 Carter 1998, Pl. 84. It is important to emphasize that the definition of the shape of this vessel is tentative due to the fragmentary state of preservation.
69 *AM* 92, 1977, taf. 60; *Kerameikos* XII, 1980, 99ff.
70 Lippolis 2004.
71 See list of the Olympic victors from Southern Italy and Sicily in Stampolidis & Tassoulas (eds.) 2004, 288-289.

tombs and prior to the democratic revolution of the 470s.⁷² No archaeological remains of gymnasia or stadia have been found in Southern Italy, but according to Strabo a gymnasion was located at Taranto and several sources indicate that local games were carried out in Southern Italy and Sicily as well.⁷³

But while the Attic imports were limited and seem to have been used exclusively by the elite for tombs of athletic importance, the local production, by contrast, made the vessels available to a broader clientele, appearing mainly in aristocratic tombs outside the Greek sphere of influence. The iconographic evidence from around 430 to 370 BC, however, indicates a special preference for using the shape for cultic activities around the tomb of heroic males. Later, as the production of the amphoras increases, the iconographic themes are often naiskoi scenes which associate the amphoras with male as well as female tombs. In this period the production of the amphoras becomes far more numerous and they probably develop a more general meaning, which can confidently be compared to the lekythos, as suggested by Jenifer Neils. Further evidence to support this theory can be found in the fact that by the end of the century the shape has in some ways mutated and become more of a lekythos than an amphora.⁷⁴

From the evidence described above, we face some interesting variations in the use of the vessels, in their iconography and in the archaeological record. This seems to point towards a duality in the interpretation of the cultural meaning of the Panathenaic amphora. While the preserved archaeological contexts, mainly from Peucetian sites, point towards a use of the vessel as part of the banquet equipment in correspondence with the tomb ideology of this Italic community, the iconography of the vessels indicates their active use in the tomb ritual around the tomb, mainly for males of heroic status. In this way the emblematic meaning of the vessel can be directly linked to the use of the Panathenaic amphoras in the Archaic tombs of Taranto.

Although the use of the vessels in the tomb ritual around the tomb has only been documented sporadically in the archaeological record, I would propose the thesis that the iconography reflects the fact that the Panathenaic amphora remained a part of the tomb ritual among the Greek communities, a tradition which was born due to the import of Attic Panathenaic amphoras in the Archaic period.

72 Lippolis 2004, esp. 49-50.
73 Strabo (VI,1,3).
74 See e.g. the amphoras depicted in naiskoi scenes on two volute kraters attributed to the late Apulian Ganymede Painter: Basel S23 (*RVAp* II,no. 8, 797, pl. 296.1) and Bari, Locente coll. 3 (*RVAp* II,no. 9, 797, pl. 296.2).

ACKNOWLEDGEMENTS

I would like to pay a special thank to my PhD-advisors Lise Hannestad and Bodil Bundgaard Rasmussen for their support and constructive criticism. I am very grateful to Dyfri Williams who turned my attention towards the pseudo-Panathenaic fragment in the collection of the National Museum of Denmark. Also, I would like to thank the following institutions for providing me with photos and permissions to illustrate vases in their possession: Museo Archeologico Nazionale di Metaponto, Allard Pierson Museum, Schwerin Staatliche Museen, Musée du Louvre, Musée Royaux d'Art et d'Historie and University of Mississippi.

Vase-painting and Narrative Logic:
Achilles and Troilos in Athens and Etruria

BY GUY HEDREEN

Vase-painting and Narrative Logic: Achilles and Troilos in Athens and Etruria

BY GUY HEDREEN

Among the many possible approaches to the problem of the reception of Athenian vase-painting in Etruria is the analysis of vase-paintings as references to traditional narratives. Such an approach is not exactly new, but the working assumptions that govern it have evolved. An important attempt to understand what Etruscan representations of Greek mythology might have to say about the stories themselves, about their plots, was undertaken some time ago by Roland Hampe and Erika Simon. Their study was limited, however, by an assumption that serious, detailed, knowledgeable representations of myths in the visual arts must have been informed, directly or indirectly, by familiarity with the texts of Archaic Greek poetry. Although their analyses of Etruscan visual representations are ingenious and productive, their argument for Etruscan familiarity with Greek poetic texts has met with relatively less acceptance.[1] It is a premise of this paper that the foundation upon which the mythological tradition was built in the Archaic and early Classical periods is oral storytelling.[2] The archaeological evidence of cultural exchange between Greece and central Italy is sufficient evidence to guarantee limited existence of one fundamental requirement for storytelling, the ability for storyteller and audience to communicate in a common spoken language.[3] Now that the oral chain of narrative transmission and interpretation has been broken, modern scholarly assessment of ancient narrative vase-painting must follow a special hermeneutic. We must work backward from surviving material objects – texts or painted vases – in order to reconstruct the dynamic oral narrative discourse that informed their creation.[4] The possibility that Greek merchants, colonists and artisans living and working in Etruria faithfully communicated the main points of their mythology orally permits us to take Etruscan narrative art seriously as a form of creative engagement with the tradition. As I hope to show in this paper, we can learn something about the manner in which the Greeks

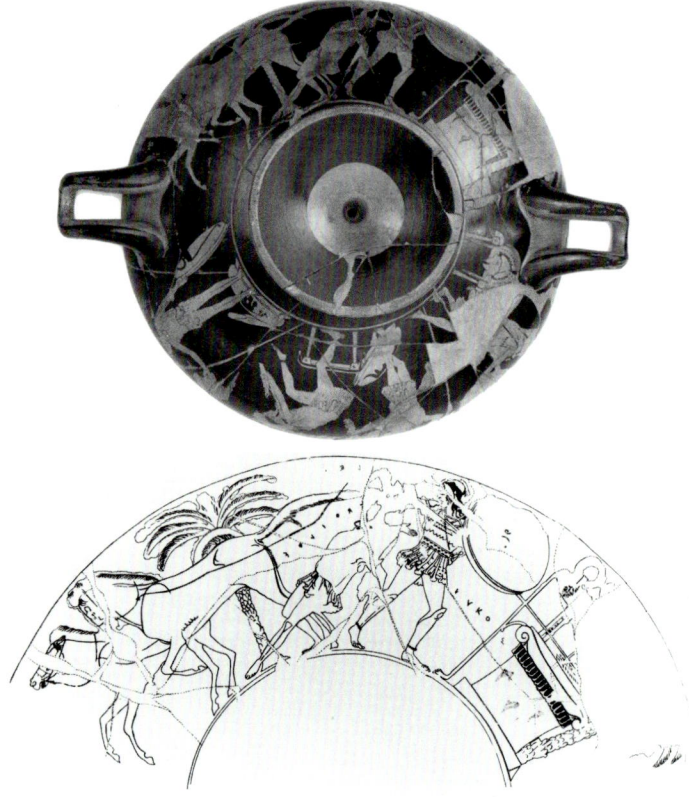

Fig. 1a. The murder of Troilos. Cup attributed to the Onesimos painter. Perugia, Museo Archeologico Nazionale inv. 89 (Photo courtesy: Museo Archeologico Nazionale, Perugia).

understood their own stories from the manner in which the Etruscans gave them visual form.

THE MURDER OF TROILOS IN ATHENIAN AND ETRUSCAN VASE-PAINTING

I begin with an Athenian red-figure vase-painting of the murder of Troilos. The Athenian vase, now in Perugia, was found in Etruria at Vulci (Fig. 1a, b). It is a late Archaic cup attributed to Onesimos.[5] On the exterior, a warrior drags a frightened boy toward an altar. The palm trees and tripod cauldron designate the sanctuary as belonging to Apollo.[6] In the bowl of the cup we can see what frightens the boy: the hero intends to slaughter him at the altar. Inscriptions identify the hero as Achilles, the boy as Troilos. The murder of Troilos was an extremely popular subject in both Greek and Etruscan art.[7] Numerous works of art depict Achilles lying in ambush for Troilos at a water source outside the

Fig. 1 b. The murder of Troilos also decorates the tondo of the cup in fig. 1a. (Photo courtesy: Museo Archeologico Nazionale, Perugia).

a

b

Fig. 2a-b. Kassandra seeks refuge by Athena statue, and Priam takes refuge on the altar of Zeus. Details of the interior of a cup by Onesimos. Rome, Villa Giulia inv. 121110 (Photo courtesy: The J. Paul Getty Museum, Malibu).

walls of Troy. Although he had the advantage of a horse, Troilos could not reach safety before Achilles ran him down. The murder itself, which is less commonly seen in art, virtually always occurs at or on an altar.

The cup in Perugia poses a serious problem for the understanding of the story of the murder of Troilos. On the one hand, the cup cannot be accounted for on the assumption that Achilles defiled the altar of Apollo unintentionally, with his victim Troilos merely taking refuge on the altar. That is not what the cup paintings show. Compare a cup in the Villa Giulia also attributed to Onesimos (Fig. 2a, b). On the exterior, Kassandra clings to a

---

1 Hampe & Simon 1964. For a critique of their assumptions about literacy and availability of texts of Greek poetry in Etruria, see Spivey & Stoddart 1990, 101.
2 For justification, see Hedreen 2001, 3-12.
3 For an overview of Greek contact with Etruria, see Bonfante 2003; for the oral basis of transmission of Greek myth in Etruria, see Spivey & Stoddart 1990, 92-106.
4 On the dynamic nature of the discourse, see Hedreen 2001, 12-18.
5 Perugia, Museo Archeologico Nazionale 89: ARV^2 320, 8; *BAPD* Vase 203224. For the inscriptions, see Immerwahr 1990, 84, no. 506.
6 Hedreen 2001, 68-74. I mistakenly assumed that the inscription Lykos on this cup referred to Apollo as titular deity of the shrine. In fact, Lykos is a well-known kalos name in the work of Onesimos: see ARV^2 1595-1596.
7 Kossatz-Deissmann 1997, 72-95, with further bibliography.

Fig. 3. Pontic amphora. Detail. Reading, Ure Museum, inv. 47.6.1 (Photo courtesy: The Ure Museum, University of Reading).

Fig. 4. La Tolfa Group amphora. Vatican City, Museo Gregoriano Etrusco Vaticano inv. 35718 (Astarita 742). (Photo courtesy: Museo Gregoriano Etrusco Vaticano, Rome).

statue of Athena, where she has obviously taken refuge; in the tondo, Priams awaits a death blow, sitting on the altar of Zeus, showing that he has taken refuge there.[8] On the cup in Perugia, Achilles is dragging Troilos toward the altar, and the boy is resisting. Nothing suggests that the boy sees the altar as anything but a kind of chopping block. On the other hand, those scholars who do recognize that Achilles is deliberately conducting the boy to the altar have not been able to explain how such a deliberate action functions within the larger underlying story.[9]

A close parallel to what is unfolding on the Athenian cup occurs on an Etruscan amphora of the so-called Pontic workshop. The vase is in Reading and dates to around 530 BC (Fig. 3).[10] On one side of the vase, a warrior packs a boy on his shoulder toward a water source that is also a cylindrical, ashlar-built altar.[11] It has been claimed that the Reading vase-painting is a "unique representation", never shown elsewhere in vase-painting, unlikely to have a Greek prototype, even incomprehensible in terms of Athenian iconography.[12] Those claims are not accurate. The image is unusual, in comparison to Athenian vase-paintings of the Troilos story, in suggesting that the water source where Achilles waited in ambush is coextensive with the sanctuary of Apollo where he killed the boy. But the idea that Achilles waited in ambush within the sanctuary is not unknown in Athenian art.[13] The main point, however, is that the vase in Reading expresses the same basic story as the vase-painting on the Perugia cup with respect to the hero's intentions. The two images differ only in the manner in which Achilles transported Troilos to the altar before killing him.

Although he incorrectly, in my view, interpreted the story unfolding on the Reading amphora as a uniquely

Fig. 5a-c. La Tolfa Group amphora. Harvard Art Museum inv. 1995.1166 (Photo courtesy: Harvard Art Museum).

Etruscan version of the story, Bruno d'Agostino rightly suggested that the crime is characterized as a human sacrifice.[14] His argument rests in part on observations made about the iconography of the ambush of Troilos in the late-sixth-century BC Etruscan Tomba dei Tori at Tarquinia[15]: Luca Cerchiai noted that the knife wielded by Achilles is a *machaira*, a sacrificial knife, not a battle sword, and Erika Simon observed that the setting is characterized as a sanctuary of Apollo by the laurel and palm trees.[16]

8 Rome, Villa Giulia 121110: *BAPD* Vase 13363, Onesimos.
9 See especially Schefold 1992, 227.
10 Reading, University 47.6.1, Pontic amphora, Tityos Painter: *CVA* Reading 1, pls. 36-37; Beazley 1947, 295.
11 For the identification of the altar, see especially Prayon 1977, 183.
12 Beazley 1947, 295; Ure 1951, 198; Schauenburg 1970, 66-67; d'Agostino 1987, 151, respectively. See also Prayon 1977, 189, n. 38; d'Agostino & Cerchiai 1999, 114.
13 Basel, Cahn 805, hydria fragment, Group E: *LIMC* 1, pl. 78, s.v. Achilleus 211; *BAPD* Vase 6902.
14 The idea that the murder of Troilos was characterized as a human sacrifice in Etruscan art is now widely held: see Camporeale 2009a, 18, with further references.
15 Steingräber 1986, 350 no. 120.
16 Simon 1973, 28-30; Cerchiai 1980, 26.

Fig. 6. Corinthian column krater. Musée du Louvre inv. E638 (Photo courtesy: Musée du Louvre, Paris).

Fig. 7. Chalkidian amphora. Musée du Louvre inv. E799 (Photo courtesy: Musée du Louvre, Paris).

THE LA TOLFA GROUP AND THE ETRUSCAN IMAGE OF APOLLO'S SANCTUARY

Since appearing in scholarly literature in 1970, three remarkable late-sixth-century BC Etruscan black-figure vases attributed to the La Tolfa Group have strengthened the sacrificial interpretation of the Troilos myth (Fig. 4-5).[17] Each vase depicts Achilles crouching behind a monumental fountain on the obverse, and Troilos approaching on horseback on the reverse. As on the Reading amphora and Tomba dei Tori, the fountain appears to take the form of an altar. The most significant new feature in the La Tolfa Group vase-paintings is the diminutive figure located on top of the fountain. The figure possesses the claws and head of an animal (either wolf or bird; see below), and the body and hands of a nude man. The figure strides in the direction of the approaching Troilos, and raises a sacrificial knife or other object (a sacrificial spit?) in a threatening manner.

The interpretation of this diminutive figure is a fascinating story, for it was originally identified as a representation of Anubis, the Egyptian god of the dead.[18] Today, a number of scholars understand it within a uniquely Etruscan framework, while a few understand it according to shared Greek and Etruscan ideas. The former group of scholars has identified the diminutive figure as a death demon of the sort familiar from Classical Etruscan tomb painting. As a death demon, the figure would be especially appropriate because the murder of Troilos, it is argued, was reinterpreted in Etruscan culture as a metaphor for the unexpected and brutal experience of death.[19] The identification of the animal-headed figure as a death demon, however, poses some difficulties. There are no generally accepted parallels for death demons in Etruscan art as early as the La Tolfa Group. The diminutive, knife-wielding figure would be the earliest known example. Death demons in later art do not resemble this figure, in part because they are usually winged.

Maurizio Harari significantly advanced the narrative understanding of this diminutive figure by suggesting that its head, which he and other scholars identified as that of a wolf, would be especially appropriate in an Apollonian context. One of Apollo's chief epithets was Lykeios, which was understood in Antiquity as related to *lykos*, the Greek word for wolf. The similarity in sound between Lykeios and Lykia, the name of a region near Troy, may have encouraged the idea that Apollo was worshipped as Lykeios at the Thymbraion, the sanctuary of Apollo outside Troy identified in literature as the setting of the death of Troilos. Cerchiai called attention in particular to a gloss in Hesychios that couples the Lykeion with the Thymbraion. Early coins from Argos depict wolves or wolf-heads, a reference to the city's cult of Apollo Lykeios, which shows that wolf imagery was understood, in one early Greek context, in relation to the Apollonian epithet.[20] The identification of the head of the diminutive figure, however, is not a matter of general scholarly agreement, for other scholars identify it as the head of a bird.[21]

Irrespective of the identity of the animal part of the diminutive figure, there is one important formal observation that should be made: the diminutive size of the part-animal figure, its striding pose, threatening gesture, and compositional arrangement on top of a base correspond closely to representations of statues of deities in late Archaic Greek art. Compare the statue of Athena on the cup by Onesimos (Fig. 2a). In Athenian art, the earliest extant representation of a statue of diminutive scale standing on a base may be the representation of the statue of Athena on a hydria by the Priam Painter of around 510 BC. This vase is more or less contemporary with the vases of the La Tolfa Group.[22] As a statue wielding a sacrificial knife, the animal-headed figure functions as an indication of the sacred, Apollonian setting of the ambush of Troilos.[23] It also emphasizes the sacrificial manner in which the boy will be killed.

THE SACRIFICE OF TROILOS IN EARLY GREEK ART
The belief that the sacrificial method was a unique Etruscan addition to the story of Troilos is unfounded, because several works of sixth-century Greek art depict the murder of Troilos as a *sphagē*, or meal-less, human sacrifice. In the images, Achilles drags Troilos to the altar and/or slits his throat so that the boy's blood flows onto the sacred stone. The slitting of the throat recalls the manner in which other victims of human sacrifice are dispatched, such as Polyxena.[24] In addition to the Athenian red-figure cup in Perugia, there is a fragmentary Corinthian column krater (Fig. 6): Achilles holds the body of Troilos by the foot

---

17 Vatican City, Museo Gregoriano Etrusco Vaticano 35718 (Astarita 742), Etruscan black-figure amphora, La Tolfa Group: *LIMC*sup. 2009, pl. 180, Monstra Anonyma (in Etruria) 23; published by Schauenburg 1970, 70, fig. 38. Once Lucerne market, Ars Antiqua A. G., Etruscan black-figure amphora, La Tolfa Group: *LIMC* 1, pl. 146, Achle 11, published by Schmidt 1971. For current whereabouts, see Woodford 2010, 99, n. 34. Harvard Art Museum 1995.1166: Zilverberg 1986, 59; d'Agostino & Cerchiai 1999, 115, n. 3; fully published by Woodford 2010.
18 Schmidt 1971.
19 Simon 1973, 39-40; Prayon 1977, 192-193 and passim; Richardson 1977, 99; Krauskopf 1987, 20-22; Camporeale 2009b, 368-369; Krauskopf 2009, 145. On the wolfman, see also Elliot 1995; Franken 2007.
20 Harari 1987, 289; d'Agostino & Cerchiai 1999, 117-118. The earliest explicit connection between the Apollonian epithet Lykeios and the wolf occurs in Soph. El. 6-7. For the coins, see Eckels 1937, 62-63; Lambrinodakis 1984, 223.
21 See most recently Woodford 2010, 100-101. For the head of the diminutive figure – on the amphora in the Vatican, at least – a close parallel occurs on the late-sixth-century Etruscan plate in Rome, Museo Nazionale Etrusco di Villa Giulia, 84444, Tityos Painter: *LIMC*sup. 2009, pl. 180, Monstra Anonyma (in Etruria) 22. The figures are comparable in the shape of the eye, the tall upright elongated ear, the long tapered nose, the long thin jaw, the visible tongue, and the general contour of the top of the head. The all-over body hair on the figure on the plate suggests that it is part-canine or part-lupine.
22 Vatican City, Museo Gregoriano Etrusco Vaticano 35698 (Astarita 733): *Para* 147, 30, Priam Painter; *BAPD* Vase 351083. Possibly earlier still is a black-figure amphora on the art market, attributed to the Leagros Group, illustrated in de Cesare 1997, 88, fig. 38, depicting a diminutive striding figure of Athena on a tall, three-step base. On the date of the La Tolfa Group, see Zilverberg 1986, 58. Schauenburg 1970, 74-76 understands the diminutive figure as a statue, but believes it to be the product of misunderstanding of the story. Schmidt 1971, 121 discounts the significance of identifying the image as a statue on the ground that the distinction between statue and living model is hardly relevant at this date. But the Priam Painter's hydria and other late-sixth-century vase-paintings of statues suggest that, by this point in time, the distinction was relevant and important in certain narrative contexts.
23 Cf. Camporeale 2009b, 368.
24 See e.g. London, British Museum 1897.7-27.2, Tyrrhenian amphora: *ABV* 97,27, Timiades Painter; *LIMC* 7, pl. 347, s.v. Polyxene 26; *BAPD* Vase 310027.

Fig. 8. Etruscan red-figure stamnos. Paris, Musée du Louvre CA 6529 (Photo courtesy: Musée du Louvre, Paris).

in preparation to slice him over a low altar; inscriptions identify the figures. There is a Chalkidian amphora on which Achilles holds Troilos upside down over the top surface of the altar and cuts through the boy's neck (Fig. 7). There are two Athenian black-figure vases on which Achilles holds the body and/or severed head of the victim in the vicinity of the altar, one of which contains identifying inscriptions.[25] Finally, there are fragments of sixth-century Cretan terracotta reliefs of a warrior dragging a resistant boy, though the identities of the figures are not explicit.[26]

The Etruscan vase-paintings of the La Tolfa Group advance the understanding of this body of imagery. They support the argument that the original intention of the hero Achilles was generally understood to be not merely to murder Troilos but more specifically to slit his throat over the altar of Apollo. Most importantly, as Steven Lowenstam put it in his recent, posthumously published book, 'despite various assertions about the uniqueness of these Archaic Etruscan paintings, they adhere closely to the Greek conception of the myth'.[27] Lowenstam identified one aspect of the imagery only as uniquely Etruscan: 'Achilles is consummating what Apollo Lykeios is intimating when the god holds up the sacrificial knife'. Lowenstam correlated Apollo's apparent acceptance of the human sacrifice in Etruscan imagery with rumors that Etruscans actually practiced human sacrifice.[28] It is hard to claim that human sacrifice is a specifically Etruscan taste, however, when so many representations of human sacrifice occur in Greek myth, literature, and art. Troilos' own sister, Polyxena, was victim of such an offering. It is not obvious that Greek art and Etruscan art differ with respect to any cardinal function of the story of Troilos. The imagery of the La Tolfa Group may support the idea that Achilles *believed* that making a human sacrifice of Troilos to Apollo was a desirable thing; but nothing in the imagery suggests that Apollo himself desired this particular offering.

THE NARRATIVE LOGIC OF THE SACRIFICE OF TROILOS

In Antiquity, the death of Achilles was in fact linked precisely to Apollo's anger over the desecration of his sanctuary. In the literary and visual traditions, Achilles dies at the hand of Apollo, with or without the assistance of Paris.[29] Although more than one motive is offered in ancient literature to account for Apollo's murder of Achilles, the earliest attested explanation is the god's anger at Achilles for defiling the Thymbraion with the murder of Troilos. Already in the early sixth century BC, in the representation of the story of Troilos on the François vase, the god Apollo himself appears, identified by inscription, gesturing emphatically – and, I think it is reasonable to infer, angrily – at Achilles, who, everyone knew, would catch the boy and murder him on Apollo's altar.[30]

The link between the unwanted sacrificial offering of Troilos and the death of Achilles was not unfamiliar to Etruscan artists. A late classical Etruscan stamnos once in the Fould collection and now in the Louvre establishes just such a link through imagery that originated in Athenian vase-painting (Fig. 8a, b).[31] The vase depicts Achilles creeping toward Troilos (not visible in the illustration), who stands with his horse before a water source, unaware of the danger. Juxtaposed to the scene of the ambush of Troilos is a representation of Ajax carrying the corpse of Achilles off the battlefield. The recovery of the body is a venerable visual image originating in seventh-century Greek art and popularized in Etruria by dozens of imported Archaic Athenian vase-paintings of the subject, such as the François vase.[32] The seamless visual transition from the ambush to the recovery on the Etruscan stamnos underscores emphatically the causal link between the involvement of Achilles in Troilos' death and the death of Achilles himself.[33]

Late literary sources claim that the death of Troilos was a prerequisite for the sack of Troy, and it is possible that the idea occurred already in the Archaic poetry of Ibykos.[34] The Fould stamnos gives visual form to that idea as well. It does so by quoting, most likely, from Athenian red-figure vase-painting. On the stamnos, Athena sits on top of the altar on which Achilles will make the unwanted sacrifice to Apollo. The image of a human figure sitting on an altar is rare in ancient art, limited by and large to Archaic and early Classical Athenian vase-painting. The most popular and significant occurrence of the motif is the figure of Priam seated on his courtyard altar at the moment when he is slain by Neoptolemos, an image that may fairly be said to epitomize the destruction of Troy (Fig. 9).[35] Significantly, the image of Priam sitting on the altar also occurs in a handful of Athenian vase-paintings of the attack on Troilos

---

25 Paris, Musée du Louvre E638bis, Middle Corinthian krater: Amyx 1988, 567, no. 44; *LIMC* 1, pl.94, Achilleus 365. Paris, Musée du Louvre E799, Chalkidean neck amphora: Rumpf 1927, 161, pl. 207. Munich, Staatliche Antikensammlungen 1426, neck amphora: *ABV* 95,5, Timiades Painter; *LIMC* 1, pl. 94, s.v. Achilleus 364; *BAPD* Vase 310005. Basel, BS 1424, Athenian black-figure band cup: *LIMC* 1, pl. 93, s.v. Achilleus 359a; *BAPD* Vase 6894.
26 Agios Nikolaos 2364: *LIMC* 8, pl. 69, s.v. Troilos 7b, and other fragments discussed in Erickson 2009, 371-373.
27 Lowenstam 2008, 143.
28 Lowenstam 2008, 145-147. See also Camporeale 2009a, 18.
29 For the literary sources, see Hom. *Il.* 19.408-417; Pind. *Paian* 6.75-86; Simonides' Plateia hymn, discussed below. For further details, see Kullmann 1960, 308-312, 320-326. For art, see e.g. London E468, Athenian red-figure volute krater: *ARV*² 206, 132, Berlin Painter; *BAPD* Vase 201941; *LIMC* 1, 181-185 [Kossatz-Deissmann].
30 Florence 4209, Athenian black-figure volute krater: *ABV* 76, 1, Kleitias and Ergotimos; *BAPD* Vase 300000. See also Vienna Inv. IV 3614, hydria: *ABV* 106, near Tyrrhenian Group; *LIMC* 1, pl. 81, s.v. Achilleus 247; *BAPD* Vase 310144, as interpreted by Bernhard-Walcher 1980, 71-72.
31 Paris, Musée du Louvre CA 6529, Etruscan red-figure stamnos: Beazley 1947, 179-180; Greifenhagen 1978, 73-75; Gaultier & Villard 1985; Harari 1988, 182-183.
32 For the iconography, see Kunze 1950, 151-154; Woodford & Louden 1980; *LIMC* 1, 185-193 [Kossatz-Deissmann]; Robertson 1983, 61.
33 Greifenhagen 1978, 75 thought that it referred to the idea that Achilles died in the same location as Troilos. In later literature, it is true, Achilles dies not at the Skaian Gate of Troy, but in the sanctuary of Apollo Thymbraios, where he arranged to meet Polyxena, with whom he was infatuated. See Gantz 1993, 628. But the juxtaposition of the two events, both in the vase-painting and in the later literary tradition, is the visual manifestation of the fatal consequentiality of the murder of Troilos in a religious sanctuary. See Harari 1995, 108-109.
34 See Robertson 1970, 12-13; Scaife 1995, 189.
35 Paris, Louvre G 152, cup: *ARV*² 369, 1; *BAPD* Vase 203900. For the iconography, see Wiencke 1954; Dugas 1960; Neils 1994.

Fig. 9. Red-figure cup, detail. Paris, Musée du Louvre G 152 (Photo courtesy: Musée du Louvre Paris).

Fig. 10. Malibu, J. Paul Getty Museum 81.AE.183.2. (Photo courtesy: J. Paul Getty Museum, Malibu).

(Fig. 10).³⁶ In the Attic vase-paintings of the story of Troilos, the quotation of the unusual motif of Priam seated on an altar visually insinuates a reminder of the sack of Troy, the specific event or narrative context in which one most frequently sees Priam seated on an altar. In that way, the vase-paintings articulate a link between the death of Troilos and the destruction of Troy. On the Etruscan stamnos, the image of Athena seated on the altar arguably serves a similar semantic function: to link the murder of Troilos with the sack of Troy. But there is further significance to this image. If the destruction of Troy depends upon the death of Troilos, then it is easier to understand why the goddess, who wished above all else to see the city of Troy in ruins, is helping her protege to accomplish a task that will result in his own destruction. Indeed, the Fould stamnos offers an answer to a question raised by the recognition that Achilles' intention in murdering Troilos was to sacrifice the boy to Apollo. The question is why Achilles thought that Apollo might have wished such a sacrifice.³⁷ The image on the Fould stamnos is significant because it suggests that

Fig. 11. Etruscan mirror, engraved. Hellenistic. London, British Museum 625 (Drawing: The British Museum, London).

the goddess was present not primarily to guard Achilles' back, as some earlier vase-paintings have suggested, but as an instigator of the sacrificial murder itself.

Although the literary sources claim that Troy could not be destroyed so long as Troilos lived, they do not explain why. Troilos himself plays no role in the Trojan War except as Achilles' victim, so it is far from clear how his death would have advanced the Achaian aim of sacking Troy. The death of Achilles, on the other hand, fundamentally altered the course of the Trojan War. It ultimately resulted in a

36 Malibu, J. Paul Getty Museum 81.AE.183.2, Athenian red-figure nestoris, Group of Polygnotos: BAPD Vase 30684. See also Louvre G 154, Athenian red-figure cup: ARV^2 369, 3, Brygos Painter; Pottier 1897-1922, 3, pl. 122; BAPD Vase 203902. Athens, NM Acropolis 355, Athenian red-figure cup: ARV^2 828, 29, Stieglitz Painter; Graef & Langlotz 1909-1933, 2, pls. 25-26; BAPD Vase 210284, as interpreted in Hedreen 2001, 153, 157.

37 For further discussion of this question, see Hedreen 2001, 158-181.

change in Achaian strategy, from direct military attack to the use of espionage. The new strategy succeeded where the old one failed. The walls of Troy, built by the gods, would have withstood direct attack indefinitely; but the walls could not prevent the Trojans from falling for the trick of the wooden horse.[38] Achilles and Odysseus were understood to hold opposing views on the question of how Troy could be sacked, whether through direct military assault or indirectly, through espionage. Ancient scholia claim that this question was the object of the dispute between Achilles and Odysseus that was the subject of Demodokos' song in the *Odyssey*.[39] Horace put it in a characteristically pithy way: hiding inside a wooden horse is something Achilles would never have done (Hor. Odes 4.6.13-16). The trouble with Achilles is that he stood in the way of the only effective means of sacking Troy.

The moment Achilles defiled the altar of Apollo with Troilos' blood, the story of the Trojan War changes direction. Achilles is destroyed by Apollo, the war-making initiative passes to Odysseus, and the Achaians infiltrate the city of Troy in the wooden horse, after ten years of futile siege warfare. One hero figures prominently in the transition between the Achillean and Odyssean phases of the war. That figure is Ajax. After Achilles, Ajax was the best of the Achaians to fight at Troy. Homer, Pindar, and many others agree on that point.[40] Ajax was the one to wrest the body and armor of Achilles from the Trojans and return it to the Achaians for burial. Understandably, Ajax believed that he deserved to inherit the arms and armor of Achilles. But that is not the way the story ended. The Achaians awarded the arms to Odysseus, Ajax ended his own life out of shame, and the strategic responsibility passed to Odysseus. The story of Ajax was governed by the larger narrative logic of the Trojan War, with the result that he too, like Achilles, needed to be neutralized.

ACHILLES AND AJAX ON THE ALTAR OF APOLLO

One work of late Etruscan art epitomizes the narrative interconnections between Achilles, Ajax, and the death of Troilos. This work of art is significant because it expresses its ideas through imagery derived, directly or indirectly, it appears, from Athenian red-figure vase-painting. It makes possible a new interpretation of a problematic Athenian vase-painting. An early Hellenistic engraved Etruscan mirror depicts the aftermath of the murder of Troilos (fig. 11).[41] Achilles takes up a defensive position, with one knee on the altar where he has just killed Troilos; he still holds the

Fig. 12. Red-figure cup signed by the Brygos Painter. From Cerveteri. Oxford, Ashmolean Museum 1911.615 (Photo courtesy: Ashmolean Museum, Oxford).

boy's severed head. Vanth, a winged female demon, marks the presence of death. Hektor arrives too late to save his brother, but perhaps not too late to avenge the death. To anyone familiar with the Athenian visual tradition of the fight over the body of Troilos, it is surprising to see a second Achaian warrior taking up a defensive position beside Achilles, kneeling on the altar. An inscription tells us that Achilles' companion is Ajax.

The image of Achilles and Ajax, taking refuge together on the altar where Troilos was sacrificed, occurs frequently on Hellenistic Etruscan urns.[42] In earlier art, I know of a single possible example: the late Archaic Athenian red-figure cup in Oxford signed by Brygos as potter (Fig. 12).[43] This cup was found in Cervetri, which is thought, as it happens, to be the home of the artist who manufactured the Etruscan mirror. In the tondo of the cup, two warriors take up defensive positions on a carved stone block, which is shown by daubs of blood to be an altar.[44] Various interpretations of this vase-painting have been offered.[45] None of the ones I have seen takes into consideration the fact that a later Etruscan artist identified two warriors very similarly posed on an altar as Achilles and Ajax, and identified the narrative context as the

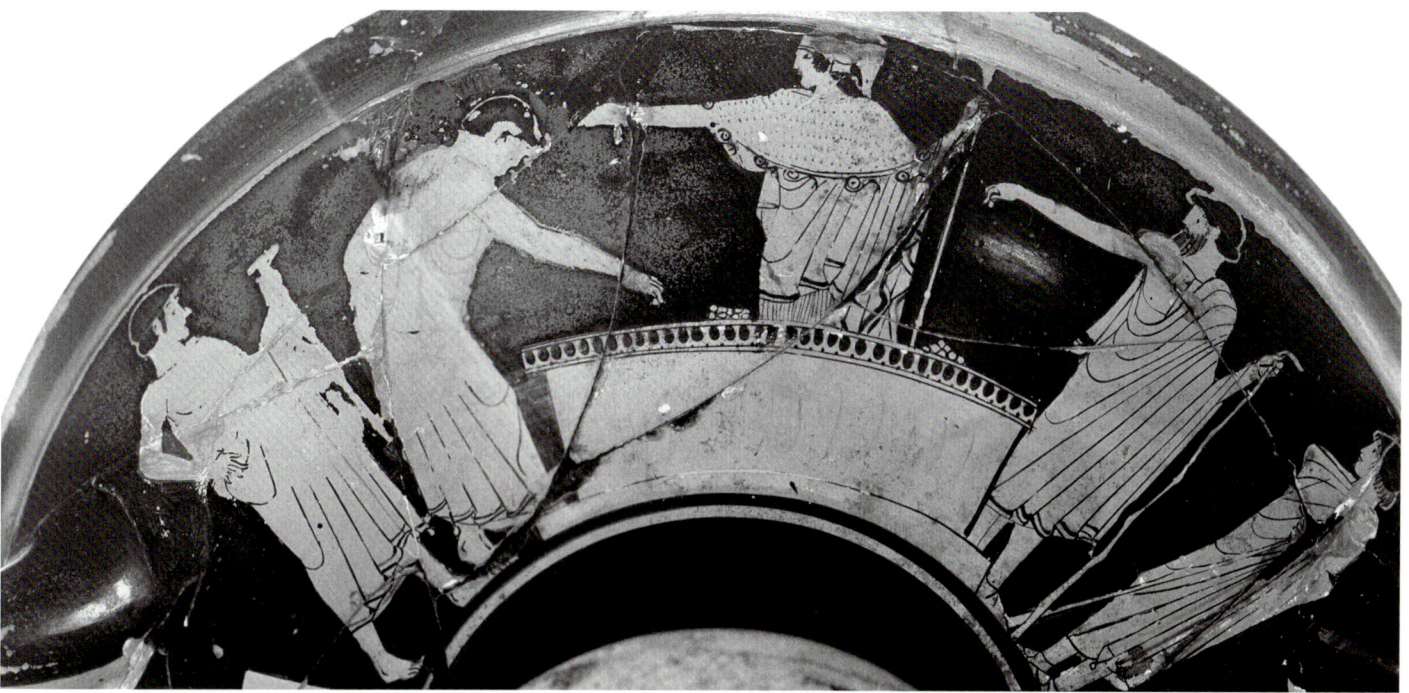

Fig. 13. Red-figure cup attributed to Painter of Louvre G265. Leiden, Rijksmuseum PC75 (Photo courtesy: Rijksmuseum, Leiden).

aftermath of the sacrifice of Troilos.[46]

As a representation of Achilles and Ajax in the aftermath of the murder of Troilos, the Athenian red-figure cup is significant, in relation to both the narrative logic governing the shift in Achaian strategy, as well as the late Archaic Athenian visual tradition. The process by which the military initiative was transferred to Odysseus was completed by the vote to award the armor of Achilles to Odysseus and not Ajax (e.g. Fig. 13).[47] Compositionally, the Oxford cup-painting evokes the representations of the vote through the central stone block with egg-and-dart molding. Compositionally, the central block and pair of warriors on the Oxford cup evoke even more insistently, however, the venerable Athenian and Etruscan image of Achilles and Ajax playing a game (e.g. Fig. 14).[48] On the Oxford cup, it is as if Ajax and Achilles, surprised during their game, have leapt up onto the block game table and taken defensive positions. The dried blood on the front of the block indicates, however, that this is not a game table but an altar. Moreover, the traditional image of the game played by Ajax and Achilles is arguably the basis for the image of the vote. This is suggested by the cup in Leiden (Fig. 13) in particular, through the blocks underneath

38 The importance of this point for understanding the logic of the entire Trojan War, as a story, is emphasized by Fehling 1989, 7-8.
39 Hom. *Od.* 8.73-82, with scholia on 75 and 77. See Nagy 1999, 22-24, 40, 42-65.
40 Hom. *Il.* 2.761-762, 768-769, 15.743-746, 16.112-113; *Od.* 11.550-551 (Odysseus); Pind. *Nem.* 7.27. For further references, see Rossbach 1894, 930–931.
41 London, British Museum 625, Etruscan engraved mirror, 3rd century BC: van der Meer 1977-1978, 59; Steuernagel 1998, 82.
42 van der Meer 1977-1978, 58-59; Steuernagel 1998, 81-87.
43 Oxford, Ashmolean Museum 1911.615, Athenian red-figure cup: *ARV*² 399, Painter of the Oxford Brygos; *BAPD* Vase 204329.
44 *CVA* Oxford 1, 3.
45 E.g. Herford 1914; Barrett & Vickers 1978; Williams 1986.
46 In early Archaic vase-painting, Achilles, like most other heroes, is bearded. In late Archaic and early Classical art, he is frequently unbearded. But there are numerous examples of late Archaic or early Classical representations of Achilles as a bearded warrior: e.g., Paris, Louvre G 154, cup: *ARV*² 369, 3, Brygos Painter; *LIMC* 1, pl. 91, s.v. Achilleus 344; *BAPD* Vase 203902. Paris, Louvre G 231, pelike: *ARV*² 581, 4, Painter of Louvre G 231; *LIMC* 1, pl. 91, s.v. Achilleus 345; *BAPD* Vase 206702. Ajax is regularly shown bearded. For short, curly hair on Ajax and other Trojan War heroes, see Vienna, Kunsthistorisches Museum 3695, cup: *ARV*² 429, 26, Douris; *LIMC* 1, pl. 240, s.v. Aias I 71; *BAPD* Vase 205070.
47 Leiden, Rijksmuseum PC 75, cup: *ARV*² 416, 7, Painter of Louvre G265. For the vase-paintings of the vote, see especially Williams 1980.

Fig. 14. Achilles and Ajax. Red-figure amphora attributed to Exekias. Vatican City, Museo Gregoriano Etrusco Vaticano 344 (Photo courtesy: Hirmer Verlag, München).

the handles that correspond to the seats used by Achilles and Ajax during the game.[49]

The compositional affinities in this set of vase-paintings have deep semantic resonance. Implicit in the story of the decision over the arms is the idea that, prior to the death of Achilles, the military initiative lay with him. Ajax and Odysseus competed not primarily for hardware but for the authority accorded to the best of the Achaians. Of the two competitors, Ajax embodied values most like those of Achilles. That idea is expressed pictorially in the images of Ajax and Achilles playing a game. The images suggest that Ajax shared the same interests, values, and abilities as Achilles – or almost the same abilities. Yet the circumstances surrounding the creation of the walls of Troy necessitated a military approach different from the one valued by Achilles and, it appears, Ajax. This is suggested by the intervention of Athena in the vote over the awarding of the arms of Achilles, ensuring that the arms, and the authority they embody, went to Odysseus. The images of Achilles and Ajax taking refuge together on the altar, in the aftermath of the slaughter of Troilos (Figs. 11 and 12), depict the two exponents of direct military action at the very moment when their power or influence begins to slip away from them for good.

The possibility that the figures in the tondo of the cup in Oxford are Trojan War heroes has been discounted, because the exterior of the cup appears to depict arming and battle in connection with the Persian War.[50] For the juxtaposition of a significant incident in the Trojan War with the more recent event of the Persian War, however, there is a good parallel in Simonides' hymn to the fallen warriors of Plateia, which is approximately contemporary with the Oxford cup.[51] The poem frames the achievements of the heroes who fought and died in the battle of Plateia with an invocation of the sack of Troy by the Achaians. The main subject of the invocation is in fact Achilles, his death at the hand of Apollo, his funeral, the perseverance of the Achaians in sacking Troy, and perhaps Achilles' continued presence after death in cult.[52] On the cup in Oxford, the collocation of Ajax and Achilles in the tondo, embodying a particular form of heroism, and the Persian War conflict on the exterior, is similar to the rhetorical structure of the Simonidean hymn.

CONCLUSION

This paper leaves unanswered questions about specifically how late Classical Etruscan artists became familiar with works of Archaic Athenian vase-painting, whether directly or through intermediary objects. But I maintain that an essential step in the process of understanding how Etruscan representations of the murder of Troilos relate to Greek art is the reconstruction of the narrative logic that governs the story. Perhaps the story of the short life of Troilos functioned differently in Etruscan culture than in Greece, as some scholars have suggested. But it does not follow that the story itself, in its cardinal functions, will have differed.

---

48 Vatican City, Museo Gregoriano Etrusco Vaticano 344, amphora: *ABV* 145, 13, Exekias; *BAPD* Vase 310395. For the Greek iconography, see Woodford 1982. For the Etruscan, Camporeale 2009a, 201, 210.
49 For further details concerning the affinities between the iconographies of the game and the vote, see Hedreen 2001, 91–119.
50 *CVA* Oxford 1, 4; Herford 1914, 109; Barrett & Vickers 1978, 19-22, 23; Williams 1986, 77-79. The cup was associated with the battle of Plateia by Barrett and Vickers, but with Marathon by Williams.
51 West 1998, 118-120, frag. 11. The poem presumably dates shortly after the battle of Plateia.
52 For the possibilities of cult, see Obbink 2001.

ACKNOWLEDGEMENTS

I thank the organizers for the kind invitation to participate in this project.

Abstracts

Abstracts

MARTIN LANGNER

MANTLE-FIGURES AND THE ATHENIZATION OF LATE CLASSICAL IMAGERY

The Athenian picture of conversing men in cloaks is regularly found on the B-sides of later red-figure kraters and pelikai as well as on cups, skyphoi and jugs. Compared to the main picture they seem to be all the same, sketchy stereotypes without any narrative content. But these mantle-figures can be connected with specific virtues of the Athenian citizen. And looking at tomb contexts from the fourth century BC, it is clear that these images were used as a means of concentrating the narrative on one main picture and as a quality feature that ensures the Attic origin.

At the end of the fifth century BC the local red-figure productions of Apulia, Lucania and Boeotia depended on and to some extent clearly imitated imported Attic red-figure vases. On this occasion, the B-sides also show the usual decoration type of youths or men in cloaks. Now the local red-figure took over and appreciated the Attic way of depicting citizens. In comparison to Alto-Adriatic, Campanian and Paestan red-figure pottery, where the pictures were actualized and altered, it becomes clear that elsewhere the originally Athenian motif turns into a very general expression of civic identity and was mostly accepted as a good way of depicting Greeks. This model conquered the world in the same way as the Attic tragedy or the typical figure style of the Attic relief art. In this sense Athens remained the 'School of Hellas', as Pericles said.

ANNIE VERBANCK-PIÉRARD

HERAKLES AND HIS ATTIC PILLARS: ICONOGRAPHICAL STUDY AND SOCIO-RELIGIOUS CONTEXT OF THE FOUR-COLUMN HERAKLEION

Some red-figure vases from the late fifth and first half of the fourth century BC represent Herakles resting in a strange and puzzling architectural setting: a four-column edifice, seen in foreshortened view. The religious purpose of this iconography is revealed by comparison with contemporary votive reliefs, representing the same structure for Herakles welcoming his worshippers. Traditionally these images have been linked with a special offering to Herakles called the oinisteria, part of the famous Apatouria festival celebrated by the Attic phratries. By relating this iconographic theme to the historical and religious context of the end of the fifth and first half of the fourth century BC, I assert that this corpus of vases and reliefs gives new evidence for the contemporary revival of local Attic cults and family cults. Moreover, it illustrates perfectly the symbolic value of the Heraklean iconography by stressing his divine patronage for the ephebes, athletes and ritual transitions. At the end of the article, I propose an enlargement of the corpus. Two other gods, Hermes and Apollo, seem to be connected with a similar tetrastyle which has until now only been documented in a few examples, such as a Lucanian Panathenaic amphora in Taranto.

ADRIENNE LEZZI-HAFTER

THE XENOPHANTOS CHOUS FROM KERCH WITH CYPRIOT THEMES

The 'Xenophantos-chous', although not signed, belongs to a late fifth-century BC group of innovative vessels, on which the figures were largely or totally inspired by repoussé works in metal. The chous was found in the Crimea; its style and iconography are thoroughly Attic. The subject, however, leads the viewer to Cyprus: Teukros and his nephew welcomed by the personified Cyprus, and Adonis courted by Peitho and Eros at Aphrodite's behest. This paper also discusses the location of the Xenophantos workshop.

ATHENA TSINGARIDA

WHITE-GROUND CUPS IN FIFTH-CENTURY GRAVES: A DISTINCTIVE CLASS OF BURIAL OFFERINGS IN CLASSICAL ATHENS?

A few Attic white-ground cups, decorated in outline technique by red-figure painters and dated from the early to the middle of the fifth century BC, serve as special offerings in some Attic tombs. Because of their rare iconographical themes and their elaborate style and technique, they form a coherent group of really individual and thus potentially personal objects from grave contexts. This paper concentrates on their iconography, technique and shapes to show that there are underlying connections in all this material, mainly through iconographic allusions to the afterlife and divination but also through a common practice of ritual breaking. It further suggests that these burial offerings were addressed to particular deceased individuals, in order to outline their distinctive status, probably that of a mantis within Athenian society. In the concluding remarks, the article discusses the workshop organization used to produce these vessels with a view to finding out whether they were special commissions or sets fashioned to respond to an expected, although occasional, demand from distinctive purchasers.

MAURIZIO GUALTIERI

LATE 'APULIAN' RED-FIGURE VASES IN CONTEXT: A CASE STUDY

This paper will address the problem of context and cultural setting of a group of 'Apulian' red-figure vases (a loutrophoros, a volute krater and a very large oinochoe) from a monumental chamber tomb in the Roccagloriosa necropolis pertaining to the second half of the fourth century BC. On the basis of a preliminary inspection of a number of fragments in the course of excavation (in the 1980's), A.D. Trendall did not hesitate to attribute the vases to the Darius-Underworld Group (RVApII, 531-532). The recent restoration of the tomb group has, on the one hand, raised some questions regarding their place of production and, on the other, allowed an in-depth analysis of the complex mythological episodes depicted on the vases within the framework of a specific cultural and social setting, provided by the extensively explored site of Lucanian Roccagloriosa. A closely related problem which will be brought up in the discussion is the possible role of the fast growing 'native' market for late Apulian red-figure vases in the selection and adaptation of such complex iconographies.

HELENA FRACCHIA

CHANGING CONTEXTS AND INTENT: THE MOURNING NIOBE MOTIF FROM LUCANIA TO DAUNIA

The Mourning Niobe motif, one of the most popular amongst the various indigenous cultures of Southern Italy, has been recognized in nine Apulian vases: five are without context, while the other four were found at Canosa (2), Ruvo and Arpi, all dated across the middle and second half of the fourth century BC. Another example, of uncertain manufacture, was found in Tomb 24 at Roccagloriosa in western Lucania. Despite a wide geographical and chronological diffusion, all the known representations of the Niobe myth share certain elements: Niobe, queen of Thebes, is shown as she turns to stone, surrounded by other members of the Royal House of Thebes. Given the disparate proveniences and the lengthy chronological popularity of the scene, Marina Mazzei postulated that the use of the myth should speak to common shared values or religious beliefs of the indigenous settlements where the motif was used. This presentation will explore the use of the Mourning Niobe motif on Apulian style vases as a conscious expression of shared values and religious beliefs, a cultural tag of the Italic aristocracies in both Daunia and some Tyrrhenian communities in the complex cultural world of Magna Graecia in the second half of the fourth century BC.

VICTORIA SABETAI

BOEOTIAN RED-FIGURED VASES: OBSERVATIONS ON THEIR CONTEXTS AND SETTINGS

This paper discusses the contexts and settings that are essential in understanding fifth century BC Boeotian red-figured pottery. Attic imports are traced in order to map artistic transmission in the region. Workshop affiliations indicate that the local red-figure production developed within the framework of Boeotian black-figure potteries that produced Kabiric and floral wares. Attic and indigenous red-figure pottery in Boeotia occurs in limited numbers: in a few graves and in the Kabirion sanctuary and the cave of the Nymphs at Helicon. The tombs that contain red-figured vases are characterized by a wealth of other pots, mainly degenerate Haimonean black-figure, black-glazed and floral ware. It is argued that graves with red-figure pottery can be associated with deceased individuals of special status and social standing, and that some of the red-figured vases, especially the monumental kantharoi, were objects of distinction imbued with heroic overtones. Boeotian red-figure imagery belongs to a formal genre that builds on gendered roles. It praised visually the male citizen as virtuous ephebe, heroic soldier/rider and mature symposiast, and the female citizen as nubile maiden and matron.

MARTIN BENTZ

ELEAN RED-FIGURE POTTERY FROM OLYMPIA

During the excavations of Olympia, about one hundred vases and fragments of local red-figure pottery have been found. The complete study of this material allows for the first time a comprehensive view of this local fabric mainly active for three generations from about 425-350 BC. Nearly 80% of the vases are bell- and calyx-kraters, and the images show mainly Dionysiac themes. While the first generation produces very Atticising images in terms of style and iconography – and thus were probably produced by emigrated Attic potters and painters – the later painters are strongly influenced by South Italian workshops. The range of shapes, the known archaeological contexts as well as the iconographic themes indicate that Elean red-figure was mainly used in daily life and rarely for ritual purposes.

THOMAS MANNACK
AN OVERVIEW OF ATHENIAN FIGURE-DECORATED POTTERY IN SOUTHERN ITALY AND SICILY

This article presents an overview of the Athenian figure-decorated pottery imported to Southern Italy and Sicily during the sixth and the fifth century BC: its use, shape and iconography. It raises the questions of whether Greeks and natives imported Attic pottery mainly for the grave and whether the Attic potters and painters were aware of the use of their containers abroad. From the analysed material it is not possible to distinguish any kind of special commissions, since the pottery seems to have sold everywhere in the region, among the Greeks as well as the indigenous population. In addition, the iconography does not indicate any special preferences, even though it should be noted that many lekythoi were decorated with scenes relating to the female world. Athenian lekythoi were probably bought exclusively for use in funerals, and the same seems to be the case for larger shapes such as kraters, amphorae and a smaller number of pelikai and hydriai, since only in rare cases can they be connected to domestic contexts or sanctuaries. Funerals with whole symposia sets are limited to the northern Apulian graves.

STINE SCHIERUP
A HEROIC EMBLEM: THE CULTURAL TRANSFORMATION OF THE PANATHENAIC AMPHORA IN SOUTHERN ITALY

The Panathenaic amphora shape seems to have held a special importance in Italiote red-figure production, where it becomes the main amphora shape from the beginning of the local red-figure production and throughout the fourth century BC. Early Italiote black-figure examples likewise indicate that the iconographic themes of the original prize vessels were reproduced in Southern Italy outside their Attic context of use and without any direct reference to their original context of use in the Panathenaic games. Through an analysis of the archaeological and iconographical evidence for the use of the amphoras in Southern Italy, this paper explores the social and cultural transformation that the Panathenaic amphora as an emblematic vessel underwent: from being an Attic prize vessel secondarily imported and used in the aristocratic tombs of Taranto and Ruvo, to being an essential part of the funerary vessels in the repertoire of the local red-figure production.

The iconographic evidence from around 430 to 370 BC indicates a special preference for using the shape for cultic activities around the tomb of heroic males. A use that can be paralleled with the use of the imported Attic Panathenaic amphoras found in early fifth century aristocratic tombs in Taranto. From the archaeological contexts there are little evidence for the use of pseudo-Panathenaic amphoras outside the tombs, which should most probably be explained by the circumstances of their preservation (usually only small and insignificant fragments can be found) and the absence of archaeological documentation. However, in a few cases examples of the use of the amphoras as semata or as remnants of cultic activities outside the tombs can be found from well-documented excavations on Greek sites. Through a comparison with the archaeological evidence in Italic communities such as Peucetia a duality in the use of the amphoras can be detected. Here the amphoras seem to have been considered part of the banquet equipment in correspondence with the tomb ideology in this area.

GUY HEDREEN
VASE-PAINTING AND NARRATIVE LOGIC: ACHILLES AND TROILOS IN ATHENS AND ETRURIA

The structural analysis of narrative affords the possibility of recognizing affinities between art even of different cultures. Identifying the cause-and-effect logic governing a story sometimes makes it possible to recognize that visual representations differing stylistically or iconographically may nonetheless refer to the same story. In this paper, I examine visual representations of the story of Troilos and Achilles in Athenian and Etruscan vase-painting. I argue that Etruscan vase-paintings represent essentially the same story as the one referred to in Athenian vase-paintings. The value of the comparison in this instance lies in the fact that the Etruscan vase-paintings are unambiguous about the intentions of Achilles in murdering Troilos. Like a handful of works of Greek art, Etruscan vase-paintings show that Achilles intended to sacrifice Troilos on the altar of Apollo. Two late Classical works of Etruscan art show that the larger narrative implications of the sacrilegious murder of Troilos were familiar to Etruscan artists, and they suggest that familiarity with the story of the Trojan War was based in part at least on earlier Athenian visual traditions. This is perhaps not surprising, since many relevant Athenian painted vases were found in Etruscan tombs. But the important implication is that some Etruscan artists were knowledgeable of the stories underlying the vase-paintings, not merely of the painted imagery.

Bibliographic Abbreviations

Bibliographic Abbreviations

AA	Archäologischer Anzeiger
AAA	Αρχαιολογικά ανάλεκτα εξ Αθηνών
ABV	Beazley, J.D. 1956, *Attic Black-figure Vase-painters*, Oxford
ActaArch	Acta Archaeologica
Add	Carpenter, T.H., with Mannack, T. and Mendonca, M. 1989, *Beazley Addenda*, (2nd edition), Oxford
ADelt	Αρχαιολογικόν Δελτίον
AJA	American Journal of Archaeology
AM	Mitteilungen des Deutschen Archäologischen Instituts, Athenische Abteilung
AnnAStorAnt	Annali di Archeologia e Storia Antica
Anodos	Anodos. Studies of the Ancient World
AntK	Antike Kunst
ArchEph	Αρχαιολογικὴ Ἐφημερίς
ARV²	Beazley, J.D. 1963, *Attic Red-figure Vase-painters* (2nd edition), Oxford
AttiMemMagnaGr	Atti e Memorie della Società Magna Grecia
AttiTaranto	Atti del Convegno de Studi sulla Magna Grecia
AW	Antike Welt
BaBesch	Bulletin Antieke Beschaving
Badd²	Carpenter, T.H. 1989, *Beazley Addenda: Additional References to ABV, ARV² & Paralipomena*, Oxford
BAPD	The Beazley Archive Pottery Database
BCH	Bulletin de Correspondance Hellénique
BICS	Bulletin of the Institute of Classical Studies
BSA	Annual of the British School at Athens
BSR	Papers of the British School in Rome
CivClCr	Civiltà Classica e Cristiana
ClAnt	Classical Antiquety
CorVP	Amyx, D.A. 1988, *Corinthian Vase-painting of the Archaic Period*, Berkeley
CVA	Corpus Vasorum Antiquorum
DialA	Dialoghi di Archeologia
EchosCl	Echos du Monde Classique
Eikasmos	Eikasmos. Quaderni Bolognesi di Filologia Classica
EtrSt	Etruscan Studies
FR	Furtwängler, A. & Rheinholdt, K.W. 1904-1932, *Griechische Vasenmalerei* I-VI, Munich
GVGetty	Greek Vases in the J. Paul Getty Museum
Hermathena	Hermathena. A Trinity College Dublin Review
Hesperia	Hesperia. Journal of the American School of Classical Studies at Athens
IG	Inscriptiones Greacae

JdI	*Jahrbuch des Deutschen Archäologischen Instituts*	*Para*	J.D. Beazley, 1974, *Paralipomena: Additions to Attic Black-figure Vase-painters and the Attic Red-figure Vase-painters*, Oxford
JHS	*The Journal of Hellenic Studies*		
JSav	*Journal des Savants*	*Prospettiva*	*Prospettiva. Rivista di Storia dell'Arte Antica e Moderna*
Kernos	*Kernos. Revue Internationale et Pluridisciplinaire de Religion Grecque Antique*	*RA*	*Revue Archéologique*
		REG	*Revue des Études Grecques*
LCS	Trendall, A.D. & Cambitoglou, A. 1967-, *The Red-figured Vases of Lucania, Campania and Sicily*, London	*RHistRel*	*Revue de l'Histoire des Religions*
		RVAp	Trendall, A.D. and Cambitoglou, A. 1978-, *The Red-figured Vases of Apulia*, London
LIMC	*Lexicon Iconographicum Mythologiae Classicae*		
MedArch	*Mediterranean Archaeology*	*StEtr*	*Studi Etruschi*
MedHistR	*Mediterranean Historical Review*	*Taras*	*Taras. Rivista di Archeologia*
MEFRA	*Mélanges de l'Ecole Française de Rome. Antiquité*	*THeSCRA*	*Thesaurus Cultus et Rituum Antiquorum*
		WürzbJb	*Würzburger Jahrbücher für die Altertumswissenschaft*
MetrMusJ	*Metropolitan Museum Journal*		
MonPiot	*Monuments et Mémoires. Fondation Eugène Piot*	*ZÄS*	*Zeitschrift für Ägyptische Sprache und Altertumskunde*
NumAntCl	*Numismatica e antichità classiche. Quaderni ticinesi*		
OlB	*Berichte über die Ausgrabungen in Olympia*		
Ostraka	*Ostraka. Rivista di Antichità*		
ÖJh	*Jahreshefte des Österreichischen Archäologischen Institutes in Wien*		
Pallas	*Pallas. Revue d'Études Antiques*		

Bibliography

Bibliography

Adriani, A., Arias, P.E. & Manni, E. 1971
Odeon ed altri monumenti archeologici, Palermo.

Akamatis, N. 2008
Ερυθρόμορφη κεραμική από την Πέλλα, *ArchEph* 147, 1-78.

Amandry, P. 1950
La mantique apollienne à Delphes. Essai sur le fonctionnement de l'Oracle, Paris.

Amandry, P. 1997
Propos sur l'oracle de Delphes, *JSav* (1997), 195-209.

Amyx, D.A. 1988
Corinthian Vase-painting of the Archaic Period, Berkeley.

Ancillotti, A. & Calderini, A. (eds.), 2009
La Città Italica. Atti del II Convegno Internazionale sugli antichi Umbri, Gubbio, 25-27 settembre 2003, Perugia.

Andreassi, G. 1992
L'ipogeo Varrese, in: Cassano, R. (ed.), *Principi Imperatori Vescovi. Duemila anni di storia a Canosa*, Bari, 238-240.

Andreioménou, A.K. 1985
Το νεκροταφείο της Ακραιφίας, *ADelt* 40, Chron. [1990], 149-152.

Andreioménou, A.K. 1994
La nécropole d'Akraiphia, in: De la Genière, J. (ed.), *Nécropoles et sociétés antiques (Grèce, Italie, Languedoc). Actes du Colloque International du centre de recherches archéologiques de l'Université de Lille III, Lille 2-3 décembre 1991*, Naples, 99-126.

Andreioménou, A.K. 2007
Τανάγρα. Η ανασκαφή του νεκροταφείου (1976-1977, 1989), Αθήνα.

Aravantinos, V. 1994
Αλίαρτος. Οικόπεδο Μαρίας Πούλου, *ADelt* 49, B1, [1999] 281-283.

Assmann, J. 1997
La memoria culturale. Scrittura, ricordo e identità politica nelle grandi civiltà antiche, Torino.

Avronidaki, C. 2007
Ο Ζωγράφος του Άργου. Συμβολή στην έρευνα της βοιωτικής ερυθρόμορφης κεραμικής στο Β' μισό του 5ου αιώνα π.Χ. Αθήνα.

Avronidaki, C. 2008
Boeotian Red-figure Imagery on Two New Vases by the Painter of the Dancing Pan, *AntK* 51, 8-22.

Baggieri, G. 1999
Un Atleta Tarantino del V sec. A.C.: Ipotesi di ricostruzione antropologica e storica, *Taras* XIX.2, 285-310.

Baldassarre, I. 1998
Discussione, in: Mazzei, M. (ed.), *Il caso Arpi. Ambiente italico e magnogreco tra primo e medio ellenismo. Atti della tavola rotonda, Foggia 8 marzo 1996*, Foggia, 31-34.

Barrett, A.A. & Vickers, M. 1978
The Oxford Brygos cup reconsidered, *JHS* 98, 17-24.

Barringer, J. 1995
Divine Escorts: Nereids in Archaic and Classical Greek Art, Ann Arbor.

Barr-Sharrar, B. 1990
Coroplast, Potter and Metalsmith, in: Uhlenbrock, J.P. (ed.), *The Coroplast's Art. Greek Terracottas of the Hellenistic World, Exhibition Princeton September 22-December 30*, New York, 31-36.

Beazley, J.D. 1918
Attic Red-figure Vases in American Museums, Cambridge.

Beazley, J.D. 1944
Some Attic Vases in the Cyprus Museum, *Proceedings of the British Academy* 33, 44-46.

Beazley, J.D. 1947
Etruscan Vase-painting, Oxford.

Bentz, M. 1998
Panathenäische Preisamphoren. Eine athenische Vasengattung und ihre Funktion von 6.-4. Jahrhundert v. Chr., Basel.

Bentz, M. 2001
Schwarzfigurige Amphoren panathenäischer Form. Typologie, Funktion und Verbreitung, in: Bentz, M. & Eschbach, N. (eds.), *PANATHENAÏKA. Symposion zu den Panathenäischen Preisamphoren, Rauischholzhausen 25.11-29.11 1998*, Mainz, 111-118.

Bentz, M. 2007
Torchrace and vase-painting, in: Palagia, O. & Choremi-Spetsieri, A. (eds.), *The Panathenaic Games. Proceedings of an International conference held at the University of Athens, May 11-12 2004*, Oxford, 73-80.

Bentz, M. 2009
Athenian Red-figure Pottery from Olympia, in: Oakley, J. & Palagia, O. (eds.), *Athenian Potters and Painters 2*, Oxford, 11-17.

Bérard, C. (ed.) 1984
La Cité des Images. Religion et société en Grèce antique, Paris.

Bérard, C. (ed.) 1987
Images et société en Grèce ancienne. L'iconographie comme méthode d'analyse. Actes du colloque international, Lausanne 8-11 fevrier 1984, Lausanne.

Bergemann, J. 1997
Demos und Thanatos. Untersuchungen zum Wertsystem der Polis im Spiegel der attischen Grabreliefs des 4. Jahrhunderts v. Chr. und zur Funktion der gleichzeitigen Grabbauten, Munich.

Bernabó-Brea, L., Cavalier, M. & Spigo, U. 1995
Lipari, Museo Eoliano, Palermo.

Bernabó-Brea, L., Cavalier, M. & Villard, F. 2001
Meligunìs Lipára, 11. Gli scavi nella necropoli greca e romana di Lipari nell'area del terreno vescovile, Lipari.

Bernhard-Walcher, A. 1980
Zwei tyrrhenische Hydrien in Wien, in: Krinzinger, F., Otto, B. & Walde-Psenner, E. (eds.), *Forschungen und Funde. Festschrift Bernhard Neutsch*, Innsbrook, 69-76.

Berti, F. & Guzzo, P.G. (eds.) 1993
Spina, Storia di una città tra Greci ed Etruschi, Ferrara.

Berti, F., Bonomi, S. & Landolfi, M. 1996
Classico. Anticlassico. Vasi alto-adriatici tra Piceno, Spina e Adria, San Giovanni in Persiceto.

Bianco, S., Bottini, A. & Pontrandolfo, A. (eds.) 1996
I Greci in Occidente. Greci, Enotri e Lucani nella Basilicata meridionale, Napoli.

Boardman, J. 1972
Herakles, Peisistratos and Sons, *RA* 1972, 57-72.

Boardman, J. 1974
Athenian Black Figure Vases, London.

Boardman, J. 1975
Athenian Red Figure Vases. The Archaic Period. A Handbook, London.

Boardman, J. 1985
Greek Sculpture. The Classical Period. A Handbook, London.

Boardman, J. 1989
Athenian Red Figure Vases. The Classical Period. A Handbook, London.

Boardman, J. 2001
The History of Greek Vases. Potters, Painters and Pictures, London.

Bonacasa, N., Braccesi, L. & De Miro, E. (eds.) 2002
La Sicilia dei due Dionisi. Atti della settimana di studio, Agrigento, 24-28 febbraio 1999, Rome.

Bonanno-Aravantinos, M. *forthcoming*
La tomba 404 della necropoli nord-orientale di Tebe (Beozia), in: Lafli, E. & Muller, A. (eds.), *Figurines de terre cuite en Mèditerranée grecque et romaine: production, diffusion, iconographie et fonction. Actes du Colloque international d'Izmir, Juin 2007, BCH* Supplement.

Bonfante, L. 2003
The Greeks in Etruria, in: Karageorghis, V. (ed.), *The Greeks Beyond the Aegean. From Marseilles to Bactria. Papers Presented at the International Symposium Held at the Onassis Cultural Center, New York, 12th October, 2002*, New York, 43–58.

Bonnet, C. (ed.) 1998
Le bestiaire d'Héraclès. IIIe Rencontre héracléenne. Actes du colloque, Liége-Namur du 14 au 16 novembre 1996, Kernos Suppl. 7, Liège.

Bonnet, C. & Jourdain-Annequin, C. (eds.) 1992
Héraclès d'une rive à l'autre de la Méditerranée. Bilan et perspectives. Actes de la table ronde de Rome 15-16 septembre 1989, Bruxelles.

Bonnet, C. & Jourdain-Annequin, C. (eds.) 1996
Héraclès, les femmes et le féminin. Actes du colloque de Grenoble, 22-23 octobre 1992, Bruxelles.

Borg, B.E. 2002
Der Logos des Mythos. Allegorien und Personifikationen in der frühen griechischen Kunst, München.

Boulter, C.G. 1963
Graves in Lenormant Street, Athens, *Hesperia* 32, 113-137.

Braccesi, L. *et al.* (eds.) 1988
"Veder Greco." Le necropoli di Agrigento. Mostra internazionale, Agrigento, 2. maggio - 31. luglio 1988, Roma.

Braun, K. & Haevernick, T.E. 1981
Bemalte Keramik und Glas aus dem Kabirenheiligtum bei Theben. Das Kabirenheiligtum bei Theben 4, Berlin.

Brun, J.P. (ed.) 2009
Artisanats antiques d'Italie et de Gaule. Mélanges offerts á Maria Francesca Buonaiuto, Naples.

Brun, J.P. (ed.) 2010
L'artigianato nel Mediterraneo, Paris and Naples.

Burn, L. 1985
Honey pots: Three white-ground cups by the Sotades Painter, *AntK* 28, 93-105.

Burn, L. 1998
Figured Vases, in: Carter, J.C. *et al.* (eds.), *The Chora of Metaponto. The Necropoleis,* Austin, 592-640.

Burn, L. 2010
The contexts of the production and distribution of Athenian painted pottery in c. 400 BC, in: Taplin, O. & Wyles, R. (eds.), *The Pronomos Vase and its Context,* Oxford, 15-31.

Burow, J. *et al.* 2000
Archaische Keramik aus Olympia. Olympische Forschungen vol. 28, Berlin.

Burrows, R.M. & Ure, P.N. 1907/1908
Excavations at Rhitsóna in Boeotia, *BSA* 14, 226-318.

Bühl, G. 1995
Constantinopolis und Roma. Stadtpersonifikationen der Spätantike, Kilchberg.

Callipolitis-Feytmans, D. 1979
La coupe apode à boutons en Attique et le Peintre d'Athénes 533, *BCH* 103, 195-215.

Camporeale, G. 2009a
Achle, *LIMC* Supplementum, 15-19.

Camporeale, G. 2009b
Monstra anonyma (in Etruria), *LIMC* Supplementum, 359-373.

Carabatea, M. 1997
Herakles and a "Man in Need", in: Palagia, O. (ed.), *Greek Offerings. Essays on Greek art in honour of John Boardman,* Oxford, 131-143.

Carpenter, T.H. 2003
The native market for red-figure vases in Apulia, *MAAR* 48, 1-24.

Carpenter, T.H. *forthcoming*
A Case for Greek Tragedy in Italic Settlements in 4th Century BC Apulia, in: Carpenter, T.H. (ed.), *Beyond Magna Graecia: New Developments in South Italian Archaeology.*

Carter, J.C. *et al.* 1998
The Chora of Metaponto. The Necropoleis, Austin.

Cassano, R. 1992
Ceramica a Figure Rosse, in: Cassano, R. (ed.), *Principi Imperatori Vescovi. Duemila anni di storia a Canosa,* Bari, 261-301

Castoldi, M. 2004
Il defunto come eroe, in: Sena Chiesa, G. & Arslan, E.A. (eds.), *Miti Greci. Archeologia e pittura della Magna Grecia al collezionismo,* Milano, 193-202.

Cerchiai, L. 1980
La *máchaira* di Achille: Alcuni osservazioni a proposito della 'Tomba dei Tori', *AnnArchStorAnt* 2, 25-39.

Ciancio, A. 1997
Silbíon. Una città tra Greci e Indigeni. La documentazione archeologica dal territorio di Gravina in Puglia dall'ottavo al quinto secolo a.C, Bari.

Cipriano, M., Longo, F. & Viscione, M. (eds.) 1996
I Greci in Occidente. Poseidonia e i Lucani. Paestum, Museo Archeologico Nazionale, 27 aprile 1996, Napoli.

Clairmont, C.W. 1993
Classical Attic Tombstones vol. 2, Kilchberg.

Clay, J.S. 1989
The Politics of Olympus. Form and meaning in the major Homeric Hymns, Princeton.

Clinton, K. 2003
Stages of initiation in the Eleusinian and Samothracian mysteries, in: Cosmopoulos, M.B. (ed.), *Greek mysteries. The archaeology and ritual of ancient Greek secret cults,* London, 50-78.

Cohen, B. 2006
The Colors of Clay. Special Techniques in Athenian Vases, Los Angeles.

Cohen, B. (ed.) 2000
Not the classical ideal. Athens and the construction of the other in Greek art, Leiden.

Cohen, E.E. 2002
The Athenian Nation, Princeton.

Coleman, J.E. 1986
Excavations at Pylos in Elis, Hesperia suppl. 21, Princeton.

Colivicchi, F. 2009
Warriors and Citizens. Models of self-representation in native Basilicata, in: Osanna, M. (ed.), *Verso la città. Forme insediative in Lucania e nel mondo italico fra IV e III sec. a.C. Atti della Giornate di studio, Venosa, 13-14 maggio 2006*, Venosa, 69-88.

Connor, W.R. 1994
The problem of Athenian civic identity, in: Boegehold, A.L. & Scafuro, A.C. (eds.), *Athenian identity and civic ideology*, Baltimore, 34-44.

Cook, R.M. 1959
Die Bedeutung der bemalten Keramik für den griechischen Handel, *JdI* 74, 114-123.

Costa, G. 1982
Hermes dio delle iniziazioni, *CivClCr* 3, 277-295.

Coulié, A. 2002
La céramique thasienne à figures noires, Etudes Thasiennes XIX, Paris.

Coumanoudis, S.N. & Gofas, D.C. 1978
Deux décrets inédits d'Eleusis, *REG* 91, 289-306.

d'Agostino, B. 1987
Achille et Troïlos: images, textes et assonances, in: *Poikilia. Études offerts à Jean-Pierre Vernant*, Paris, 145-154.

d'Agostino, B. & Cerchiai, L. 1999
Il mare, la morte, l'amore. Gli etruschi, i Greci e l'immagine, Roma.

Dakaris, S.I. 1993
The Nekyomanteion of the Acheron, Athens.

Dakoronia, F. & Bouyia, P. 2002
Ο δρόμος είχε τη δική του ιστορία... (Exhibition guide), Λαμία.

De Cesare, M. 1997
Le statue in immagine. Studi sulle raffigurazioni di statue nella pittura vascolare greca, Rome.

De Juliis, E.M. 2004
Origine della ceramica italiota a figure rosse e sua diffusione in Puglia, in: Sena Chiesa, G. & Arslan, E.A. (eds.), *Miti greci. Archeologia e pittura dalla Magna Grecia al collezionismo, Mostra Milano 3 ottobre 2004 - 16 gennaio 2005*, Milano, 145-150.

De La Genière, J. (ed.) 2006
Les Clients de la Céramique Grecque. Actes du Colloque de l'Académie des Inscriptions et Belles-Lettres Paris, 30-31 janvier 2004. Cahiers du Corpus Vasorum Antiquorum vol. 1. Paris.

De La Genière, J. 2009
Quelques réflexions sur l'ouvrage 'La céramique Apulienne, bilan et perspectives', in: Brun, J.P. (ed.), 2009, *Artisanats antiques d'Italie et de Gaule. Mélanges offerts á Maria Francesca Buonaiuto*, Naples, 239-242.

Delorme, J. 1960
Gymnasion. Étude sur les monuments consacrés à l'éducation en Grèce, Bibliothèque des Écoles Françaises d'Athènes et de Rome 196, Paris.

Demakopoulou, K. & Konsola, D. 1981
Αρχαιολογικό Μουσείο της Θήβας, Αθήνα.

Denoyelle, M. 1997
Attic or non-Attic? The Case of the Pisticci Painter, in: Palagia, O., Coulson, W.D.E. & Oakley, J.H. (eds.), *Athenian Potters and Painters*, Oxford, 395-405.

Denoyelle, M. *et al.* (eds.) 2005
La Céramique Apulienne. Bilan et perspectives. Actes de la Table Tonde organisée par l'École française de Rome en collaboration avec la Soprintendenza per i Beni Archeologici della Puglia et le Centre Jean Bérard de Naples (Naples, Centre Jean Bérard, 30 novembre - 2 décembre 2000), Naples.

Denoyelle, M. & Iozzo, M. 2009
La céramique grecque d'Italie méridionale et de Sicile. Productions coloniales et apparentées du VIIIe au IIIe siècle av. J.-C., Paris.

Deonna, W. 1935
'Monokripides', *RHistRel* 12, 50-72.

De Palma, G. 1992
Ceramica dorata, in: Cassano, R. (ed.), *Principi Imperatori Vescovi. Duemila anni di storia a Canosa,* Bari, 302-309.

Desantis, P. 1993
Altre tombe di IV secolo a.C., in: Berti, F. & Guzzo, P.G., *Spina. Storia di una città tra Greci ed Etruschi,* Ferrara, 308-320.

Descoeudres, J.P. (ed.) 1990
EUMOUSIA. Ceramic and iconographic studies in honour of Alexander Cambitoglou, Sydney.

Diez del Corral Corredoira, P. 2007
"Y Dioniso desposó a la rubia Ariadna". Estudio iconográfico de la cerámica ática (575-300 a.C.). British archaeological reports. International series 1719, Oxford.

Dodds, E.R. 1951
The Greeks and the Irrational, Berkeley.

Dolci, M. 2004
Il *rhyton*: vaso potorio rituale, in: Sena Chiesa, G. & Arslan, E.A. (eds.), *Miti Greci. Archeologia della Magna Grecia al collezionismo. Mostra Milano 3 ottobre - 16 gennaio 2005,* Milano, 183-185.

Dugas, C. 1960
Tradition littéraire et tradition graphique dans l'antiquité grecque, in: *Recueil Charles Dugas,* Paris, 59-74.

Eckels, R.P. 1937
Greek wolf-lore [Ph.D. dissertation], University of Pennsylvania, Philadelphia.

Ekroth, G. 2002
The sacrificial rituals of Greek hero-cults in the archaic to the early Hellenistic periods, Kernos suppl. 12, Liège.

Elliot, J. 1995
The Etruscan wolfman in myth and ritual, *EtrSt* 2, 17-33.

Elliot, M. 1998
Black-glazed pottery, in: Carter, J.C. *et al.* (eds.), *The Chora of Metaponto. The Necropoleis,* Austin, 642-693.

Erickson, B. 2009
Roussa Ekklesia, part 1: Religion and politics in East Crete, *AJA* 113, 353-404.

Esposito, A.M. / De Tommaso, G. (eds.) 1993
Museo archeologico nazionale di Firenze. Antiquarium. Vasi attici, Firenze.

Fehling, D. 1989
Die ursprüngliche Geschichte vom Fall Trojas, oder Interpretationen zur Troja-Geschichte, *WürzbJb* 15, 7-16.

Felletti Maj, B.M. 1940
La cronologia della necropoli di Spina e la ceramica alto-adriatica, *StEtr* 14, 43-87.

Ferrari, G. 2002
Figures of speech. Men and maidens in Ancient Greece, Chigaco.

Fialko, E.E. 2004
Atticheskij krater kak simbol skifskogo nomarcha, in: Chochorowski, J. (ed.) *Kimmerowie Scytowie Sarmaci. Ksi ga po wi cona pami ci Professora Tadeusza Sulimirskiego* [Cimmerians Scythians Sarmatians. In memory of Professor Tadeusz Sulimirski], Cracow, 149-160.

Flashar, M. & Wohlfeil, J. (eds.) 2003
Adolf Furtwängler. Der Archäologe, München.

Fless, F. 2002
Rotfigurige Keramik als Handelsware. Erwerb und Gebrauch attischer Vasen im mediterranen und pontischen Raum während des 4. Jhs. v.Chr, Rahden/Westfalen.

Flower, M.A. 2008
The seer in ancient Greece, Berkeley.

Fornasier, J. & Böttger, B. (eds.) 2002
Das Bosporanische Reich. Der Nordosten des Schwarzen Meeres in der Antike, Mainz.

Fortunelli, S. (ed.) 2007
Sertum Perusinum Gemmae Oblatum. Docenti e allievi del Dottorato di Perugia in onore di Gemma Sena Chiesa, Quaderni di Ostraka 13, Napoli.

Fortunelli, S. & Masseria, C. (eds.) 2009
Ceramica attica da santuari della Grecia, della Ionia e dell'Italia. Atti convegno internazionale Perugia 14-17 marzo 2007, Venosa.

Fracchia, H. 1984
Two new mythological scenes from Western Lucania, in: Hackens, T. (ed.), *Crossroads of the Mediterranean. Papers delivered at the international conference on the archaeology of early Italy,* Louvain, 291-300.

Fracchia, H. 1987
The Mourning Niobe Motif in South Italian Art, *EchosCl* 6, 199-208.

Fracchia, H. 1993
The Votive Deposit, in: Gualtieri, M. (ed.), *Fourth Century BC. Magna Graecia: a case study,* Göteborg, 108-140.

Fracchia, H. 2011
Family and community: Self-representation in a Lucanian chamber tomb, in: Gleba, M. & Horsnæs, H. (eds.), *Communicating Identity in Italic Iron Age Communities*, Oxford, 90-98.

Fracchia, H. & Gualtieri, M. 2004
Committenza e mito. Un caso di studio dalla Lucania occidentale, *MEFRA* 116, 301-326.

Fracchia, H. & Gualtieri, M. 2009
Roccagloriosa (SA). Organizzazione insediativa e sviluppi istituzionali (IV-III sec. a.C.), in: Osanna, M. (ed.), *Verso la città. Forme insediative in Lucania e nel mondo italico fra IV e III sec a.C., Atti delle Giornate di Studio, Venosa, 13-14 maggio 2006*, Venosa, 119-143.

Fracchia, H. & Gualtieri, M. 2010
La produzione artigianale fra IV e II secolo a.C. in Magna Grecia. Un caso di studio dall'area italica, in: Brun, J.P. (ed.), *Artisanats antiques d'Italie et de Gaule. Mélanges offerts à Maria Francesca Buonaiuto*, Naples, 99-114.

Franken, N. 2007
Rückkehr aus dem Schattenreich. Zu einem etruskischen Todesdämon in Berlin, *RM* 113, 241-246.

Frazer, J.G. 1927
The golden Bough. Taboo and the Perils of the Soul. A Study in Magic and Religion, London.

Frickenhaus, A. 1911
Das Herakleion von Melite, *AM* 36, 113-144.

Froning, H. 1996
Un Eracle attico in Sicilia, *CronA* 29, 107-119.

Fröhner, W. 1892
Collection A. Van Branteghem, Vases peints et terre cuites antiques dont la vente aux enchères aura lieu à Paris, Hôtel Drouot, 16-18 juin 1892, Paris.

Furtwängler, A. 1881
Thongefässe aus Athen, *AM* 6, 112-118.

Furtwängler, A. 1893
Meisterwerke der griechischen Plastik. Kunstgeschichtliche Untersuchungen, Leipzig/Berlin.

Gantz, T. 1993
Early Greek myth. A guide to literary and artistic sources, Baltimore.

Gaultier, F. & Villard, F. 1985
Les stamnoi Fould. Un dernier éclat de la peinture sur vases en Etrurie, *MonPiot* 67, 1-30.

Gebauer, J. 2002
Pompe und Thysia. Attische Tieropferdarstellungen auf schwarz- und rotfigurigen Vasen, Münster.

Gehrke, H.J. 2004
Eine Bilanz. Die Entwicklung des Gymnasions zur Institution der Sozialisierung in der Polis, in: Kah, D. & Scholz, P. (eds.), *Das hellenistische Gymnasion*, Berlin, 413-419.

Gerhard, E. 1856
Thongefäss des Xenophantos, *AZ* 1856, 163-169.

Gernet, L. 1928
Frairies antiques, *REG* 41, 313-359

Gex, K. & McPhee, I. 1995
The Painter of the Eretria Cup. A Euboian red-figure vase-painter, *AntK* 38, 3-10.

Giudice, F. & Giudice, I. 2009
Seeing the Image. Constructing a Data-Base of the Imagery on Attic Pottery from 635 to 300 BC., in: Oakley, J.H. & Palagia, O. (eds.), *Athenian Potters and Painters 2*, Oxford, 48-62.

Giudice, G. 2007
Il tornio, la nave, le terre lontane. Ceramografici attici in Magna Grecia nella seconda meta del V sec. aC. Rotte e vie di distribuzione, Roma.

Giudice, G., Tusa, S. & Tusa, V. (eds.) 1992
La collezione archaeologica del Banco di Sicilia, Palermo.

Giudice, R. & Panvini, R. (eds.) 2003
Il greco, il barbaro e la ceramica attica. Proceedings of an International Colloquium, Catania 2001, vol. 2, Rome.

Giuliani, L. 1996
Rhesus between dream and death. On the relation of image to litterature in Apulian vase-painting, *BICS* 41, London.

Gleba, M. & Horsnæs, H. (eds.) 2011
Communicating Identity in Italic Iron Age Communities, London.

Godart, L. & De Caro, S. (eds.) 2007
Nostoi. Capolavori ritrovati. Roma, Palazzo del Quirinale, Galleria di Alessandro VII. 21 dicembre 2007 - 2 marzo 2008, Roma.

Graef, B. & Langlotz, E. 1909-1933
Die antiken Vasen von der Akropolis zu Athen, Berlin.

Graf, F. 2009
Apollo, possession, and prophecy, in: Athanassaki, L. et al. (eds.), *Apolline Politics and Poetics*, Athens, 587-605.

Graf, F. & Iles Johnston, S. 2007
Rituals texts for the afterlife. Orpheus and the Bacchic gold tablets, London.

Greco, E. & Guzzo, P.G. (eds.) 1992
La Tomba a camera di Marcellina, Taranto.

Greifenhagen, A. 1972
Neue Fragmente des Kleophradesmalers, Heidelberg.

Greifenhagen, A. 1978
Zeichnungen nack etruskischen Vasen im deutschen archäologischen Institut, Rom, *RM* 85, 59-90.

Groß-Albenhausen, K. 2004
Bedeutung und Funktion der Gymnasien für die Hellenisierung des Ostens, in: Kah, D. & Scholz, P. (eds.), *Das hellenistische Gymnasion*, Berlin, 313-322.

Gualtieri, M. 1982
Cremation among the Lucanians, *AJA* 86, 475-481.

Gualtieri, M. 1990
Rituale funerario di una aristocrazia lucana. Fine V-inizio III secolo a.C., in: Tagliente, M. (ed.), *Italici in Magna Grecia, insediamenti e strutture*, Venosa, 161-197.

Gualtieri, M. 2003
Elites lucane ed immagini. Niobe a Roccagloriosa, in: Giudice O. & Panvini, R. (eds.), *Il greco, il barbaro e la ceramica attica. Immaginario del diverso, processi di scambio e autorappresentazione degli indigeni 2. Atti del convegno internazionale di studi, 14-19 maggio 2001, Catania, Caltanissetta, Gela, Camarina, Vittoria, Siracusa*, Roma, 147-154.

Gualtieri, M. 2006
La committenza della ceramica a figure rosse tardo-apula: un caso di studio, in: De La Genière, J. (ed.), *Les clients de la céramique grecque. Actes du colloque de l'Académie des inscriptions et belles-lettres, Paris, 30-31 janvier 2004*, Paris, 97-106 and 221-230.

Gualtieri, M. 2007
Un gruppo di vasi 'apuli' dalla Lucania occidentale, in: Fortunelli, S. (ed.), *Sertum perusinum Gemmae oblatum. Docenti e allievi del Dottorato di Perugia in Onore di Gemma Sena Chiesa*, Napoli, 259-272.

Gualtieri, M. 2009
Un'anonima touta della Lucania tirrenica: l'abitato ed i nuovi documenti epigraficii, in: Ancillotti, A. & Calderini, A. (eds.), *La Città Italica. Atti del II Convegno interna-zionale sugli antichi Umbri, Gubbio, 25-27 settembre 2003*, Perugia, 157-178.

Gualtieri, M. (ed.) 1993
Fourth Century B.C. Magna Graecia: a case study, Göteborg.

Gualtieri, M. & Fracchia, H. (eds.) 1990
Roccagloriosa I. L'abitato, scavo e ricognizione topografica (1976-1986), Naples.

Gualtieri, M. & Fracchia, H. (eds.) 2001
Roccagloriosa II. Il territorio e la regione dall' terzo secolo a.C. al tardo antico, Rome.

Gualtieri, M. & Jackes, M. 1993
The cemetery areas: material culture and social organization, in: Gualtieri, M. (ed.), *Fourth Century B.C. Magna Graecia: a case study*, Göteborg, 140-226.

Hackens, T. & Ross Holloway, R. (eds.) 1984
Crossroads of the Mediterranean. Papers delivered a the international conference on the archaeology of early Italy, Haffenreffer Museum Brown University, 8-10 May 1981, Louvain-la-Neuve and Providence.

Hall, J.M. 2002
Hellenicity. Between ethnicity and culture, Chicago.

Hampe, R. & Simon, E. 1964
Griechische Sagen in der frühen etruskischen Kunst, Mainz.

Hannestad, L. 1991
Athenian Pottery in Corinth c. 600-470 BC, *ActaArch* 62, 151-163.

Harari, M. 1987
Dibattito, in: *Tarquinia. Richerche, scavi e prospettive. Atti del Convegno internazionale di studi La Lombardia per gli Etruschi, Milano, 24-25 giugno 1986*, Milan, 288-291.

Harari, M. 1988
Les gardiens du paradis. Iconographie funéraire et allégorie mythologique dans la céramique étrusque à figures rouge tardive, *NumAntCl* 17, 169-191.

Harari, M. 1995
Ipotesi sulle regole del montaggio narrativo nella pittura vascolare etrusca, in: *Modi e funzioni del racconto mitico nella ceramica greca, italiota ed etrusca dal VI al IV secolo a.C. Atti del convegno internazionale, Raito di Vietri sul Mare 29-31 maggio 1994,* Salerno, 103-135.

Hardie, A. 2004
Muses and mysteries, in: Murray, P. & Wilson, P. (eds.), *Music and the muses. The culture of 'mousike' in the classical Athenian city,* New York, 11-37.

Hart, M.L. 2010
The art of ancient Greek theater, Los Angeles.

Hawhee, D. 2004
Bodily arts. Rhetoric and Athletics in Ancient Greece, Austin.

Hedreen, G. 2001
Capturing Troy. The narrative functions of landscape in Archaic and Early Classical Greek art, Ann Arbor.

Heilmeyer, W-D. (ed.) 1988
Antikenmuseum Berlin. Die ausgestellten Werke, Berlin.

Hemelrijk, J.M. 1988
CVA Amsterdam, Allard Pierson Museum, University of Amsterdam, Amsterdam.

Herbert, S. 1977
The Red-figure Pottery, Corinth VII.4, Princeton.

Herford, M.A.B. 1914
A cup signed by Brygos at Oxford, *JHS* 34, 106-113.

Hesberg, H. von 1995
Das griechische Gymnasion im 2. Jh. v. Chr., in: Wörrle, M. & Zanker, P. (eds.), *Stadtbild und Bürgerbild im Hellenismus, Kolloquium, München, 24. bis 26. Juni 1993, veranstaltet von der Kommission zur Erforschung des Antiken Städtewesens der Bayerischen Akademie der Wissenschaften,* Munich, 13-27.

Himmelmann, N. 1994
Realistische Themen in der griechischen Kunst der archaischen und klassischen Zeit, Berlin.

Hoepfner, W. 2006
Die griechische Agora im Überblick, in: Hoepfner, W. & Lehmann, L., *Die griechische Agora. Bericht über ein Kolloquium am 16. März 2003 in Berlin,* Mainz, 1-28.

Hoff, R. von den 2009
Hellenistische Gymnasia: Raumgestaltung und Raumfunktionen, in: Matthaei, A. (ed.), *Stadtbilder im Hellenismus. Die hellenistische Polis als Lebensform 1,* Berlin, 245-275.

Hoff, R. von den & Schmidt, S. 2001
Bilder und Konstruktion. Ein interdisziplinäres Konzept für die Altertumswissenschaften, in: Hoff, R. von den & Schmidt, S. (eds.), *Konstruktionen von Wirklichkeit. Bilder im Griechenland des 5. und 4. Jahrhunderts v. Chr.,* Stuttgart, 11-25.

Hoffmann, A. 2002
Grabritual und Gesellschaft. Gefässformen, Bildthemen und Funktionen unteritalisch-rotfigurige Keramik aus der Nekropole von Tarent, Rahden/Westphalen.

Hoffmann, H. 1966
Tarentine rhyta, Mainz.

Hoffmann, H. 1997
Sotades. Symbols of Immortality on Greek Vases, Oxford.

Hollein, H.G. 1988
Bürgerbild und Bildwelt der attischen Demokratie auf den rotfigurigen Vasen des 6.-4. Jahrhunderts v. Chr., Frankfurt am Main.

Houby-Nielsen, S. 1996
The archaeology of ideology in the Kerameikos: new interpretations of the 'Opferinnen', in: Hägg, R. (ed.), *The Role of Religion in the Early Greek Polis,* Stockholm, 41-54.

Hölscher, T. 1998
Images and Political Identity: The Case of Athens, in: Boedeker, D. & Raaflaub, K.A. (eds.), *Democracy, Empire, and the Arts in Fifth-Century Athens,* Cambridge, 153-183.

Hölscher, T. 1999
Immagini mitologiche e valori sociali nella Grecia arcaica, in: Muth, S. & De Angelis, F. (eds.), *Im Spiegel des Mythos. Bilderwelt und Lebenswelt. Lo specchio del mito. Immaginario e realtá,* Wiesbaden, 11-30.

Iles Johnston, S. 2008
Ancient Greek Divination, Oxford.

Immerwahr, H.R. 1990
Attic script. A survey, Oxford.

Isler-Kerényi, C. 2009
The Study of Figured Pottery Today, in: Nørskov *et al.* (eds.), 2009, *The World of Greek Vases,* Roma.

Junker, K. 2003
Namen auf dem Pronomoskrater, *AM* 118, 317-335.

Kaempf-Dimitriadou, S. 1979
Die Liebe der Götter in der attischen Kunst des 5. Jhs. v.Chr. Beiheft zur Antiken Kunst 11, Basel.

Kaeser, B. 1990
Zuschauerfiguren, in: Vierneisel, K. & Kaeser, B. (eds.), *Kunst der Schale – Kultur des Trinkens,* München, 151-156.

Kathariou, K. 2007a
New attributions to the Painter of the New York Centauromachy, *Egnatia* 11, 209-212.

Kathariou, K. 2007b
Two new Boeotian cups at the Benaki Museum: Potters and painters, *Μουσείο Μπενάκη* 7, 9-32.

Kaufman-Samara, A. 1997
"Οὐκ ἀπόμουσον τὸ γυναικῶν" (Ευριπ. Μηδ. 1089). Γυναίκες μουσικοί στα αττικά αγγεία του 5ου αι. π.Χ., in: Oakley, J.H. et al. (eds.), *Athenian Potters and Painters,* Oxford, 285-296.

Kenzler, U. 1999
Studien zur Entwicklung und Struktur der griechischen Agora in archaischer und klassischer Zeit, Frankfurt am Main.

Kerényi, C. 1974
The Gods of the Greeks, London.

Kilinski II, K. 1990
Boeotian black-figure vase-painting of the Archaic Period, Mainz am Rhein.

Kilinski II, K. 2004
Attic Influences on Boiotian Cups, in: Fossey, J.M. & Francis, J.E. (eds.), *The Diniacopoulos Collection in Québec: Greek and Roman Antiquities*, Montréal, 53-61.

Kistler, E. 1998
Die Opferrinne-Zeremonie. Bankettideologie am Grab, Orientalisierung und Formierung einer Adelsgesellschaft in Athen, Stuttgart.

Koch-Harnack, G. 1983
Knabenliebe und Tiergeschenke. Ihre Bedeutung im päderastischen Erziehungssystem Athens, Berlin.

Konstantinou, I. 1970
Λευκή δελφική κύλιξ, *ArchEph* (1970), 27-46.

Kopcke, G. 1969
Attische Reliefkeramik klassischer Zeit, *AA* (1969), 545-551.

Kossatz-Deissmann, A. 1997
Troilos, *LIMC* 8, 91-94.

Kowalzig, B. 2007
Singing for the Gods, Oxford.

Kraiker, K. 1934
Ausgrabungen der Kerameikos, *AM* 59, 1-20.

Krauskopf, I. 1987
Todesdämonen und Totengötter im vorhellenistischen Etrurien: Kontinuität und Wandel, Florence.

Krauskopf, I. 2009
Daemones Anonymi (in Etruria), *LIMC* Supplementum 143-155.

Kullmann, W. 1960
Die Quellen der Ilias (Troischer Sagenkreis), Hermes Einzelschriften 14, Wiesbaden.

Kunze, E. 1950
Archaische Schildbänder: Ein Beitrag zur frühgriechischen Bildgeschichte und Sagenüberlieferung, *Olympische Forschungen* 2, Berlin.

Kunze, E. 1964
Ausgrabungen in Olympia 1963/4, *ADelt* 19.2.

Kurke, L. 2007
Visualizing the Choral. Epichoric Poetry, Ritual, and Elite Negotiation in Fifth-Century Thebes in: Kraus, K. et al. (eds.), *Visualizing the Tragic. Drama, Myth and Ritual in Greek Art and Literature. Essays in Honour of Froma Zeitlin,* Oxford, 63-101.

Kurtz, D.C. & Boardman, J. 1971
Greek Burial Customs, London.

La Sorsa, S. (ed.) 1979
Storia della Puglia I, Bari.

La Torre, G.F. 2009
Da Blanda a Temesa: fenomeni di urbanizzazione lungo la fascia tirrenica della Lucania meridionale e del Bruzio settentrionale, in: Osanna, M. (ed.), *Verso la città. Forme insediative in Lucania e nel mondo italico fra IV e III secolo a.C. Atti delle Giornate di studio, Venosa, 13-14 maggio 2006,* Venosa, 181-195.

La Torre G.F. & Mollo, F. 2006
Blanda Julia sul Paecastro di Tortora. Scavi e ricerche (1990-2003), Pelorias XIII, Messina.

Lambert, S.D. 1998
The Phratries of Attica, Ann Arbor.

Lambrinodakis, W. 1984
Apollon, *LIMC* 2, 183-327.

Landolfi, M. 1988
I Piceni, in: *Italia. Omnium terrarum alumna. La civiltà dei Veneti, Reti, Liguri, Celti, Piceni, Umbri, Latini, Campani e Iapigi,* Milano, 315-372.

Landolfi, M. (ed.) 2000
Adriatico tra IV e III sec. a.C. Vasi alto-adriatici tra Piceno, Spina e Adria, Rome.

Langner, M. 2005
Barbaren griechischer Sprache? Die Bildwelt des Bosporanischen Reiches und das Selbstverständnis seiner Bewohner in: Fless, F. & Treister, M. (eds.), *Bilder und Objekte als Träger kultureller Identität und interkultureller Kommunikation im Schwarzmeergebiet,* Rahden/Westfalen, 53-66.

Larson, S.L. 2007
Tales of Epic Ancestry. Boiotian collective identity in the late Archaic and early Classical periods, Historia Einzelschriften 197, Stuttgart.

Laurens, A.-F. 1987
Identification d'Hèbè? Le nom, l'un et le multiple, in: Bérard, C., *Images et société en Grèce ancienne,* Cahiers d'Archéologie romande 36, Lausanne, 59-72.

Leblond, P. 1990
Les loutrophores apuliennes à figures rouges: morphologie et iconographie, M.A. Thesis, Université Laval, Québec.

Lévêque, P. & Verbanck-Piérard, A. 1992
Héraclès, héros ou dieu?, in: Bonnet, C. & Jourdain-Annequin, C. (eds.), *Héraclès d'une rive à l'autre de la Méditerranée, Etudes de philologie, d'archéologie et d'histoire ancienne de l'Institut historique belge de Rome* 28, Bruxelles-Rome, 43-65.

Leypold, C. 2008
Bankettgebäude in griechischen Heiligtümern, Wiesbaden.

Lezzi-Hafter, A. 1976
Der Schuwalow-Maler. Eine Kannenwerkstatt der Parthenonzeit, Kerameus 2, Mainz.

Lezzi-Hafter, A. 1988
Der Eretria-Maler. Werke und Weggefährten, Kerameus 6, Mainz.

Lezzi-Hafter, A. 1997
Offerings made to Measure: Two Special Commissions by the Eretria Painter for Apollonia Pontica, in: J.H. Oakley *et al.* (eds.), *Athenian Potters and Painters,* Oxford, 353-369.

Libertini, G. 1930
Il Museo Biscari, Milano.

Lippolis, E. 1994
La tipologia dei semata, in: Lippolis, E. (ed.), *Catalogo del Museo Nazionale Archeologico di Taranto I, 3. Atleti e Guerrieri. Tradizioni Aristocratiche a Taranto tra VI e V sec. A.C. Catalogo della mostra Taranto, Museo Nazionale Archeologico,* Taranto, 111-112.

Lippolis, E. 2004
The cultural framework of the polis and the sports in the Greek West. Competition and social status among the italiots, in: Stampolidis, N.C. & Tassoulas, Y. (eds.), *Magna Graecia. Athletics and the Olympic spirit on the periphery of the Hellenic world,* Athens, 39-53.

Lippolis, E. (ed.) 1994
Catalogo del Museo Nazionale Archeologico di Taranto I, 3. Atleti e Guerrieri. Tradizioni Aristocratiche a Taranto tra VI e V sec. A.C. Catalogo della mostra Taranto, Museo Nazionale Archeologico, Taranto.

Lippolis, E. *et al.* (eds.) 1995
Culti Greci in Occidente I, Taranto.

Lippolis, E. (ed.) 1996
I Greci in Occidente. Arte e Artigianato in Magna Grecia, Naples.

Lissarrague, F. 1999
Vases grecs. Les Athéniens et leurs images, Paris.

Lissarrague, F. 2008
Image and representation in the pottery of Magna Graecia, in: Revermann, M. & Wilson, P. (eds.), *Performance, iconography, reception. Studies in honour of Oliver Taplin,* Oxford, 439-449.

Lo Porto, F.G. 1967
Tombe di Atleti Tarentini, *AttiMemMagnaGr* VIII, 31-68.

Lohmann, H. 1979
Grabmäler auf unteritalischen Vasen, Berlin.

Lohmann, H. 1982
Zu technischen besonderheiten Apulischer Vasen, *JdI* 97, 191-249.

Loraux, N. 1986
The Invention of Athens. The Funeral Oration in the Classical City, Cambridge.

Low, P. (ed.) 2008
The Athenian empire, Edinburgh.

Lowenstam, S. 2008
As witnessed by images. The Trojan war tradition in Greek and Etruscan art, Baltimore.

Lullies, R. 1940
Zur boiotisch rotfigurigen Vasenmalerei, *AM* 65, 1-27.

MacDonald, B.R. 1981
The Emigration of Potters from Athens in the Late Fifth Century BC and its Effects on the Attic Pottery Industry, *AJA* 85, 159-168.

Maffre, J.-J. 1975
Collection Paul Canellopoulos (VIII). Vases Béotiens, *BCH* 99, 409-520.

Maggiani, A. *et al.* 1997
Vasi attici con dediche a divinità etrusche, Rome.

Mann, C. 2009
Kalokagathia in der Demokratie. Überlegungen zur Medialität der politischen Kommunikation im klassischen Athen, in: Mann, CH., Haake, M. & Hoff, R. von den (eds.), *Rollenbilder in der athenischen Demokratie. Medien, Gruppen, Räume im politischen und sozialen System*, Wiesbaden, 147-170.

Mannack, T. 2012
Liebesverfolgungen in Unteritalien, in: Schmidt, S. & Stähli, A. (eds.), *Vasenbilder im Kulturtransfer: Zirkulation und Rezeption griechische Keramik im Mittelmeerraum*, Munchen, 51-58.

Mannino, K. 2005
I contesti della ceramica protoitaliota in Messapia, in: Denoyelle, M. *et al.* (eds.), *La céramique apulienne. Bilan et perspectives*, Naples, 27-38.

Marino, D. & Corrado, M. 2009
Luoghi e testimonianze del sacro dentro le mura, Crotone.

Massa Pairault, F.H. 1996
Le peintre de Darius et l'actualité politique, in: Mele, A. & Breglia Pulci Doria, L. (eds.), *L'incidenza dell'antico II. Studi in memoria di Ettore Lepore*, Napoli, 235-262.

Massa Pairault, F.H. (ed.) 1999
Le Mythe Grec dans L'Italie Antique. Fonction et Image, Rome.

Massa Pairault, F.H. 2008
Philippos Laos, in: Volpe, G. *et al.* (eds.), *Storia e archeologia della Daunia in ricorda di Marina Mazzei*, Bari, 195-203.

Massei, L. 1978
Gli askoi a figure rosse nei corredi funerari delle necropoli di Spina, Milan.

Mastronuzzi, G. 2005
Repertorio dei contesti culturali indigeni in Italia Meridionale 1. Eta arcaica, Bari.

Matheson, S.B. 1989
Panathenaic amphorae by the Kleophrades Painter, *GVGetty* 4, 95-112.

Mazzei, M. 1990
L'ipogeo Monterisi Rossignoli di Canosa, *AnnAStorAnt* 12, 123-167.

Mazzei, M. 1992a
Notiziario delle attività di tutela, a cura della Soprintendenza Archeologica della Puglia, *Taras* 1992, 239-241.

Mazzei, M. 1992b
La Daunia dal V al II secolo a.C., in: Cassano, R. (ed.), *Principi Imperatori Vescovi. Duemila anni di storia a Canosa*, Bari, 587-590.

Mazzei, M. 1992c
L'ipogeo Monterisi Rossignoli, in: Cassano, R. (ed.), *Principi Imperatori Vescovi. Duemila anni di storia a Canosa*, Bari, 163-175.

Mazzei, M. 1996
Lo stile apulo tardo, in: Lippolis (ed.), *I Greci in Occidente. Arte e artigianato in Magna Grecia*, Naples, 403-406.

Mazzei, M. 1999
Committenza e Mito. Esempi dalla Puglia Settentrionale, in: Massa Pairault, F.H. (ed.), *Le Mythe Grece dans l'Italie Antique. Fonction et Image*, Roma, 467-483.

Mazzei, M. 2003
Condottieri Epiroti nella Daunia Ellenistica: l'evidenza archeologica, in: *Allesandro il Molosso e i 'condottieri' in Magna Grecia. Atti del quarantatreesimo convegno di studi sulla Magna Grecia, Taranto-Cosenza 26-30 settembre 2003*, Taranto, 243-261.

Mazzei, M. 2005
La ceramica apula a figure rosse: aspetti e problemi, in: Denoyelle, M. et al. (eds.), *La céramique apulienne. Bilan et perspectives*, Naples, 15-18.

Mazzei, M. (ed.) 1995
Arpi. L'ipogeo della Medusa e la necropoli, Bari.

Mazzei, M. (ed.) 1998
Il caso Arpi. Ambiente italico e magno-greco tra primo e medio ellenismo. Atti della tavola rotonda, Foggia 8 marzo 1998, Foggia.

McNiven, T. J. 2000
Behaving Like an Other. Telltale Gestures in Athenian Vase Painting, in: Cohen, B. (ed.), *Not the Classical Ideal. Athens and the Construction of the Other in Greek Art*, Leiden, 71-97.

McPhee, I. 1981
Some Red-figure Vase-painters of the Chalcidice, *BSA* 76, 297-308.

McPhee, I. 1983
Local Red Figure from Corinth, 1973-1980, *Hesperia* 52, 137-153.

McPhee, I. 1990
Local Red-figured Pottery from Ancient Elis. The Austrian Excavations of 1910-1914, *ÖJh* 60, 17-52.

Mele, A. & Breglia Pulci Doria, L. (eds.) 1996
L'incidenza dell'antico II. *Studi in memoria di Ettore Lepore*, Napoli,

Mertens, J. R. 1974
Attic white-ground cups. A special class of vases, *MetrMusJ* 9, 91-108.

Mertens, J. 1977
Attic White-ground. Its development on shapes other than lekythoi, New York.

Metzger, H. 1951
Les représentations dans la céramique attique du IVe siècle, Paris.

Metzger, H. 1977
APOLLON SPENDON. A propos d'une coupe attique à fond blanc trouvée à Delphes, *Etudes Delphiques*, BCH suppl. IV, 421-428.

Miller, M.C. 1997
Athens and Persia in the fifth Century BC, Cambridge.

Miller, S.G. 2004
Ancient Greek Athletics, New Haven.

Miro, E. de 2000
Agrigento I. I santuari urbani. La area sacra tra il tempio di Zeus e porta V, Roma.

Miro, E. de 2003
Agrigento II. I santuari exurbani. L'Asklepieion, Roma.

Mitchell, A.G. 2009
Greek Vase-painting and the Origins of Visual Humour, Cambridge.

Mollo, F. 2009
Dinamiche insediative e popolamento sparso in ambito brettio-italico: il quadro territoriale lungo la fascia tirrenica tra i fiumi Lao e Savuto, in: Osanna, M. (ed.), *Verso la città. Forme insediative in Lucania e nel mondo italico tra IV e III sec. a.C.*, Lavello, 195-214.

Monbrun, Ph. 2007
Les voix d'Apollon. L'arc, la lyre et les oracles, Rennes.

Montanaro, A.C. 2007
Ruvo di Puglia e il suo territorio. Le necropoli, i corredi funerari tra la documentazione del XIX secolo e gli scavi moderni, Roma.

Moore, M.B. 1997
Attic Red-figured and White-ground Pottery, Agora XXX, Princeton.

Morard, T. 2002
Les Troyens à Metaponte, Mainz.

Morel, J.P. 2009
La céramique apulienne vue par un céramologue 'd'un autre monde', in: Brun, J.P. (ed.), *Artisanats antiques d'Italie et de Gaule. Mélanges offerts á Maria Francesca Buonaiuto*, Naples, 243-255.

Moret, J.M. 2009
Review of A. Bottini and E. Setari (eds.), *Il Sarcofago delle Amazzoni* (Milan 2007), *RA* 2009, 390-392.

Mugione, E. 1996
Le importazioni di ceramica figurata, in: Bianco *et al.* (eds.), *I Greci in Occidente. Greci, Enotri e Lucani nella Basilicata meridionale*, Napoli, 215-218.

Mugione, E. 2000
Miti della ceramica attica in Occidente, Taranto.

Murray, O. & Tecusan, M. (eds.) 1995
In Vino Veritas, London.

Musti, D. 2005
Magna Grecia. Il quadro storico, Roma

Muth, S. & de Angelis, F. (eds.) 1999
Im Spiegel der Mythos. Bilderwelt und Lebenswelt. Lo specchio del mito. Immaginario e realtá, Wiesbaden.

Mylonas, G.E. 1961
Eleusis and the Eleusinian Mysteries, Princeton.

Nagy, G. 1999
The Best of the Achaeans. Concepts of the Hero in Archaic Greek Poetry, Baltimore.

Neer, R.T. 2002
Style and Politics in Athenian Vase-Painting. The Craft of Democracy, ca. 530-460 BCE, Cambridge.

Neils, J. 1992
Panathenaic Amphoras: Their meaning, makers and markets, in: Neils, J. (ed.), *Goddess and Polis. The Panathenaic Festival in Ancient Athens*, New Hampshire, 29-52.

Neils, J. 1994
Priamos, *LIMC* 7, 507–522.

Neils, J. 2001
Panathenaics in the West, in: Bentz, M. & Eschbach, N. (eds.), *PANATHENAÏKA, Symposion zu den Panathenäischen Preisamphoren, Rauischholzhausen 25.11-29.11 1998*, Mainz, 125-130.

Neils, J. *et al.* 2001
List of Attic red-figured amphorae of Panathnaic form, in: Bentz, M. & Eschbach, N. (eds.), *PANATHENAÏKA, Symposion zu den Panathenäischen Preisamphoren, Rauischholzhausen 25.11-29.11 1998*, Mainz, Appendix 3.

Nelson, M. & Todd, R.B. 2000
E.R. Dodds. Two Unpublished Letters on Ancient "Irrationalism", *Eikasmos* XI, 401-408.

Neutsch, B. (ed.) 1967
Archäologischen Forschungen in Lukanien II. Herakleiastudien, Heidelberg.

Nilsson, A. 1999
The Function and Reception of Attic Figured Pottery: Spina, a Case Study, *Analecta Romana* 26, 7-23.

Nørskov *et al.* (eds.) 2009
The World of Greek Vases, Roma.

Oakley, J.H. 1990
The Phiale Painter, Mainz.

Oakley, J.H. 2004
Picturing Death in Classical Athens. The Evidence of the White-ground Lekythoi, Cambridge.

Oakley, J.H. 2009a
Attic Red-Figured Beakers. Special Vases for the Thracian Market, *AntK* 52, 66-74

Oakley, J.H. 2009b
Greek Vase Painting, *AJA* vol. 113, no. 4, 599-627.

Oakley, J.H. & Palagia, O. (eds.) 2009
Athenian Potters and Painters 2, Oxford.

Obbink, D. 2001
The genre of Plateia: Generic unity in the new Simonides, in: Boedeker, D. & Sider, D. (eds.), *The new Simonides: Contexts of praise and desire*, Oxford, 65-85.

Ogden, D. 2001,
Greek and Roman Necromancy, Princeton.

Osborne, R. (ed.) 2007
Debating the Athenian Cultural Revolution. Art, Literature, Philosophy, and Politics 430-380 BC, Cambridge.

Osanna, M. (ed.) 2009
Verso la cittá. Forme insediative in Lucania e nel mondo italico fra IV e III sec. a.C., Lavello.

Osanna, M. *et al.* 2010
Ninfe ad Heraklea Lucana? Il santuario extra-urbano di Masseria Petrulla nella Valle del Sinni, *Kernos* 23, 239-270.

Paleothodoros, D. 2007
Commercial Networks in the Mediterranean and the Diffusion of Early Attic Red-figure Pottery (525-490 BCE), *MedHistR* 22, 165-182.

Paleothodoros, D. 2009
Archaeological context and iconographic Analysis: Case studies from Greece and Etruria, in: Nørskov, V. *et al.* (eds.), *The World of Greek Vases*, Rome, 45-62.

Pani, M. 1979
Politica e amministrazione in età romana, in: La Sorsa, S. (ed.), *Storia della Puglia* I, Bari, 83-98.

Panvini, R. 2004
Ceramiche attiche figurate del Museo Archeologico di Gela. Selectio vasorum, Venezia.

Panvini, R. 2005
Lavinia Sole, L'acropoli di Gela: stipi, depositi o scarichi. Corpus delle stipi in Italia, Roma.

Panvini, R. & Giudice, F. (eds.) 2003
Ta Attika. Veder greco a Gela. Ceramiche attiche figurate dall'antica colonia. Gela, Sirucusa, Rodi 2004, Roma.

Papadopoulos, J.K. 2009
The Relocation of Potters and the Dissemination of Style: Athens, Corinth, Ambrakia, and the Agrinion Group, in: Oakley, J. & Palagia, O. (eds.), *Athenian Potters and Painters 2*, Oxford, 232-240.

Parke, H.W. 1981
Apollo and the Muses, or prophecy in Greek verse, *Hermathena*, vol. 130-131, 99-112.

Parker, R. 1996
Athenian Religion. A History, Oxford.

Pelagatti, P. 1970
Enciclopedia dell' arte antica, Supplement, s.v. Beotici, Vasi, 146-148.

Pélékidis, C. 1962
Histoire de l'éphébie attique, Paris.

Pemberton, E.G. 2003
Classical and hellenistic pottery from Corinth and its Athenian connections in: Williams II, C.K. & Bookidis, N. (eds.), *Corinth, The Centenary 1896-1996, Corinth XX*, Princeton, 167-179.

Pfisterer-Haas, S. 2004
Eroten und junge Frauen beim Knobeln. Morraspiel, in: Wünsche, R. & Knauss, F. (eds.), *Lockender Lorbeer. Sport und Spiel in der Antike*, München, 419-420.

Philippaki, B., Symeonoglou, S. & Pharaklas, N. 1967
Αρχαιότητες και μνημεία Βοιωτίας, *ADelt* 22, B1 [1968], 225-257.

Pianu, G. 1990
La necropoli meridionale di Eraclea 1. Le tombe di secolo IV e III a.C, Roma.

Plat Taylor, J. du *et al.* 1977
Gravina-di-Puglia III. Houses and cemetery of the Iron Age and Classical periods, *BSR* 45, 69-137.

Pontrandolfo, A. 1995a
Il Mito di Cadmo nella Ceramica Attica e Italiota: in *Modi e Funzioni del Racconto Mitico nella Ceramica Greca, Italiota ed Etrusca dal VI al IV secolo a.C. Atti del convegno internazionale, Raito di Vietri sul Mare 29-31 maggio 1994*, Salerno, 215-231.

Pontrandolfo, A. 1995b
Simposio e Elites Sociali nel Mondo Etrusco e Italico, in: Murray, O. & Tecusan, M. (eds.), *In vino veritas*, London, 176-195.

Pontrandolfo, A. *et al.* 1988
Semata e naiskoi nella ceramica italiota, *AnnAStorAnt* 10, 181-202.

Pontrandolfo, A. & Rouveret, A. 1992
Le tombe dipinte di Paestum, Modena.

Pottier, E. 1895
Deux coupes à fond blanc de style attique. Musée du Louvre, *MonPiot* 2, 39-56.

Pottier, E. 1897-1922
Vases antiques du Louvre, Paris.

Pouzadoux, C. 1999
Usages du mythe dans la peinture apuliennne de la seconde moitié du IVe siècle av. J.-C. Mythe et histoire à Canosa: la tombe des Perses et le Peintre de Darius (Thèse de Doctorat, Paris-X-Nanterre), Paris.

Pouzadoux, C. 2008
Immagine, cultura e società in Dauncia e in Peucezia nel IV sec. a.C., in: Volpe, G. *et al.* (eds.), *Storia e archeologia della Daunia in ricorda di Marina Mazzei*, Bari, 205-220.

Prange, M. 1989
Der Niobidenmaler und seine Werkstatt. Untersuchungen zu einer Vasenwerkstatt frühklassischer Zeit, Frankfurt.

Prayon, F. 1977
Todesdämonen und die Troilossage in der frühetruskischen Kunst, *RM* 84, 181-197.

Raeck, W. 2004
Archäologische Randbemerkungen zum griechischen Gymnasion, in: Kah, D. & Scholz, P. (eds.), *Das hellenistische Gymnasion*, Berlin, 363-371.

Ramage, N. 1983
A merrythought cup from Sardis, *AJA* 87, 435-460.

Reusser, C. 2002
Vasen für Etrurien. Verbeitung und Funktionen attischer Keramik in Etrurien des 6. und 5. Jahrhunderts vor Christus, Zürich.

Rhodes, P.J. 2010
A history of the classical Greek world, 478-323 B.C., Malden Mass.

Richardson, E. 1977
The Wolf in the West, *The Journal of the Walters Art Gallery* 36, 91-101.

Ritter, S. 2002
Bildkontakte. Götter und Heroen in der Bildsprache griechischer Münzen des 4. Jahrhunderts v. Chr., Berlin.

Riva, C. 2010
The Urbanisation in Etruria. Funerary Practices and Social Change 700-600 BC, Cambridge.

Robertson, M. 1970
Ibycus. Polycrates, Troilos, Polyxena, *BICS* 17, 11-15.

Robertson, M. 1983
The Berlin Painter at the Getty Museum and some others, *GVGetty* 1, 55-72.

Robertson, M. 1992
The art of vase painting in classical Athens, Cambridge.

Robinson, E.G.D. 1990
Workshops of Apulian red-figure outside Taranto, in: Descoeudres, J-P (ed.), *EUMOSIA. Ceramic and iconographic studies in honour of Alexander Cambitoglou*, Sydney, 179-193.

Robinson, E.G.D. 2011
Identity in the Tomb of the Diver at Poseidonia, in: Gleba, M. & Horsnæs, H. (eds.), *Communicating Identity in Italic Iron Age Communities*, London.

Robinson, E.G.D. *et al.* 1997
Analysis of South-Italian Pottery by PIXE-PIGME, *MedArch* 9-10, 1996-97, 113-125.

Roscino, C. 2009.
Il rapimento di Persefone nella ceramica attica da Eleusi, in: Fortunelli, S. & Masseria, C. (eds.), *Ceramica attica da santuari della Grecia, della Ionia e dell'Italia. Atti convegno internazionale, Perugia 14-17 marzo 2007*, Venosa, 133-148.

Rosen, R.M. & Sluiter, S. (eds.) 2003
Andreia, Studies in Manliness and Courage in Classical Antiquity, Leiden.

Rossbach, O. 1894
Aias 3, *RE* 1, 930–936.

Rotroff, S.I. & Oakley, J.H. 1992
Debris from a Public Dining Place in the Athenian Agora, Hesperia Supplement 25.

Rouveret, A. 1997
Dibattito, *AttiTaranto* 36, 387-388.

Rumpf, A. 1927
Chalkidische Vasen, Berlin.

Rystedt, E. 2006
Athens in Etruria. A note on Panathenaic amphorae and Attic ceramic imagery in Etruria, in: Herring, E. *et al.* (eds.), *Across Frontiers. Etruscans, Greeks, Phoenicians & Cypriots. Studies in honour of David Ridgway and Francesca Romana Serra Ridgway*, London, 497-506.

Sabetai, V. 1995
ADelt 50, B1 [2000], 301-302.

Sabetai, V. 1998
Marriage Boiotian Style, *Hesperia* 67, 323-334.

Sabetai, V. 2000
Παιδικές Ταφές Ακραιφίας, in: Aravantinos, V. (ed.), Επετηρίς της εταιρείας Βοιωτικών μελετών 3, Α, Αθήνα, 494-535.

Sabetai, V. 2009
Marker vase or burnt offering? The clay loutrophoros in context, in: Tsingarida, A. (ed.), *Shapes and Uses of Greek Vases (7th - 4th centuries B.C.)*, Brussels, 291-306.

Sabetai, V. 2011
Eros Reigns Supreme: Dionysos' Wedding on a new Krater by the Dinos Painter in: Schleiser, R. (ed), *A different God? Dionysos and ancient polytheism*, Berlin/Boston, 137-160.

Sabetai, V. 2012
Looking at Athenian vases through the eyes of the Boeotians: copies, adaptations and local creations in the social and aesthetic culture of an Attic neighbour in: Schmidt, S. & Stähli, A. (eds.), *Vasenbilder im Kulturtransfer: Zirkulation und Rezeption griechischer Keramik im Mittelmeerraum*, München, 121-137.

Sabetai, V. forthcoming
Female protomes from Chaeroneia (Boeotia), in: Lafli, E. & Muller, A. (eds.), *Figurines de terre cuite en Méditerranée grecque et romaine: production, diffusion, iconographie et fonction. Actes du Colloque international d'Izmir, juin 2007*, BCH Supplément.

Sabetai, V. & Karakitsou, E. *forthcoming*
Κεραμική και τμήμα κεράμωσης των κλασικών χρόνων από την Θηβαϊκή Καδμεία: Διάσπαρτα τεκμήρια ενός ιερού, *AAA* 42.

Salapata, G. 2006
The Tippling Serpent in the Art of Laconia and Beyond, *Hesperia* 75, 541-560.

Savostina, E. & Simon, E. (eds.) 1999
Taman Relief. Greek Stele with two Warriors from the North of Black Sea Area, Moskow.

Scaife, R. 1995
The Kypria and its early reception, *ClAnt* 14, 164-191.

Schachter, A. 1994
Gods in the service of the state: the Boiotian experience, in: Aigner Foresti, L. (ed.), *Federazioni e federalismo nell' Europa antica*, Milano, 67-86.

Schauenburg, K. 1960
Perseus in der Kunst des Altertums, Bonn.

Schauenburg, K. 1970
Zu griechischen Mythen in der etruskischen Kunst, *JdI* 85, 28–81.

Schauenburg, K. 1976
Erotenspiele, *AW* 7.3, 39-52.

Schauenburg, K, 1988
Zu einer Loutrophoros in der Kieler Antikensammlung, *Jahrbuch des Museum fur Kunst und Gewerbe Hamburg* 6-7, 41-44.

Schäfer, A. 1997
Unterhaltung beim griechischen Symposion. Darbietungen, Spiele und Wettkämpfe von homerischer bis in spätklassische Zeit, Mainz.

Schefold, K. 1992
Gods and heroes in late Archaic Greek art, Cambridge, 1992.

Schefold, K. & Jung, F. 1988
Die Urkönige, Perseus, Bellerophon, Herakles und Theseus in der klassischen und hellenistischen Kunst, München.

Scheibler, I. 2000
Attische Skyphoi für attische Feste, *AntK* 43, 17-43.

Schiering, W. 1964
Rotfigurig bemalte Keramik, in: Mallwitz, H. & Schiering, W., *Die Werkstatt des Phidias in Olympia, Olympishe Forschungen* 5, Berlin, 248-266.

Schilardi, D.U. 1977
The Thespian Polyandrion (424 B.C.). The Excavations and Finds from a Thespian State Burial, Diss. Princeton University.

Schilbach, J. 1995
Elische Keramik des 5. und 4. Jahrhunderts, Olympische Forschungen 23, Berlin.

Schilbach, J. 1999
Datierung der Schichten im Südostgebiet, *OlB* 11, 75-79.

Schild-Xenidou, V. 2008
Corpus der boiotischen Grab- und Weihreliefs des 6. bis 4. Jahrhunderts v. Chr., AM Beih. 20, Mainz am Rhein.

Schmaltz, B. 1974
Terrakotten aus dem Kabirenheiligtum bei Theben. Menschenähnliche Figuren, menschliche Figuren und Gerät. Das Kabirenheiligtum bei Theben V, Berlin.

Schmidt, M. 1971
Ein ägyptischer Dämon in Etrurien, *ZÄS* 97, 118-125.

Schmidt, M. 2002
La ceramica italiota del IV secolo a.C. in Italia meridionale. Problemi di botteghe e cronologia archeologica, in: Bonacasa, N. *et al.* (eds.), *Sicilia dei due Dionisi. Atti della settimana di studio, Agrigento 24-28 febbraio 1999,* Roma, 252-264.

Schmidt, M. 2005
Livello culturale di singoli pittori, dalla erudizione individuale all'automatismo artigianale?, in Denoyelle, M. *et al.* (eds.), *La Ceramique Apulienne. Bilan et perspectives,* Naples, 201-206.

Schmidt, M., Trendall, A.D. & Cambitoglou, A. 1976
Eine Gruppe Apulischer Grabvasen in Basel, Magonza.

Schmidt, S. & Oakley, J.H. 2009 (eds.)
Hermeneutik der Bilder, Beiträger zur Ikonographie und Interpretation griechischer Vasenmalerei, München.

Schmidt, S. & Stähli, A. 2012
Vasenbilder im Kulturtransfer: Zirkulation und Rezeption griechischer Keramik im Mittelmeerraum, München.

Schneider-Herrmann, G. 1980
Red-figured Lucanian and Apulian nestorides and their ancestors, Amsterdam.

Scholl, A. 2002
Geschlossene Gesellschaft. Die Bewohner des klassischen Athen in den Bildern und Inschriften ihrer Grabmäler, in: *Die griechische Klassik. Idee oder Wirklichkeit. Eine Ausstellung im Martin-Gropius-Bau, Berlin, 1. März-2. Juni 2002 und in der Kunst- und Austellungshalle der Bundesrepublik Deutschland, Bonn, 5. Juli-6. Oktober 2002*, Mainz, 179-190.

Schöne-Denkinger, A. 2012
Import und Imitation attischer Bilder in Böotien, in: Schmidt, S. & Stähli, A. (eds), *Vasenbilder im Kulturtransfer: Zirkulation und Rezeption Griechischer Keramik im Mittelmeerraum*, München, 139-149.

Sedita Migliore, M. 1991
Sabucina, Caltanissetta.

Sena Chiesa, G. & Arslan, E.A. (eds.) 2004
Miti Greci. Archeologia e pittura dalla Magna Grecia al collezionismo, Milan.

Settis, S. & Parra, M.C. (eds.) 2005
Magna Grecia. Archaeologia di un sapere, Milano.

Shapiro, H.A. 1990
Oracle-mongers in Peisistratid Athens, *Kernos* 3, 335-345.

Shapiro, H.A. 1993a
Personifications in Greek Art. The Representation of Abstract Concepts. 600-400 BC, Kilchberg.

Shapiro, H.A. 1993b
Pottery, Private Life, and Politics in Democratic Athens, in: Ober, J. (ed.), *The birth of democracy. An exhibition celebrating the 2500th anniversary of democracy at the National Archives, Washington, DC, June 15, 1993 - January 2, 1994*, Athens, 21-27.

Shapiro, H.A. 2001
Red-figure Panathenaic amphoras: Some iconographical problems, in: Bentz, M. & Eschbach, N. (eds.), *PANATHENAÏKA, Symposion zu den Panathenäischen Preisamphoren Rauischholzhausen 25.11-29.11 1998*, Mainz, 119-124.

Shapiro, H.A. 2009a
Looking at Sculpture and Vases Together: The Banqueting Hero, in: Schmidt, S. & Oakley, J.H. (eds.), *Hermeneutik der Bilder. Beiträge zu Ikonographie und Interpretation griechischer Vasenmalerei*, München, 177-186.

Shapiro, H.A. 2009b
Alcibiades. The Politics of Personal Style, in: Palagia, O. (ed.), *Art in Athens during the Peloponnesian War*, Cambridge, 236-263.

Shear, T.L. Jr. 1994
The Agora and the Democracy, in: Coulson, W.D.E. *et al.* (eds.), *The Archaeology of Athens under the Democracy, International Conference Celebrating 2500 Years since the Birth of Democracy in Greece held in Athens 1992*, Oxford, 225-248.

Siewert, P. 1977
The Ephebic Oath in Fifth-Century Athens, *JHS* 97, 102-111.

Simon, E. 1953
Opfernde Götter, Berlin.

Simon, E. 1972
Hera und die Nymphen. Ein böotischer Polos in Stockholm, *RA* 1972, 205-220.

Simon, E. 1973
Die Tomba dei Tori und der etruskische Apollonkult, *JdI* 88, 27-42.

Sourvinou-Inwood, C. 1979
Theseus as son and stepson: a tentative illustration of Greek mythological mentality, London.

Söldner, M. 2007
ΒΙΟΣ ΕΥΔΑΙΜΩΝ. Zur Ikonographie des Menschen in der rotfigurigen Vasenmalerei Unteritaliens. Die Bilder aus Lukanien, Möhnesee.

Sparkes, B.A. 1967
The Taste of a Boeotian Pig, *JHS* 87, 116-130.

Spatafora, F. & Vassallo, S. (eds.) 2002
Sicani, Elimi e Greci, Palermo.

Spivey, N. 1991
Greek vases in Etruria, in: Rasmussen, T. & Spivey, N. (eds.), *Looking at Greek Vases*, Cambridge, 131-150.

Spivey, N. & Stoddart, S. 1990
Etruscan Italy, London.

Stamoudi, A. 2006
Η έκφραση της κλασικής πόλης στη Θεσσαλία. Το παράδειγμα της Πελασγίας, in: *1º διεθνές συνέδριο ιστορίας και πολιτισμού Θεσσαλίας. Πρακτικά Συνεδρίου 9-11 Νοεμβρίου 2006*, Θεσσαλονίκη, 138-151.

Stampolidis, N.C. & Tassoulas, Y. (eds.) 2004
Magna Graecia. Athletics and the olympic spirit on the periphery of the hellenic world, Athens.

Stansbury-O'Donnell, M. 2006
Vase-painting, gender, and social identity in archaic Athens, Cambridge.

Stehle, E. 2007
Thesmophoria and Eleusinian mysteries. The fascination of women's secret ritual, in: Parca, M. & Tzanetou, A. (eds.), *Finding Persephone. Women's rituals in the ancient Mediterranean,* Bloomington, 165-188.

Steingräber, S. 1986
Etruscan painting: Catalogue raisonné of Etruscan wall paintings, New York.

Steuernagel, D. 1998
Menschenopfer und Mord am Altar. Griechische Mythen in etruskischen Gräbern, Palilia 3, Wiesbaden.

Stewart, A. 1995
Rape?, in: Reeder, E.D. (ed.), *Pandora. Women in Classical Greece,* Princeton, 74-90.

Stissi, V. 2009
Why did they end up there? The role of iconography in the distribution, purchase and use of Siana cups, in: Moormann, E.M. & Stissi, V. (eds.), *Shapes and Images. Studies on Attic Black Figure and Related Topics in Honour of Herman A.G. Brijder,* Leuven, 21-36.

Stroszeck, J. 2006
Lakonisch-rotfigurige Keramik aus den Lakedaimoniergräbern am Kerameikos von Athen (403 v. Chr.), *AA,* 101-120.

Tagalidou, E. 1993
Weihreliefs an Herakles aus klassischer Zeit, Jonsered.

Tagliente, M. (ed.) 1990
Italici in Magna Grecia, Venosa.

Taplin, O. 2007
Pots and Plays. Interactions between tragedy and Greek vase-painting of the fourth century BC, Los Angeles.

Thompson, E.L. 2006
Images of Ritual Mockery, online Diss., New York.

Tiverios, M. 1997
Die von Xenophantos Athenaios signierte große Lekythos aus Pantikapaion: Alte Funde neu betrachtet, in: Oakley, J.H. et al. (eds.), *Athenian Potters and Painters,* Oxford, 269-284

Tiverios, M. 2009
Αγγεία-αναθήματα από το μεγάλο Ελευσινιακό ιερό, in: Oakley, J.H. & Palagia, O. (eds.), *Athenian Potters and Painters 2,* Oxford, 280-290.

Tomei, D. 2008
I *kantharoi* greci a figure nere e rosse, *Ostraka* 17, 111-180.

Torelli, M. 1992
Aspetti materiali e ideologici della romanizzazione della Daunia, *DialA* I-II, 47-64.

Torelli, M. 2004
Principes indigeni e classi dirigenti italiote. Per una storia della committenza dei vasi apuli, in: Sena Chiesa, G. Arslan, E.A. (eds.), *Miti Greci. Archeologia e pittura dalla Magna Grecia al collezionismo,* Milan, 190-193.

Trantalidou, K. & Kavoura, I. 2006/2007
Astragali in caves. The contribution of the archaeozoology in the understanding of some ancient Greek cult practices, *Anodos* 6-7, 459-473.

Trendall, A.D. 1967
Phlyax Vases, *BICS* 19, London.

Trendall, A.D. 1972
The Mourning Niobe, *RA* (1972), 309-316.

Trendall, A.D. 1985
An Apulian Loutrophoros Representing the Tantalidae, *GVGetty* II, Malibu, 129-144.

Trendall, A.D. 1987
The Red-figured Vases of Paestum, Rome.

Trendall, A.D. 1991
Farce and Tragedy in South Italian vase-painting, in: Rasmussen, T. & Spivey, N. (eds.), *Looking at Greek Vases,* Cambridge, 151-182.

Trendall, A.D. & McPhee, I. 1982
An Elean Red-figured Pelike in Liverpool and Early South-Italian Vase-painting, in: *Aparchai. Nuove ricerche e studi sulla Magna Grecia e la Sicilia antica in onore di Paolo Enrico Arias,* Pisa, 471-472.

Trendall, A.D. & McPhee, I. 1986
The Painter of Louvre M 85, *Quaderni Ticinesi* 15, 155-160.

Trofimova, A.A. (ed.) 2007
Greeks on the Black Sea. Ancient Art from the Hermitage, Los Angeles.

Tsingarida, A. 2002
Nul ne sait qui n'essaye. Alphonse van Branteghem et sa collection de vases grecs, in: Tsingarida, A. & Kurtz, D.C., *Appropriating Antiquity. Saisir l'Antique, Collections et collectionneurs d'antiques en Belgique et en Grande Bretagne au XIXe siècle*, Bruxelles, 245-273.

Tsingarida, A. 2003
Des offrandes pour l'éternité. Les vases de la Tombe Sotades, in: Rouillard, P. & Verbanck, A. (eds.), *Le vase grec et ses destins*, Munich, 67-74.

Tsingarida, A. 2008
Color for a market? Special techniques and distribution patterns in Late Archaic and Early Classical Greece, in: Lapatin, K. (ed.), *Papers on Special Techniques in Athenian Vases*, Los Angeles, 199-204.

Tsingarida, A. *forthcoming*
Special vases for the Etruscans? Reception and Uses of outsized Athenian drinking vessels, in: Mannack, Th. *et al.* (eds.), *Greek Pots Abroad*, Oxford.

Ure, A.D. 1958
The Argos Painter and the Painter of the Dancing Pan, *AJA* 62, 389-395.

Ure, A.D. 1959
Un-incised Black Figure, *BICS* 6, 1-4.

Ure, A.D. & Ure, P.N. 1933
Boeotian Vases in the Akademisches Kunstmuseum in Bonn, *AA* (1933), 1-42.

Ure, P.N. 1951
A new Pontic amphora, *JHS* 71, 198-202.

Valenza Mele, N. 1991
Solo 'tombe di atleti' a Taranto?, *Prospettiva* 63, 4-16.

Van der Meer, L.B. 1977-1978
Etruscan urns from Volterra: Studies on mythological representations, *BABesch* 52-53, 57-131.

Van Straten, F.T. 1979
The lebes of Herakles, *BaBesch* 54, 189-191.

Van Straten, F.T. 1995
Hiera Kala. Images of Animal Sacrifice in Archaic and Classical Greece, Leiden.

Verbanck-Piérard, A. 1989
Le double culte d'Héraclès: légende ou réalité?, in: Laurens A.F. (ed.), *Entre hommes et dieux*, Paris, 43-65.

Verbanck-Piérard, A. 1992
Herakles at Feast in Attic Art: a Mythical or Cultic Iconography?, in: Hägg, R. (ed.), *The Iconography of Greek Cult in the Archaic and Classical Periods, Kernos* Suppl. 1, Athènes-Liège, 85-106.

Verbanck-Piérard, A. 1995
Héraclès l'Athénien, in: Verbanck-Piérard, A. & Viviers, D. (eds.), *Culture et Cité*, Bruxelles, 103-125.

Verbanck-Piérard, A. 1998
Héros attiques au jour le jour: les calendriers des dèmes, in: Pirenne-Delforge, V. (ed.), *Les Panthéons des cités, Kernos* suppl. 8, Liège, 109-127.

Verbanck-Piérard, A. & Massar, N. (eds.) 2008
Parfums de l'antiquité. La rose et l'encens en Méditerranée. Catalogue d'exposition (Musée royal de Mariemont), Morlanwelz.

Viviers, D. 2006
Signer une œuvre en Grèce ancienne: Pourquoi? Pour qui?, in: De la Genière, J. (ed.), *Les Clients de la céramique grecque. Actes du Colloque*, Paris, 141-154.

Vollkommer, R. 1988
Herakles in the Art of Classical Greece, Oxford.

Volpe, G. *et al.* (eds.) 2008
Storia e archeologia della Daunia in ricorda di Marina Mazzei, Bari.

Walter, O. 1937
Der Säulenbau des Herakles, *AM* 62, 41-51.

Webster, T.B.L. 1972
Potter and Patron in Classical Athens, London.

Wehgartner, I. 1983
Attisch weissgrundige Keramik, Maltechniken, Werkstätten, Formen, Verwendung, Mainz am Rhein.

Wehgartner, I. 1987
Das Ideal massvoller Liebe auf einem attischen Vasenbild. Neues zur Lekythos F 2705 im Berliner Antikenmuseum, *JdI* 102, 185-197.

West, M.L. 1983
The Orphic Poems, Oxford.

West, M.L. 1998
Iambi et elegi graeci ante Alexandrum cantati: Editio altera, Oxford.

Wiencke, M.I. 1954
An epic theme in Greek art, *AJA* 58, 285-306.

Williams, D. 1980
Ajax, Odysseus and the arms of Achilles, *AntK* 23, 137-145.

Williams, D. 1986
A cup by the Antiphon Painter and the Battle of Marathon, in: Boehr, E. & Martini, W. (eds.), *Studien zur Mythologie und Vasenmalerei: Konrad Schauenburg zum 65. Geburtstag am 16. April 1986*, Mainz, 75-81.

Williams, D. 1999
Greek Vases, London.

Williams, D. 2004
Sotades: Plastic and white, in: Keay, S. & Moser, S. (eds.), *Greek Art in View. Essays in honour of Brian Sparkes*, Oxford, 95-120.

Williams, D. 2006
The Sotades Tomb, in: Cohen, B. (ed.), *The Colors of Clay. Special Techniques in Athenian Vases*, Los Angeles, 291-300.

Williams, D. & Ogden, J. 1994
Greek Gold. Jewelry of the Classical World [Exhibition catalogue], London.

Wolters, P. & Bruns, G. 1940
Das Kabirenheiligtum bei Theben I, Berlin.

Woodford, S. 1982
Ajax and Achilles playing a game on an Olpe in Oxford, *JHS* 102, 173-185.

Woodford, S. 2010
An Etruscan Twist to the Story of Troilos, in: Brauer, A. (ed.), *Teaching with Objects: The Curatorial Legacy of David Gordon Mitten*, Cambridge, 92-104.

Woodford, S. & Louden, M. 1980
Two Trojan themes: The iconography of Ajax carrying the body of Achilles and of Aeneas carrying Anchises in black figure vase painting, *AJA* 84, 25-40.

Zampiti, A. & Vassilopoulou, V. 2008
Κεραμική αρχαϊκής και κλασικής περιόδου από το Λειβήθριο άντρο του Ελικώνα in: V. Aravantinos (ed.) 2008, Επετηρίς της εταιρείας Βοιωτικών μελετών 4, Α, Athens, 445-472.

Zanker, P. 1995
The mask of Socrates. The image of the intellectual in antiquity, Sather Classical Lectures 59, Berkeley.

Zervoudaki, E. 1968
Attische polychrome Reliefkeramik des späten 5. und des 4. Jahrhunderts v. Chr., *AM* 83, 1-88.

Zumbrunnen, J.G. 2008
Silence and Democracy. Athenian Politics in Thucydides' "History", University Park.

Zilverberg, M. 1986
The La Tolfa Painter: Fat or thin?, in: Brijder, H.A.G., Drukker, A.A. & Neeft, C.W. (eds.), *Enthousiasmos. Essays on Greek and related pottery presented to J. M. Hemelrijk*, Amsterdam, 49-60.

List of Authors

List of Authors

Martin Bentz
Universität Bonn
Abteilung für Klassische Archäologie
Am Hofgarten 21
D-53113 Bonn
Germany
m.bentz@uni-bonn.de

Helena Fracchia
Department of History and Classics
University of Alberta
Edmonton, Alberta
Canada
Helena.Fracchia@ualberta.ca

Maurizio Gualtieri
Dipartimento di Studi Storico-Artistici
Sezione di Studi Comparati sulle
Società Antiche
Università degli Studi di Perugia
Via Armonica 3
06123 Perugia
Italy
mgualt@unipg.it

Guy Hedreen
Department of Art
Williams College
Lawrence Hall
Williamstown, Massachusetts 01267
USA
Guy.M.Hedreen@williams.edu

Martin Langner
Institut für Klassische Archäologie
Freie Universität Berlin
Otto-von-Simson-Straße 11
D-14195 Berlin
Germany
langnerm@zedat.fu-berlin.de

Adrienne Lezzi-Hafter
AKANTHVS. Verlag Für Archäologie
Böndlerstrasse 49
CH-8802 Kilchberg
Switzerland
akanthus@bluewin.ch

Thomas Mannack
The Beazley Archive
Ioannou School for Classical and
Byzantine Studies
66 St Giles
Oxford
United Kingdom
thomas.mannack@beazley.ox.ac.uk

Bodil Bundgaard Rasmussen
Collection of Classical and Near
Eastern Antiquities
The National Museum of Denmark
Frederiksholms Kanal 12
DK-1220 Copenhagen K
Denmark
bodil.bundgaard.rasmussen@
natmus.dk

Victoria Sabetai
Research Centre for Antiquity
Academy of Athens
14, Anagnostopoulou Str.
10673 Athens
Greece
vsabetai@academyofathens.gr

Stine Schierup
Collection of Classical and Near
Eastern Antiquities
The National Museum of Denmark
Frederiksholms Kanal 12
DK-1220 Copenhagen K
Denmark
stine.schierup@natmus.dk

Athena Tsingarida
Université Libre de Bruxelles
CP175/01, avenue F.D. Roosevelt 50
B-1050 Bruxelles
Belgium
atsingar@ulb.ac.be

Annie Verbanck-Piérard
Collection of Greek and Roman
Antiquities
Musée Royal de Mariemont
Chaussée de Mariemont 100
B-7140 Morlanwelz
Belgium
annie.verbanck@musee-mariemont.be

GÖSTA ENBOM MONOGRAPHS are published in connection with the research programme "Pots, Potters and Society in Ancient Greece" (2008-2013) at the Collection of Classical and Near Eastern Antiquities, the National Museum of Denmark.

The research programme and its publications are supported by the "Foundation of Consul General Gösta Enbom".

VOLUME 1
POTTERY IN THE ARCHAEOLOGICAL RECORD: GREECE AND BEYOND
Edited by Mark L. Lawall & John Lund.
Aarhus University Press 2011.

VOLUME 2
RED-FIGURE POTTERY IN ITS ANCIENT SETTING
Edited by Stine Schierup and Bodil Bundgaard Rasmussen
Aarhus University Press 2012.